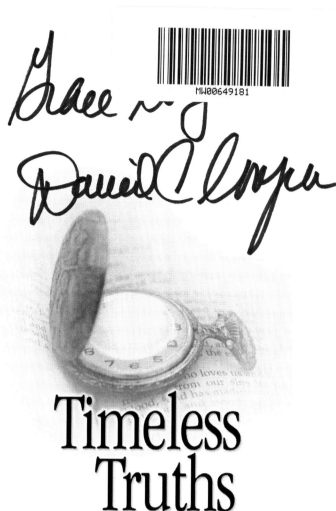

Timeless Truths

in Changing Times
366 Daily Devotions

PATHWAY PRESS
WE ARE THINKING DIFFERENTLY.
Cleveland, TN

David C. Cooper

Timeless Truths
in Changing Times
366 Daily Devotions

Book Editor: Wanda Griffith
Editorial Assistant: Tammy Hatfield
Copy Editors: Esther Metaxas
Jessica Sirbaugh

Library of Congress Catalog Card Number: 2007920976
ISBN: 978-1-59684-250-2
Copyright © 2007 by Pathway Press
Cleveland, Tennessee 37311
All Rights Reserved
Printed in the United States of America

Dedication

This book is dedicated
to the loving memory of my father

William H. Cooper, Jr.

who taught me to
"be still and know"
that God is sovereign
(Psalm 46:10).

Contents

Introduction

As World War II was drawing to a close, C.S. Lewis, British professor at Oxford, lectured to a group of students. He paused and asked the class, "How can you go to college and study literature when London is under siege?"

He then answered his own question. "We're always under siege. The real question then is, Will you spend your life dealing with the immediate or the eternal?"

Our lives can get so cluttered with the demands of the day that we fail to spend time focusing on the things that are most important.

I have prepared this daily devotional to help individuals focus on the more important matters of faith. Great things happen little by little. So it is with spiritual growth.

As you take time each day to contemplate spiritual truths and focus on the presence of God in your life, you will grow in His grace and His knowledge.

Jesus said His words are "spirit and . . . life" (John 6:63). Each devotional article is based on Scripture as it applies to the daily issues each of us face.

I pray you find new strength to face life's challenges and opportunities with faith, hope and love.

—David C. Cooper, D.Min.

New Mercies Every Morning   DAY 1

Have you ever come to a place in your life when you felt you needed a fresh start? Maybe you have made a mess of everything . . . failed to reach your goals . . . had a relationship breakup . . . fallen away from God . . . made unwise decisions . . . suffered loss.

This was the experience of Jeremiah and the people of Judah. They needed a new start. Jeremiah had forewarned that Babylon would invade Judah if they persisted in their sin. And his word came to pass. In 588 B.C., Nebuchadnezzar's army laid siege to Jerusalem. Two years later the city fell and the people of Judah were deported to Babylon. The city was burned. The Temple was destroyed. The holy articles were confiscated. For 70 years they would be in captivity in Babylon.

One day Jeremiah sat viewing the ruins of Jerusalem. He wept and prayed. He struggled with his faith and battled his own disillusionment with life. Then came the promise of a new beginning: "Yet this I call to mind and therefore I have hope: Because of the Lord's great love we are not consumed, for his compassions never fail. They are new every morning; great is your faithfulness. . . . therefore I will wait for him" (Lamentations 3:21-24).

The morning speaks of a new beginning. We awaken every day to new opportunities afforded us by the mercy of God. God gives mercy for our sins and for our mistakes and poor decisions. The past does not have to determine the present or the future.

Move forward this new year. Press on in the faithfulness of God. "Great is your faithfulness. . . . The Lord is my portion; therefore I will wait for him" (vv. 23, 24). Wait for what? Waiting involves time and trust. Wait for His timing and trust Him to accomplish His will in your life.

Jeremiah got up from his place of disillusionment and got on with his life and ministry because he believed God was faithful to His promises. Are you actively taking steps of faith, believing God will bless you because He is faithful? God is faithful to His word, but we have to believe His Word to receive the benefits.

This Is the Day the Lord Has Made   DAY 2

In his book, *To See the World in a Grain of Sand*, C.L. James tells the fable of a wise old cat that notices a kitten chasing its tail. "Why are you chasing your tail so?" asked the wise old cat. The kitten replied, "I have learned that the best thing for a cat is happiness, and happiness is my tail. Therefore, I am chasing it; and when I catch it, I shall have happiness."

The wise old cat said, "My son, I too have paid attention to the problems of the universe. I too have judged that happiness is in my tail. But, I noticed that whenever I chase after it, it keeps running away from me, and when I go about my business, it just seems to come after me wherever I go."

Jesus promised us real happiness and true joy. "I have told you this so that my joy may be in you and that your joy may be complete" (John 15:11).

Happiness results from positive emotions such as joy, gratitude and hope. Negative attitudes are toxic to the mind and body. Research shows that negative emotions narrow thought. We can't dream or envision new possibilities when we are filled with negative emotions such as fear, resentment and pessimism. Positive emotions make thinking more creative and resourceful.

Every day is a celebration of life. Begin every day with this affirmation of faith: "This is the day the Lord has made; we will rejoice and be glad in it" (Psalm 118:24, *NKJV*). First, today is the day the Lord has made, so receive it with joy and gratitude. "In everything give thanks" (1 Thessalonians 5:18, *NKJV*).

Second, God only gives you today, not tomorrow, so focus on today. Don't get distracted by the failures of yesterday or the worries of tomorrow.

Third, He has made this day especially for you. Today is not an accident; not just another 24 hours.

Fourth, everything in each day is made for you—the ups and the downs, the joys and the sorrows. God is involved in every aspect of your today. So, "give thanks for everything" (see Ephesians 5:20).

Finally, expect something good to happen today. Then go out and make something good happen. You've got to make something happen in order to be happy.

Making a Difference

It's absolutely amazing to think about the difference we can make in life when we fulfill God's calling on our lives. President Reagan used to tell the story of Telemachus, a fourth-century Christian, whose courage for Christ made a difference in his generation.

Telemachus lived in a remote village and spent much of his time in prayer. One day he heard the voice of God telling him to go to Rome, so he obeyed. Weeks later, he arrived in the city at the time of a great celebration. The monk followed the crowd down the streets into the Coliseum. He saw the gladiators stand before the emperor and say, "We who are about to die salute you." When he realized these men were going to fight to the death for the entertainment of the crowd, he cried out, "In the name of Jesus, stop!"

As the games began, he pushed his way through the crowd, climbed over the wall, and jumped to the floor of the arena. When the crowd saw him running toward the gladiators and saying "In the name of Jesus, stop!" they thought it was part of the show and began laughing.

When they realized it wasn't, the laughter turned to anger. As he pleaded with the gladiators to stop, one of them plunged a sword into his body. As he was dying, he cried, "In the name of Jesus, stop!"

Then a strange thing happened. The gladiators gazed at his lifeless body. A hush fell over the crowd. Way up in the upper rows, a man stood and made his way to the exit. Others began to follow, until everyone left the Coliseum in silence.

The year was A.D. 391. That was the last battle to the death between gladiators in the Coliseum. All because of one voice that could hardly be heard above the tumult.[1]

One voice—one life—that spoke the truth in God's name.

You, too, can make a difference for Christ by following the admonition: "So whether you eat or drink or whatever you do, do it all for the glory of God" (1 Corinthians 10:31).

Visions for God

The noted missionary C.T. Studd asked, "Are gamblers for gold so many and gamblers for God so few?"

Accomplishing great things for God begins with possessing a vision. Vision is the ability to see the challenges and opportunities ahead. It is the willingness to take a step of faith to see the vision turn to reality. It is the courage and fortitude to press on until the vision is fulfilled.

Vision demands that we take the risk of faith, or what some call the leap of faith. I don't mean to imply that faith is risky. The risk of faith is based on the sure promises of God that promise us success. Nor is faith blind; it sees clearly the opportunities ahead and seizes them.

The prophet Ezekiel experienced visions *of* God (Ezekiel 1:1). What we need are visions *for* God. We have received so much *from* God; now let's do something *for* God. What are you doing for the kingdom of God with your life and your resources? Maybe you've never had a vision of God—I certainly have not. But, you can have a vision for God.

Solomon reminds us, "Where there is no vision, the people perish" (Proverbs 29:18, KJV). Jesus turned the world upside down with His vision of the coming kingdom of God as a here-and-now reality. "The kingdom of heaven is near" (Matthew 4:17). Multitudes followed Christ because they shared His vision.

You need a vision for your life—a vision so great it inspires others to follow you. Now, let's not confuse greatness with grandiosity. Visions for God are not the same as delusions of grandeur. Telling every child in a kindergarten class they can all be the president of the United States borders more on delusions of grandeur than it does inspiring them to reach their potential. Likewise, telling every Christian they can be the next Billy Graham is equally discouraging.

Sometimes we feel pressured to be great. Your greatness is not something that can be compared with someone else's greatness. Greatness means something different for everyone. So, rise to your level of greatness. After all, life is not a competition with others. You're only competing with yourself.

"May the God of peace . . . equip you with everything [you need] for doing his will, and may he work in us what is pleasing to him, through Jesus Christ" (Hebrews 13:20, 21).

All Sail and No Anchor DAY 5

The English historian Thomas Macauley warned the American people decades ago that our Constitution ran the risk of being "all sail and no anchor." In other words, the lofty ideals of the Constitution would only have merit as they remained anchored to moral absolutes. George Washington remarked, "It is impossible to rightly govern the world without God and the Bible."

As opposed to being firmly anchored to the truth of God, we as a society are being blown back and forth by the winds of secular ideologies that threaten to shipwreck our hearts, homes and nation.

This is why Alan Bloom, professor of philosophy at the University of Chicago, has indicted the American educational system for failing to teach moral truth to its students. In his book, *The Closing of the American Mind*, he points out that our educators utilize a new language of "value relativism," which prevents us from "teaching with any conviction about good and evil." He goes on to say that our universities offer "disconnected disciplines" without a focus on developing the whole person. Hence, students obtain degrees, but they are "unfurnished persons," lacking the moral base needed for sound judgment.

The family has forsaken its once-held position as the seat of religious and moral teaching. The eternal conflict of good and evil has now been replaced with the language "I'm OK, you're OK." Instead of paying for our choices, Bloom tells us that "America today has no-fault automobile accidents, no-fault divorces, and is moving with the aid of modern philosophy toward no-fault choices."

As a result, most Americans are dissatisfied with the moral tenor of the times. According to the Princeton Research Center, 64 percent of Americans are dissatisfied with ethics and morals; 73 percent are dissatisfied with the level of honesty and standards; 83 percent are dissatisfied with care for the poor and needy. In times of moral confusion, we hold to the moral absolutes found in God's Word. "The law of the Lord is perfect" (Psalm 19:7).

Let us resolve anew to keep our faith and values anchored firmly to the unchanging Word of God.

The Temptation Trap   DAY 6

The temptation experience of Jesus is recorded in Scripture so that we may learn how to be victorious over temptation. "Then Jesus was led by the Spirit into the desert to be tempted by the devil" (see Matthew 4:1-11). The account of Jesus' battle with Satan is especially meaningful because the only way the disciples knew of His temptation was that He told them. Jesus was alone in the desert when He faced the devil. He shared the experience of His struggle to help them face their struggles.

The devil tempted Him in an effort to defeat Him from carrying out the will of God. Christ's temptation was real. It was not playacting. He faced greater temptations than we do. Satan doesn't have to use his full force against us, but he did against Christ. Yet, Jesus overcame him! The temptations He faced are the ones we, too, must face and defeat if we are to do the will of God.

Christ overcame, and He will enable us to overcome if we follow His example. Because Christ lives in us, He gives us His victory and power. He lives out His victory in us. It is a mystery but a great reality—"Christ lives in me" (Galatians 2:20).

Victory is a process. The more we face temptation, the stronger we become. We all yield to temptation at times. When we do, let us go to God and confess our sins. Then get back up and "press toward the mark for the prize of the high calling of God" (Philippians 3:14, KJV).

May you grow stronger as you face the tempter through the power of the Word of God. Face every temptation with confidence: "Greater is He who is in you than he who is in the world" (1 John 4:4, *NASB*).

Measuring Success   DAY 7

Everyone wants to be successful. The question is, how do you measure success? Webster says that *success* is "a favorable or desired outcome of something attempted; a prosperous or advantageous issue or the attainment of wealth, fame, and so forth."

I like Winston Churchill's definition better: "Success is going from one failure to another without losing your enthusiasm."

A Gallup Poll conducted on 1,500 prominent people revealed five common traits of successful people—common sense, knowing one's field, self-reliance, general intelligence, and the ability to get things done. Is that all there is to success? Jesus responds with a heart-penetrating question, "What good will it be for a man if he gains the whole world, yet forfeits his soul?" (Matthew 16:26).

There are two sides to the coin of success. First, success means to become the person God created you to be. Success is internal before it is external. It is measured by character, not circumstances. God's greatest work is not in what He does for us, but what He does in us: "For those God foreknew he also predestined to be conformed to the likeness of his Son" (Romans 8:29). Theodore Roosevelt said, "If you are not actively pursuing the person you want to be, then you are pursuing the person you don't want to be."

Second, success is a matter of accomplishing what you set out to accomplish. It is reaching for your goals. If you find you have the wrong goals, then change them. If your strategy isn't working, then change it. Success is largely a matter of hard work and determination to accomplish what you set out to do. Don't merely try—do! As Yoda tells Luke Skywalker in *Star Wars*, "There is no try, only do!"

Go out and face the challenges of life with the will to win, the desire to succeed, and the goal to please the Lord.

Be Angry and Sin Not DAY 8

Historians may very well label our age as the "age of anger." Nearly everyone seems to be mad about something today. For example, we have "women's rage," "gangsta rap," angry talk-show guests, and radio hosts hurling insults. Anger is a popular theme in movies, music, art and television. Some call it *attitude*. We all have to deal with anger. Anger is part of our emotional makeup and serves a vital role in our lives, if we keep it in check. The important thing is how we process anger internally and how we express it outwardly.

Scripture reveals four fundamental truths about anger:

First, *anger is not a sin*. That's a relief. The apostle Paul says "Be angry and sin not." Or, "In your anger do not sin" (Ephesians 4:26). Paul tells us to vent our anger, but cautions us to express it appropriately. Even

God gets angry. There are 375 Old Testament references to God's anger. The Gospels record that Jesus experienced anger over those who were spiritually arrogant. Appropriate anger has been shown in research to be very healthy.

Second, *anger can lead us into sin if we don't deal with it properly.* In the last part of verse 26, Paul warns us of the consequences of unbridled anger: "Do not let the sun go down while you are still angry" (v. 26). Anger can lead to high blood pressure, depression, psychological disturbances, violence and can damage our relationships.

Third, *unresolved anger opens the door to spiritual bondage.* Paul's next statement is thought-provoking: "And do not give the devil a foothold" (v. 27). Anger can provoke destructive attitudes and actions that lead to resentment and rage. And these emotions are toxic.

Fourth, *anger hinders spiritual maturity.* The apostle James gives us invaluable advice: "Everyone should be quick to listen, slow to speak and slow to become angry, for man's anger does not [produce] the righteous life that God desires" (James 1:19, 20). Failing to surrender our anger to the control of the Holy Spirit prohibits our growth in Christlikeness.

Today, bring your angry feelings into the light of God's presence in prayer. Ask Him to forgive you for any inappropriate anger and to give you wisdom to resolve your anger issues.

Steps out of Anger DAY 9

As we saw yesterday, we are to "be angry but sin not" (see Ephesians 4:26). Here are five important steps to get out of the anger trap:

Step 1: Sort it out. Seek to understand why you are angry. Remember, there is a difference between the normal irritations of life and a persistent state of anger. Reflect on the causes and motivations of the angry feelings you have.

Step 2: Count the cost. One of the predominant causes of divorce today is negative behavior such as unkind words, abuse and constant fighting. One psychologist says that an angry confrontation can erase 20 acts of kindness. The point is, anger can cost us dearly if we do not keep it in check. Persistent anger is a luxury we can't afford.

Step 3: Let it out. Release your anger to God in prayer. Tell God how you feel. He can handle it. Then go talk about it with a friend—or, even the person you're angry at, if you can do it constructively. Whatever you do, don't keep your anger bottled up in your heart. Repressed anger brings in a host of emotional and relational problems.

Step 4: Set limits. This means to control your words and behavior. God tells us to get a grip on our communication: "When words are many, sin is not absent, but he who holds his tongue is wise" (Proverbs 10:19). Don't cross the line of verbal or physical abuse, no matter how frustrated you get.

Step 5: Give it up. As Christians, we do not have the right to remain angry. In Christ, we have given up that right. We surrender our anger to Him and forgive others as He has forgiven us. When we forgive, we are free indeed—free from resentment, bitterness and anger. Remember to pray, "Forgive us our debts, as we forgive our debtors" (Matthew 6:12, KJV).

As you face the complexities of your relationships and the misunderstandings that often come, put the Word into practice. "In your anger do not sin: Do not let the sun go down while you are still angry" (Ephesians 4:26).

Conquering Criticism   DAY 10

It has been said that the only deserved criticism is a better deed. How pleasant our lives would be if everyone practiced this adage. The truth, however, is that criticism flows freely in the forms of complaints, petty gripes, put-downs, unrealistic demands and judgmental attitudes. Criticism causes fractured friendships, strained marriages, discouraged employees and organizational confusion.

Solomon addressed the issue of criticism with a word of wisdom in Ecclesiastes 7:21, 22: "Do not pay attention to every word people say, or you may hear your servant cursing you—for you know in your heart that . . . you yourself have cursed others."

Who hasn't felt the crushing blow of criticism that left our hearts broken? And who hasn't dealt that death blow to another by lashing out with a critical word either to them or about them?

So, how can we conquer criticism?

First, *own up to the problem.* We dare not label criticism as discernment, strong leadership, or being opinionated. We know full well when we are being critical of others—questioning their character, judging their motives, second-guessing their intentions, and picking to pieces their performance to see if it passes the scrutiny of perfectionist standards (which, by the way, they do not even meet). We have all fallen into the deadly sin.

Second, *realize what criticism costs.* When Paul exhorts us, "Do not let any unwholesome talk come out of your mouths," he does so because such negative communication grieves the Holy Spirit (see Ephesians 4:29, 30). We hinder the work of the Holy Spirit in our lives by being critical of others. Criticism accomplishes nothing beneficial. It costs us close friendships, unity and divine blessings. Critical people hurt themselves the most when criticizing others.

Third, *cultivate the art of encouragement.* Point out what is good in others and let God take care of the rest. One of the primary ministries God has given every believer is the ministry of encouragement. "Let us encourage one another" (Hebrews 10:25).

Make it a point today to encourage someone as you fulfill God's calling to encouragement.

Treasuring Traditions DAY 11

A lot is made today over the pros and cons of traditions. A tradition is a belief, custom or narrative transmitted from generation to generation. Some traditions stifle creativity and productivity, keeping individuals, families and organizations from reaching their full potential. This is certainly true of certain religious traditions that are contrary to Scripture. Jesus confronted the empty traditions of His day: "You nullify the word of God for the sake of your tradition" (Matthew 15:6).

On the other hand, however, traditions provide a valuable, indispensable foundation for our lives.

Healthy traditions give us a sense of history, connecting our lives and experiences with those who have lived before us. We then become part of a larger story of faith being told over many generations. The writer of Hebrews says, "Since we are surrounded by such a great cloud of witnesses, let us . . . run with perseverance the race marked out for us" (12:1).

Tradition also brings stability to life, work, play and faith. In the South, we have some wonderful cultural traditions (like grits!). In the church, we have meaningful traditions of worship and community life. Tradition helps define who we are as the church—the people of God. Without traditions, we lose our sense of identity.

Tradition gives our children a legacy. Paul instructed Timothy, "Continue in what you have learned and have become convinced of, because you know those from whom you learned it" (2 Timothy 3:14).

Good traditions need to be passed on to the next generation. While things do change and progress needs to be made, good and wholesome traditions need to be treasured and preserved.

Take time today to offer thanksgiving to God for the rich traditions of life and faith that give us our unique history, identity and legacy for the next generation.

All Things New   DAY 12

One of the greatest needs in our lives is the need for restoration. To *restore* means "to bring something back into existence or effect again; to bring back to a former or original condition; to put back in a former place or position; to reinstate; to return."

We talk about restoring relationships, renovating antique furniture, reinstating a political leader and returning something that was stolen or lost. These all demonstrate the idea of restoration.

The essential meaning of salvation is restoration. To be saved means that we have experienced the miraculous restoring power of God to make all things new in our lives spiritually, psychologically, emotionally and relationally.

From Genesis to Revelation, we see the God of restoration. We hear God's message to the nation of Judah: "I will restore your judges as in days of old, your counselors as at the beginning. Afterward you will be called the City of Righteousness, the Faithful City" (Isaiah 1:26).

The psalmist prayed, "Restore to me the joy of your salvation and grant me a willing spirit, to sustain me" (Psalm 51:12). God promises, "I will restore you to health and heal your wounds" (Jeremiah 30:17). Paul the apostle declares, "Therefore if any man be in Christ, he is a new creature: old things are passed away; behold, all things are become new" (2 Corinthians 5:17, KJV).

When the apostle John received the Revelation on the isle of Patmos concerning the restoration of all things and the beauty of the new heaven and the new earth, he says, "And he that sat upon the throne said Behold, I make all things new" (Revelation 21:5, KJV).

As you surrender your failures, problems and challenges to your heavenly Father in faithful prayer, He will make all things new for you.

Mercy Triumphs Over Judgment   DAY 13

One of the most moving of all Biblical accounts is the woman caught in the act of adultery (John 8:1-11). A number of persons asked me why the study notes in their Bibles make reference to the fact that this story does not appear in some of the ancient Greek manuscripts of the New Testament. So, let me explain.

The oldest New Testament manuscripts date back to between the fourth and sixth centuries A.D. The scholars hand-copied from the originals. We call them the "Uncial Manuscripts," because they are written in all capital letters. The story of the woman caught in adultery only appears in one of the earliest manuscripts, while six omit it completely and two leave a blank where it should appear. However, it emerges strongly in the later manuscripts of the medieval times.

Jerome included the story in his Latin translation of the Bible (A.D. 400), and Augustine and Ambrose comment on it in their writings. It appears in all the later manuscripts. It is quoted in a third-century book called *The Apostolic Constitutions*, where it was given as a warning to bishops who were too strict. Eusebius, the church historian, traced its origin back as far as A.D. 100.

Why was it omitted in early manuscripts? Augustine says some removed it because of its scandalous nature. Some thought the story showed Jesus being too soft on immorality and thought people might use it as a justification for sin. After all, the early church was a small island in the ocean of paganism, and needed to learn how to live a holy life. But over time, the story arrived by word of mouth, confirmed by one early manuscript and found its way back into the Gospel of John, where it rightly belongs.

The story teaches us how to handle matters of judgment. The story underscores Jesus' statement that follows: "You judge by human standards; I pass judgment on no one. But if I do judge, my decisions are right, because I am not alone. I stand with the Father, who sent me" (John 8:15, 16).

There will always be those among us who try to make Christianity too strict and rigid, so that we always feel like we fall short of the mark. But the good news of Jesus is the message of grace. This magnificent story of grace reminds us that "mercy triumphs over judgment" (James 2:13).

I Will Give Thanks DAY 14

I will "give thanks to the Lord, for he is good; his love endures forever" (Psalm 106:1) . . . for the Father and His inescapable presence . . . for Jesus and His amazing grace . . . for the Holy Spirit, my companion and guide.

I will give thanks in all things . . . for God works in all things . . . and God works for the good of those who love Him and who are called according to His purpose (Romans 8:28). There are no coincidences, only divine opportunities.

I will give thanks for all things . . . for things pleasant and for things painful. In pleasant times, I experience the heights of happiness; in painful times, I learn to lean on Him.

I will give thanks for the overlooked blessings of life . . . the serendipitous grace . . . the kind word . . . the encouraging letter . . . the daily provisions I tend to take for granted . . . the opportunity to work and to be productive . . . the common routines of every ordinary day.

I will give thanks for my family and my friends . . . those who care enough to tell me the truth . . . those who love me enough to make sure I have everything I need . . . those who believe in me through the ups and downs.

I will give thanks for the hassles of life . . . a demanding schedule . . .

traffic jams . . . daily stresses . . . personal responsibilities . . . meaningless tasks . . . inspiring challenges . . . interruptions . . . cell phones that make me ubiquitous . . . . all these remind me of the sacred privilege of being alive.

I will give thanks for the household of faith . . . my spiritual family which surrounds me with favor and love . . . the source of God's grace . . . the body of Christ that enables me to share my gifts . . . the sanctuary of grace that calls me upward and onward in my spiritual walk.

I will give thanks for the Bible . . . the enduring Word of God . . . a lamp unto my feet and a light unto my path (Psalm 119:105) . . . a sure word in an age of confusion . . . a timely word in seasons of pain . . . a reassuring word in the prison of fear . . . a healing word for the wounds of the soul.

I will give thanks for America . . . for the cost of freedom . . . the promise of opportunity . . . the courage of patriotism . . . the sacrifice of warriors . . . the glory of the Constitution . . . and a government of the people, by the people, and for the people.

I will give thanks for this day . . . for it is a gift of God . . . it is the only day I have . . . it is a day filed with endless opportunities and bright promises . . . and I shall get everything I can from it and give everything I have to it.

The Final Challenge DAY 15

The Bible tells us that Jesus Christ will return to Earth again. We call this glorious event the second coming of Christ. Jesus said that no one knows the day nor the hour when He will return; thus, we need to be watchful, ready and faithful (see Matthew 24:36-44). What will it be like to stand face-to-face before the Lord of eternity? We fall short of the mark. We stumble and fall. Yet we are assured: "We . . . have confidence on the day of judgment" (1 John 4:17).

We battle changing emotions. The good news is that we live by faith, not by feelings. Don't make the mistake of measuring your relationship to God by your feelings. Remember, "we live by faith, not by sight" (2 Corinthians 5:7). God is faithful regardless of your feelings. He promises: "Never will I leave you; never will I forsake you" (Hebrews 13:5).

God doesn't call us to perfection, but to faith. "When the Son of Man comes," Jesus asked, "will he find faith on the earth?" (Luke 18:8). The greatest assurance we have is declared beautifully by Paul when he asks, "Who shall separate us from the love of Christ?" (Romans 8:35). Then he answers the question: "No, in all these things we are more than conquerors through him who loved us. For I am convinced that neither death nor life, neither angels nor demons, neither the present nor the future, nor any powers, neither height nor depth, nor anything else in all creation, will be able to separate us from the love of God that is in Christ Jesus our Lord" (vv. 37-39).

Christ is coming. We will meet Him either in death or when He comes; therefore, be faithful.

You Will Receive Power   DAY 16

W ho is the Holy Spirit and why was He sent? He is the third member of the triune Godhead, coexistent, eternal, and equal with the Father and Son. The Holy Spirit is not an impersonal force, emotionalism or psychic phenomenon. He is the divine guest. That's what the old term Holy Ghost actually means. The word ghost is from the Anglo-Saxon word meaning "guest." He is the divine Guest of honor who makes His home in our hearts.

Our openness to the Spirit's work is the pathway to God's power in our lives. "You will receive power when the Holy Spirit comes on you" (Acts 1:8). What, exactly, is the power of the Spirit? The word *power* (Greek, *dunamis*) means "dynamic ability." We get our word *dynamite* from this word.

1. *The power of transformation.* The Holy Spirit works in us and on us to conform us to the image of Christ. The Spirit convicts us of areas in our lives and motivates us to change our behavior to imitate Christ.

2. *The power of transcendence.* He gives us inner strength and joy to rise above pressure, adversity and stress. "We have this treasure in jars of clay to show that this all-surpassing power is from God and not from us" (2 Corinthians 4:7).

3. *The power of translation.* Our ultimate purpose in life is to share the good news of Christ with others. The Spirit gives us the words

to say. He opens the human heart to receive the grace of God in Christ.

As you face the challenges of the day, remember you are not alone. The Holy Spirit is with you. Pray and ask the Father to give you a fresh infilling of the Holy Spirit so that you face today triumphantly. "Be filled with the Spirit" (Ephesians 5:18).

Spiritual Synergism   DAY 17

Several years ago a new breed of horse was tested in Canada. Researchers found that one horse could pull an 8-ton load. When they teamed two horses together, they anticipated that the pair would pull 16 or 18 tons. To their surprise, they pulled a 30-ton load.

This is the principle of synergism. *Synergism* states that two or more objects working together can produce a greater effect than the objects working independently of each other.

Spiritually, the Holy Spirit works in our relationships, creating a spiritual synergism, referred to in Scripture as the principle of unity. Paul says, "Make every effort to keep the unity of the Spirit through the bond of peace" (Ephesians 4:3).

Accomplishing your goals in life depends on your ability to work with others. The word *unity* means "a state of oneness, agreement and coherence; the combination of separate parts into a connected whole; and different people working together for a common purpose."

Jesus underscored the principle of synergism in prayer: "Again, I tell you that if any two of you on earth agree about anything you ask for, it will be done for you by my Father in heaven. For where two or three come together in my name, there am I with them" (Matthew 18:19, 20).

An unusual event occurred at the Special Olympics in Seattle. Nine mentally and physically handicapped runners took their places at the starting line of the 400-meter race. The race began and they ran as hard and as fast as they could. About halfway through the race, one boy fell. He got up and started to run again. Then he fell again.

This time he lay there and started to cry. The other runners heard him, and one by one they stopped running and went back to help him. They picked him up and all of them had to give him a reassuring hug. Then they joined hands and finished the race together.

The crowd and the judges were puzzled. Who won the race? After deliberation, the judges decided to award all nine runners the gold medal.

Don't be a "lone ranger." Get connected with others and discover God's amazing power of spiritual synergism.

Believe in God—Believe in You!   DAY 18

Justice Oliver Wendell Holmes said, "Most people die with their music still in them." You have incredible, untapped potential. You are made in the image of God.

God created you with the potential for greatness. Unfortunately, we get caught in the Charlie Brown syndrome. One day Charlie Brown was talking with Linus about his feelings of inadequacy. "You see, Linus," Charlie moaned, "it goes all the way back to the beginning. The moment I was born and set foot on the stage of life, they took one look at me and said, 'Not right for the part.'"

The truth is, you *are* right for the part. God has given you a part to play in life. So, play it well. God is counting on you. And so are we. Besides, God believes in you, or else He wouldn't have created you. It's time for you to start believing in yourself.

Jesus took 12 of the most unlikely men, transformed them from fishermen, tax collectors and political zealots, into an army of leaders who made the greatest spiritual impact in history. How did Jesus do it? Simple—in the company of sinners, He dreamed of saints. He convinced them they were capable of achieving more with their lives than they ever dreamed possible. And you know what? They did. They not only believed in Him—they believed in themselves.

Here Comes That Dreamer!   DAY 19

Joseph was the young man made famous in the Bible because of his ornamental coat of many colors. He was also a young man with a dream. Nothing can stop a person who has a dream. One day Joseph's brothers, who were jealous of him, commented, "Here comes that dreamer!" (Genesis 37:19). They meant it as a criticism, but it was a great compliment. If you are going to succeed, you need a dream. People need to say about you, "Here comes that dreamer!"

You too need a dream for your life. Martin Luther King Jr. rallied the Civil Rights Movement behind one clarion call, "I have a dream!"

We use the word *dream* in a variety of ways. When we think of dreams, we usually think of dreams in the night. But dreams are also visions, goals and aspirations. George Bernard Shaw said, "Some men see things and say 'Why?' But I dream of things that never were, and I say, 'Why not?'"

Don't think your dreams are beyond your grasp. They're not if you have submitted your dreams to the will of God for your life and if you trust God to help you make your dreams a reality for His glory. Jesus said, "With man this is impossible, but with God all things are possible" (Matthew 19:26).

Make this your affirmation for today: "With God all things are possible!" And your dreams will come true.

You are capable of more than you realize. You are made in God's image (Genesis 1:26), crowned with glory and honor (Psalm 8:5), and given gifts and callings (Romans 11:29).

Jesus says to you, "Follow Me." As you do, He will keep His promise to "make you." We follow—He makes. He shapes us, molds us, and empowers us to reach our God-created potential.

Give your life to Christ today in full surrender to His will. He will give you back your life refined, renewed and refueled to accomplish great things for His glory.

As the great missionary William Carey said, "Expect great things from God—attempt great things for God."

Keep On Dreaming! DAY 20

Yesterday, we talked about the power of youth. Today, let's look at the other side of the coin. The prophet said, "Your old men will dream dreams" (Joel 2:28). It's been said that a man is never old until regrets take the place of his dreams. It's OK to retire from your job, but never retire from life.

Don't be like the man who wrote: "I get up each morning, dust off my wits, pick up the paper, and read the obits. If my name is missing, I know I'm not dead, so I eat a good breakfast—and go back to bed."

You're younger than you think! Moses was 80 when God called him to lead Israel out of Egypt. Michelangelo was writing poetry and designing architecture until the time he died. He painted the ceiling of the Sistine Chapel on his back on a scaffold at nearly 90. Goethe wrote a part of *Faust* at age 60 and finished it at 82.

Daniel Webster wrote his monumental dictionary when he was 70. Verdi produced the famous piece "Ave Maria" at 85. John Wesley preached for 40 years, produced 400 books, knew 10 languages and, at age 86, complained that he was unable to preach more than twice a day. I have a close friend whose father received his doctorate at the "young" age of 76. So, keep on dreaming!

The Fountain of Youth — DAY 21

Augustine searched without success for the fountain of youth. He looked for it around him, when it was actually within him. It is in us all for a brief season. Many people waste their youth. Someone remarked, "Youth is wasted on the young." But young people need to be encouraged to tap into the power of the fountain of youth God has given them. You don't have to wait until you get older to make your life count.

Did you know that most of the people who become Christians do so before they reach age 18? And most people who decide to enter Christian ministry as a career and calling do so before they reach age 21.

Raphael painted his works at a very young age and died at 37. Alfred Tennyson wrote his first work at 18. Victor Hugo was only 17 when he received prizes at a poetry competition and earned the title "Master" before he was 20.

John Calvin joined the Reformation at 21, and at 27 he wrote *The Institutes of the Christian Religion*. Isaac Newton was 24 when he formulated the law of gravity and made some of his greatest discoveries before he was 25. Charles Dickens wrote *Pickwick Papers* at 24 and *Oliver Twist* at 25.

Charles Spurgeon was a powerful preacher in his early 20s, and by age 25 he pastored the largest church in London. Martin Luther King Jr. shook the nation with his call for civil rights while he was still a young man, before being cut down in the prime of his life. And don't forget that Jesus himself had transformed the course of human history by the time He was 33.

God has a special message for young people: "Remember now your Creator in the days of your youth" (Ecclesiastes 12:1). Don't waste your youth—your most valuable years. "Don't let anyone look down on you because you are young, but set an example for the believers in speech, in life, in love, in faith and in purity" (1 Timothy 4:12). So, tap the fountain of youth and use your best years to serve the Lord.

The Lord's Prayer and You   DAY 22

E.M. Bounds observed, "Every Christian who ever did anything for the Lord was characterized by that notable quality called prayer." Everyone wants to pray with power. But how? The Lord's Prayer is our guide. The way we pray shapes the way we live. This anonymous piece explains it best:

I cannot say *Our*, if my religion has no room for others, and their needs.

I cannot say *Father*, if I do not demonstrate this relationship in my daily living.

I cannot say *Who art in heaven*, if all my interests and pursuits are in earthly things.

I cannot say *Hallowed be Thy name*, if I, who am called by His name, am not holy.

I cannot say *Thy kingdom come*, if I am unwilling to give up my own sovereignty and accept the righteous reign of God.

I cannot say *Thy will be done*, if I am unwilling or resentful of having it in my own life.

I cannot say *On earth as it is in heaven*, unless I am truly ready to give myself to His service here and now.

I cannot say *Give us this day our daily bread*, without expending honest effort for it, or by ignoring the genuine needs of my fellowmen.

I cannot say *Forgive us our trespasses, as we forgive those who trespass against us,* if I continue to harbor a grudge against anyone.

I cannot say *Lead us not into temptation,* if I deliberately choose to remain in a situation where I am likely to be tempted.

I cannot say *Deliver us from evil,* if I am not prepared to fight in the spiritual realm with the weapon of prayer.

I cannot say *Thine is the kingdom,* if I do not give the King the disciplined obedience of a loyal subject.

I cannot say *Thine is the power,* if I fear what my neighbors and friends may say or do.

I cannot say *Thine is the glory,* if I am seeking my own glory first.

I cannot say *Forever,* if I am too anxious about each day's affairs. I cannot say *Amen,* unless I honestly say, "Come what may, this is my prayer."

Whatever circumstance, challenge or difficulty you're facing, remember Jesus' promise: "If you believe, you will receive whatever you ask for in prayer" (Matthew 21:22).

A Treasured Possession DAY 23

The greatest challenge every person faces is the identity crisis. Who am I? Where did I come from? Why am I here? These are the basic questions of life we all seek to answer. The way we answer these questions determines how we live.

We all have a working philosophy of life comprised of how we answer these and other vital questions about God, ourselves and the world around us.

If any group of people ever had an identity crisis, it was the Hebrew people. For 400 years they had been slaves in Egypt. They were the labor force for the Egyptian empire, helping to build many of the majestic structures that remain to this day. Generation after generation of Hebrews grew up knowing nothing else but subjugation to the will of Pharaoh.

Then Moses came along. He announced to them that the God of heaven was calling them out of Egypt and would make them into a great and powerful nation. He even backed up his strange message with an elaborate display of miracles.

Sure enough, he brought them out of Egypt. That was easy. The real challenge was getting them into the Promised Land. It's one thing to get out of your problem and another altogether to get into your possession.

After only three months of traveling in the desert, they arrived at the mountain of God, Mount Sinai. Here God gave Moses a message for them that would once and forever resolve their identity crisis so that they would know they were indeed His special people. The Lord said to them, "You will be my treasured possession . . . a kingdom of priests and a holy nation" (Exodus 19:5, 6).

God chose them by grace to be His people. To be chosen means to be special. We are also chosen for a purpose. They were not chosen to the exclusion of others. "The whole earth is mine," God says (v. 5).

The apostle Peter uses this passage from Exodus to describe believers: "You are a chosen people, a royal priesthood, a holy nation, a people belonging to God" (1 Peter 2:9).

Face the opportunities and the challenges of life knowing who you are. You are the Lord's treasured possession. You belong to Him. You can do anything but fail!

The Creation Song   DAY 24

In its broadest definition, *scientific evolution* postulates that the universe and life came into existence by the operation of naturalistic process. Many historians view Darwin's concepts and their application to other areas of life as having fostered racism, devalued human life, and defined the workplace as one of antagonism in which only the fittest survive and excel.

The fossil records, genetics and the reproduction cycle refute the notion that life descended from lower to higher forms through gradual evolutionary changes or even through "punctuated equilibria." Colin Patterson, senior paleontologist at the British Museum of Natural History, has called into question evolutionary theory. He states:

> For the last 18 months or so I have been kicking around non-evolutionary or even anti-evolutionary ideas. For over 20 years I had thought I was working on evolution in some way. One morning I woke up and something had happened in the night,

and it struck me that I had been working on this stuff for more than 20 years, and there was not one thing I knew about it. It's quite a shock to learn that one can be misled for so long. For the last few weeks I have tried putting a simple question to various people and groups: Can you tell me anything you know about evolution? Any one thing . . . that is true?

When he asked that question at the Evolutionary Morphology Seminar in the University of Chicago, all he received was silence for a long time until one person eventually said, "I do know one thing—it ought not be taught in high school."

British astronomer Sir Fred Hoyle, famous for his research on the origins of the universe, claims that believing the first cell originated by chance is like believing a tornado could sweep through a junkyard filled with airplane parts and form a Boeing 747.

Let us begin the day with praise to our heavenly Father, who is our Creator. "In him we live and move and have our being" (Acts 17:28).

Genesis Revisited — DAY 25

Everyone faces the crisis of faith at some point in life. Who is God? What is He like? What is my relationship to God? The crisis of faith is resolved in the Book of Genesis. "In the beginning God created the heavens and the earth" (Genesis 1:1).

At some point, evolution and science part company. Science is limited to research on empirical data postulated philosophically as to how life originated. In this regard, evolution becomes a philosophical or even religious worldview, which calls upon a person to make a faith commitment as to what he or she believes about the origin of life.

In many respects, the Book of Genesis is the most important book in the Bible. Genesis lays the foundations of our faith. Every spiritual question in answered in the Book of Genesis.

Genesis has a profoundly important message for our times. In the midst of a culture that has been baptized in evolutionary philosophy, which has produced widespread negative effects—socially and spiritually—Genesis guides our way back to the fundamental truth of God, His creative power and His redemptive love, which gives our world meaning, purpose and hope.

The Creation song needs to be sung again in our world, which gives us the fundamental facts of faith:

1. God is the ultimate cause and designer of the universe.
2. God created the world ex nihilo—out of nothing—by His own omnipotent word (Genesis 1:3; Hebrews 11:3).
3. God created all living organisms to exist and reproduce within the confines of their species—"after their own kind."
4. God created the earth through both event and process as is illustrated in the account of the seven days of Creation.
5. Humankind reflects a unique quality of life—the image of God—which endows them with transcendence and dominion.
6. God created the world and humanity for the express purpose of bringing glory to Himself (Ephesians 1:3-14).
7. God not only creates life but sustains life, redeems humanity from sin, and watches over creation.

The very beginning point of worship is the response of our love to a loving God who is our Creator, Sustainer, Redeemer and Father.

Born Again   DAY 26

Time magazine once carried a cover story titled "Born Again Faith." A Gallup Poll revealed that in the United States, "more than one-third of those who are old enough to vote have experienced 'born-again' religious conversions."

Jesus spoke of both the possibility and necessity of being born again. Only God can change the emotion of the human heart. A well-to-do religious leader of Judaism approached Jesus to gain a better understanding of His teaching. Christ told him, "Unless one is born again, he cannot see the kingdom of God." Again He said, "You must be born again" (see John 3:1-8).

To be "born again" or, more technically, "born from above" means to experience a spiritual change. This change is a miraculous transformation of human nature by the power of God. The moment we confess our sins to God, repent of that sin and accept Jesus Christ as Lord, the Holy

Spirit works in us the miracle of the new birth. We are changed from death to life, from sin to righteousness, from darkness to light, and from eternal condemnation to eternal life.

To be a Christian is not a self-effort program whereby we attempt to turn over a new leaf and seek to live morally pure. I've listened to people say, "I am going to start trying to be a Christian." I respond, "That's impossible!" A person becomes a Christian by trusting in Jesus' death for sins. It is in trusting, not trying, that we are saved.

John writes, "Yet to all who received him [Jesus], to those who believed in his name, he gave the right to become children of God—children born not of natural descent, nor of human decision or a husband's will, but born of God" (John 1:12, 13).

Salvation is based on four words: "by grace through faith" (Ephesians 2:8). *Grace* simply means that God freely gives us the gift of salvation, the forgiveness of sins and the promise of eternal life when we confess our sins and ask Him to save us. Real life begins at that moment. No amount of good works, religious deeds or spiritual endeavors can save a person. It is only "by grace through faith."

Heaven Can Wait   DAY 27

A growing body of research confirms what the people of God have known for centuries—healing and faith go hand in hand. The medical community is rediscovering the wonderful healing power of faith in God.

Jesus said, "If you believe, you will receive whatever you ask for in prayer" (Matthew 21:22). While charlatans and manipulative "faith healers" will always be around who seek to merchandise the gospel, the healing power of God will always be the inheritance of God's people.

The first letter written in the New Testament is the Book of James. The apostle James teaches us the process of divine healing: "Is any one of you sick? He should call the elders of the church to pray over him and anoint him with oil in the name of the Lord. And the prayer of faith will make the sick person well; the Lord will raise him up" (5:14, 15).

Note the connection between prayer, faith and healing. Hundreds of studies link faith and health. According to research the positive benefits of faith include longer life, overall well-being, better recovery from illness, less chances of heart disease, lower blood pressure, positive mental health including lower rates of anxiety and depression, and reduced stress.

Sickness tends to get our attention. We wake up spiritually, which means trusting God, getting connected with others in a community of support, and getting our priorities in order. There is nothing quite like an illness to cause us to reevaluate our lives in light of eternity.

God uses medical means. The promise of divine healing involves both faith and medicine. God is not limited to human means. But He does choose to use them, and so should we. The first promise of healing is given in Exodus 15:26: "If you listen carefully to the voice of the Lord your God and do what is right in his eyes . . . I will not bring on you any of the diseases I brought on the Egyptians, for I am the Lord, who heals you."

This promise came when God told Moses to cast a piece of wood into the bitter waters of Marah and the waters were healed. Elisha used salt and minerals to cure the waters of Jericho (2 Kings 2:19-22). Isaiah used a poultice of figs to cure the illness of King Hezekiah in conjunction with God's promise of healing (20:4-7). Paul told Timothy to use some wine for his stomach condition (1 Timothy 5:23).

While medical science brings great benefits to our lives, only God can heal. He is Jehovah-Rapha, the Lord our healer.

Quiet Desperation DAY 28

Blaise Pascal wrote, "All men seek happiness. This is without exception. Whatever different means they employ, they all tend to this end. . . . This is the motive of every action of every man, even of those who hang themselves."

Whether you are 7, 17 or 70, you want to be happy. We may call it by different names—success, joy, fulfillment, peace of mind, significance—but we all want it. Americans are preoccupied with happiness. The Declaration of Independence states that we have "the right to life, liberty and the pursuit of happiness." Sadly, many never find happiness. Thoreau remarked, "The mass of men lead lives of quiet desperation."

What is happiness? *Happiness* can be defined as "contentment; satisfaction; being pleased with one's state in life." What does it take to be happy? According to psychological research, Americans identify four key ingredients to happiness: (1) to be loved and accepted, (2) to be comfortable, (3) to have security, and (4) to make a difference.

When the Scripture refers to happiness, it uses the word *blessed.* The Scripture is clear that the key to the secret of happiness is to experience the blessings of God. The blessing of the Lord means the favor of the Lord, literally, "to speak well of." It conveys gifts upon another. The blessing opposes and nullifies the curse of the law and sin. The blessing speaks of the abundance and the enjoyment of life.

David expresses this truth in the first psalm. He begins with "Blessed is the man" (v. 1). *Blessedness* is a gift from God. It is not contingent on one's life situation. No level of adversity or trouble can take away God's blessings.

Here's the key to happiness: "Blessed is the man who does not walk in the counsel of the wicked or stand in the way of sinners or sit in the seat of mockers. But his delight is in the law of the Lord, and on his law he meditates day and night" (vv. 1, 2).

Words That Win   DAY 29

"I know you believe you understand what you think I said, but I'm not sure you realize that what you heard is not what I meant."

This statement illustrates the complexity of communication. *Communication* is "a process by which someone or something is made common, or shared." Communication is verbal and nonverbal. It includes what we say and what we mean, plus what others say to us and what we actually hear. We all listen through personal filters that blur our perception of things.

Healthy communication provides us with richer, fuller and more meaningful relationships. On the other hand, poor communication sours our relationships by division, strife and misunderstanding. Poor communication is a contributing factor in domestic violence, business losses, parent/child conflicts, marital unhappiness, and broken friendships.

Families, friendships, businesses, churches, and even governments rise or fall based on the quality of communication. So how do we improve our communication skills? The Bible speaks forthrightly to the issue. The apostle Paul says, "Do not let any unwholesome talk come out of your mouths, but only what is helpful for building others up according to their needs, that it may benefit those who listen" (Ephesians 4:29).

We have a three-step plan for improving communication skills. First, the quality of our speech should be wholesome. We should avoid inappropriate, unfit, corrupt words. We are to be in the business of building others up, not tearing them down. Second, the motivation of our speech should be to meet each other's needs. All of us share the need to be, to belong and to do. Strive to meet those needs in others. Third, the goal of communication is to build others up. Everyone needs to be encouraged and uplifted.

Some of you grew up like I did hearing your parents say, "If you can't say something good about someone, don't say it at all." That is sound advice we all need to take to heart.

Seek to communicate in this way and watch your relationships flourish. Words are very powerful. Make a new commitment to use the gift of words to advance the kingdom of God and to make the world a better place. "Death and life are in the power of the tongue" (Proverbs 18:21, *NKJV*).

Oct. 2

Inner Peace DAY 30

One day Charlie Brown of the cartoon *Peanuts* noticed that Lucy was in a bad mood. He remarked, "Hey, Lucy, I thought you told me you had inner peace." She snapped back, "I do have inner peace, but I still have outer obnoxiousness."

Jesus promises us inner peace that results in outer pleasantness: "Peace I leave with you; my peace 1 give you. I do not give to you as the world gives. Do not let your hearts be troubled and do not be afraid" (John 14:27).

Dr. Jeff Rockwell identifies important symptoms of inner peace:
1. A tendency to think and act spontaneously rather than from fears based on past experiences

2. An unmistakable ability to enjoy each moment
3. A loss of interest in judging self
4. A loss of interest in judging others
5. A loss of interest in conflict
6. A loss of interest in interpreting the actions of others
7. A loss of ability to worry (a very serious symptom)
8. Frequent, overwhelming episodes of appreciation
9. Contented feelings of connectedness with others and nature
10. Frequent attacks of smiling through the eyes of the heart
11. Increasing susceptibility to love extended by others as well as the uncontrollable urge to extend it

How can we cultivate peace? First, *be at peace with God.* Sin troubles our relationship with our heavenly Father. When we confess our sin and receive His forgiveness, we experience peace. "Therefore being justified by faith, we have peace with God" (Romans 5:1, KJV).

Second, *calm your fears by surrendering your worries to God.* "Do not be anxious about anything, but in everything, by prayer and petition, with thanksgiving, present your requests to God." When you do, "the peace of God, which transcends all understanding, will guard your hearts and your minds in Christ Jesus" (Philippians 4:6, 7).

I once heard if you don't bother God, everything else will bother you. Bother God with your problems, and His peace will guard your heart.

"May the Lord of peace himself give you peace at all times and in every way" (2 Thessalonians 3:16).

Making Decisions   DAY 31

Decisions . . . decisions . . . decisions. Every day we make them. Big ones. Small ones. Significant ones. Insignificant ones. Our chief concern is making right decisions. By *right* we mean God's *best* for our lives.

The central issue in making decisions is gaining the wisdom of God. *Wisdom* is the ability to know what to do in a given situation. In the Old Testament the Hebrew word *chokmah* means the ability to handle life in a God-honoring way and the skill for godly living.

Some important basic principles need to be underscored. The will of

God must be differentiated from the wisdom of God. God does not have a specific will for every decision we face; therefore, more than one "right" choice often exists. The Holy Spirit gives a sense of direction regarding which choices are best for us as opposed to making our decisions for us. We must still take the "leap of faith" after hearing from God. This is why James talks about faith after he talks about wisdom (James 1:5, 6).

The Holy Spirit directs us into the specific will of God in those matters related to Kingdom work, as seen in God specifically sending Jonah to preach in Nineveh. Finally, God created us with the freedom and responsibility of choice. He desires for us to exercise these privileges based on the counsel of His Word. So how can we make wise decisions?

First, submit to the will of God in every area of your life (Matthew 26:36-42). Second, search the Scriptures (2 Timothy 3:14-17) on personal, family, financial and career issues. Third, seek godly counsel (Proverbs 11:14). Fourth, sort out your options by . . .

- Listing options in priority of choice
- Analyzing pros and cons, rewards and consequences
- Evaluating the plausibility of each option
- Playing out mentally the long-term outcome of possibilities
- Selecting the best option and assuming responsibility and ownership of your choice.

Several questions are always appropriate when making decisions. Ask yourself: Is this decision Scripturally sound? Is this the proper time? What do wise counselors say? What will be the results of my decision? Do I have a sense of peace and satisfaction about my decision?

When you have asked these questions and prayed about each choice, you will make the right decision.

Making Peace With Your Past   DAY 32

Since the day of modern psychology, much attention has been given to the study of human behavior. The field of psychology continues to make advancements in this area. *Psychology* can be defined as the study of human behavior in a social context. What motivates human behavior? Why do we act the way we do?

Several schools of thought exist. Some say we act the way we do because of the influence of the past, especially our childhood. Others say we act the way we do because of environmental conditioning of behavior learned through the process of positive and negative reinforcement. Others theorize we act the way we do in order to have our needs met. Still others state that we act the way we do because of future goals. There is truth in each of these approaches. We act the way we do because of the past, environmental conditioning, our basic needs and our future goals.

Let's focus on the role the past plays in influencing present behavior. The role of the past is often overemphasized. Many people blame their past for their present problems and conflicts. As a result, they never really face up to their personal responsibilities. Statements like, "I'm this way because . . ." fill their vocabulary.

Even though a person's past may have been difficult, each individual must decide the extent to which his or her past will continue to influence the present. In reality, the only influence the past has on us is the manner in which we choose to let it influence us. A person who was criticized as a child does not have to criticize his or her children. Because someone was raised with alcoholic parents does not mean that person is destined to become an alcoholic. On the other hand, because someone was raised in a good, stable, loving home does not ensure that his or her home life will follow suit. The real issue of life is the choices we make. The past can have either a positive or negative impact on our present choices.

Emotional, social and spiritual adjustment is not a matter of "working through" the past, but deciding to what extent and in what ways these adjustments will influence your life today. You are free in Christ to forget the things that are behind and reach for the things that are ahead (Philippians 3:13, 14).

Remember, where you're going is more important than where you've been.

Oct 5th

Managing Time   DAY 33

Mill Rogers used to say, "It's not so much what you do each day, it's what you get done that counts." Aristotle Onassis was asked to share the secret of his success. He replied, "I have learned the value and importance of time; therefore, I work two additional hours each day and in that way I gain the equivalent of one additional month each year."

Time is our most valuable commodity. Success boils down to time management. "Be very careful, then, how you live—not as unwise but as wise, making the most of every opportunity, because the days are evil" (Ephesians 5:15, 16).

I will always remember the first sermon I preached. I was 15 years old. I preached in a youth service at our church. The sermon was titled "Time." About the only thing I remember is the overwhelming sense of anxiety awaiting my time to deliver the sermon. I felt like I was walking the green mile to my tragic end.

Time management is important to us all. Many "time robbers" threaten us every day: procrastination, poor scheduling, lack of clear priorities, unconcern about time management.

Partners With God   DAY 34

After graduating from college, I headed out west to California. I became an evangelist, preaching revivals from church to church. I lived for the first few months in the small town of Lakeside, outside of San Diego. I assisted the pastor and his wife—who were well up in years—with their small congregation. They were affectionately known as Brother and Sister Thompson. The church facilities consisted simply of a small sanctuary, fellowship hall and two Sunday school classrooms—all on two acres of land.

The Thompsons were great people—salt-of-the-earth types—who had given everything they owned for the gospel. They lived in the back of that little church, in one of the Sunday school classrooms. Reverend Thompson had grown up in a life of crime. He told me one day about some money that his gang had stolen from a bank that was still buried on Lookout Mountain and had been lost. His wife was the spiritual influence in his life when they were first married.

I was given a sofa bed to sleep on in the fellowship hall, but I only got to use it three nights. I arrived back to the church one afternoon only to find that she had sold my bed in a rummage sale to make some money for the church. They gave me an army cot in its place.

Every morning I woke up with a backache from sleeping on that cot with the sound of *Good Morning America* blaring from the television. She cooked a hot breakfast in the kitchen of the fellowship hall every morning with bacon, eggs and homemade biscuits.

Pastor Thompson and I were always working on the church, building something or fixing something. One day I casually remarked, "You know, it's fantastic what God has done here. He has developed this property and established this church."

He spun around and looked at me as though he was offended by what I said. He said rather assuredly, "Let me tell you something, young man, you should've seen this place when God had it by Himself!" That was the day I learned that we are partners with God.

"Then God said, 'Let us make man in our image, in our likeness, and let them rule over the fish of the sea and the birds of the air, over the livestock, over all the earth, and over all the creatures that move along the ground'" (Genesis 1:26).

In His Image   DAY 35

One of the most magnificent statements that validates our human dignity is found in Genesis 1:27: "God created man in his own image."

What does it mean to be made in the image of God? The word *create* is used in the Creation account only three times—and only in reference to God. But we are to partner with Him in the ongoing stewardship of the Earth. Man is the servant of God to care for the earth. Humanity bears the likeness of God in four primary ways:

1. *The mental image.* We have the capacity of intellect, emotion and will.
2. *The moral image.* We are endowed with conscience; an innate sense of right and wrong; the law of God is written on our hearts.
3. *The social image.* We are created for personal interaction with God and others. "It is not good for the man to be alone" (2:18).

4. *The spiritual image.* We have a need for communion with God. Augustine prayed: "Our hearts were made for You, O God, and they will not rest until they rest in You."

Just as God is our Creator, He has given us the power to create. We can dream, plan, build, develop and invent. He expects us to use what He has given us to build a better world. Everything in the world today, beyond all God made in the seven days of Creation, has been built by human hands, guided by the Spirit of God.

You have unlimited potential, but it takes creativity, hard work and perseverance to reach your potential. The Genesis Commission is God's purpose and blessing for everyone. God expects us to do four things by which to honor Him: "Be fruitful . . . increase . . . fill . . . and subdue" (1:28).

Overcoming Temptation DAY 36

Known as the silver-tongued orator of Rome, he was a great statesman and a courageous warrior. As far as personal qualities are concerned, he could have been a world ruler. His name was Mark Anthony. In spite of his notable qualities, he possessed a great moral flaw. On one occasion his personal tutor shouted in his face, "Oh, Marcus, Oh colossal child! Able to conquer the world, but unable to resist a temptation!"

Temptation. Now there's a word we all know about. We've all been there when we have vowed to say no but, in the hour of temptation, said yes. We've felt the guilt, the shame and the disappointment. The hour of temptation reveals the strength of our character. *Character* has been defined as what you would do in a given situation if you knew you would never be caught.

Can we do what Mark Anthony failed to do? I'm sure we all remember the story of Joseph. His brothers were jealous of him and sold him into slavery. Eventually he became the personal steward of Potiphar, one of Pharaoh's officials in Egypt.

Then his commitment to God was severely tested. Potiphar's wife tried to seduce him. Joseph learned to say no. From his example we learn principles for overcoming temptation (see Genesis 39:1-12).

1. *Be on guard.* When we become too self-reliant, overconfident, and lack discernment, we yield to temptation. Jesus said, "Watch and pray so that you will not fall into temptation" (Matthew 26:41).
2. *Look beyond immediate gratification to the ultimate consequences.* Sure, there is pleasure in sin for a short time. Then comes the aftermath of sin. Living for immediate gratification results in long-term negative consequences.
3. *Avoid vulnerable situations.* Do not set yourself up for a fall. Watch the company you keep, the places you go, and the activities in which you participate. Stay away from tempting situations.
4. *Run.* Joseph ran out of the house when Potiphar's wife grabbed him and said, "Come to bed with me!" There is one word for people who stay around and try to reason with temptation: *victim.* Don't be a victim, be a victor!

"So, if you think you are standing firm, be careful that you don't fall!" (1 Corinthians 10:12).

Stillness Under Stress   DAY 37

A recent survey indicated that 82 percent of Americans felt they needed less stress in their lives. The following statistics are attributed to the real or imagined stress confronting people today:

- More than 1 million people have heart attacks each year.
- One out of every 10 Americans is an alcoholic.
- It is estimated that 8 million people have ulcers.
- Some 25 million people have high blood pressure.
- Stress-related mental disorders account for a $17 billion decline in production annually.
- More than $60 billion have been lost due to stress-related physical disorders.
- One out of five Americans will experience a heart attack before age 60.

It's stressful just reading a list of statistics like that! We deal with stress from the moment we enter this world until the moment we leave. Children face the stress of learning, parental demands, and entry into school. Teenagers are continually exposed to the unrelenting stress of peer pressure, identity issues, and the search for meaning. Young adulthood brings the stress of career choices, marriage and early parenting. Singles face the stress of delayed marriage, divorce and single-parenting. The executive faces the pressure of increasing demands to stay on top. The factory worker faces the pressure of monotony. Retirement sees the stress of financial security. On and on the list goes.

God has something to say about our stress: "Keep silence before me, O islands; and let the people renew their strength" (Isaiah 41:1, KJV). We need a sense of inner strength to combat the external stress of our times.

One of the earliest definitions of the word *cope* was "to meet and contend with in combat." Life is like a fight, and constant pressure is an enemy that we must master before it masters us.

How do we maintain such inner strength so that we do not collapse under pressure? God says, "Keep silent before Me." We need to be still, silent and restful. We need to pull away from the hustle and bustle of life and reevaluate our priorities, restructure our lives and replenish our resources.

Find time today for stillness and silent meditation before the Lord, and renew your strength.

In All Circumstances! DAY 38

Cicero, the Roman poet, said, "Thanksgiving is not only the greatest virtue, it is the parent of all other virtues."

Gratitude is a discipline that has to be developed. It is so easy to fall into patterns of negativism. Criticism, complaining and ingratitude seem to come so easy. Being thankful is a virtue we have to cultivate and a habit we need to develop.

The apostle Paul gave the following admonition to the Thessalonian believers: "Give thanks in all circumstances, for this is God's will for you in Christ Jesus" (1 Thessalonians 5:18). We might have liked that admonition better if Paul had left out the words "in all circumstances."

We are all taught to express gratitude when we receive a gift. Anyone can be positive when everything is going right. Can we be as positive "in all circumstances"? Now that's a different story.

The only way to develop the gratitude attitude is to change our perspective on life. When faced with adversity, criticism or an unpleasant circumstance, our focus must never be on the circumstances but on God who reigns over all.

The Old Testament prophet Habakkuk suffered a crisis of faith, asking God why had bad things happened to God's people. But he resolved his crisis by faith, by giving thanks, and by changing his perspective:

Though the fig tree does not bud and there are no grapes on the vines, though the olive crop fails and the fields produce no food, though there are no sheep in the pen and no cattle in the stalls, *yet* I will rejoice in the Lord, I will be joyful in God my Savior (3:17, 18).

That little word *yet* contains a wealth of truth. We can choose to exercise faith and maintain a thankful spirit, regardless of the circumstances. When we do, we experience joy unspeakable. The choice is ours.

Attitude Determines Altitude   DAY 39

Let me share some sound advice with you—your attitude determines your altitude. You and I never rise any higher than our attitude toward God, others, life and even ourselves.

Gratitude is the attitude that elevates your altitude to a new level. "Rejoice evermore" (1 Thessalonians 5:16, KJV). "Always giving thanks to God the Father for everything" (Ephesians 5:20).

Thankful people are happy. We tend to look in the wrong place for happiness. Happiness comes from giving, not receiving. As we express gratitude, give the gift of encouragement, and maintain a positive stance in life, happiness comes our way.

Thankful people are healthy. It is amazing to consider that 50 percent to 70 percent of all beds in hospitals are filled with individuals suffering emotional and psychological hurts. There is no way to be physically healthy if our attitudes are sick. Attitudes of ingratitude, criticism, cynicism, negativism and doubt impair health. Healthy living starts on the inside with a thankful heart.

Thankful people are helpful. When we withdraw into a shell of isolation, we get depressed. We view the world in a negative fashion, and we grow cynical, critical and judgmental. We come up with a long list of gripes and grievances against others.

A thankful spirit brings us out of ourselves. The only way to keep negative attitudes out is to keep positive attitudes in. Gratitude takes our eyes off ourselves and places them on the needs of others.

You can develop the gratitude attitude by a simple act of obedience: "Give thanks in all circumstances" (1 Thessalonians 5:18).

As a Man Thinks   DAY 40

Solomon wrote, "As [a man] thinks in his heart, so is he" (Proverbs 23:7, *NKJV*). How we think determines our attitudes, values, beliefs, behavior and life philosophy. There is simply no way to overstate the power of our thoughts.

People throughout the ages have continued to recognize the power of thoughts. Virgil, the Roman poet, said, "They can because they think they can." Ralph Waldo Emerson said, "A man is what he thinks about all day long," and "the key to every man is his thoughts."

The key to a triumphant thought life is controlling the input. The human brain is like a computer. It functions only on programmed data. We receive cognitive data from everything we experience.

For example, think about the power of television to shape our thoughts. The A.C. Nielsen Company, major broadcast rating firm in the United States, reports: The average amount of television viewing time per individual in the United States is 24 hours weekly. Children average over 30 hours per week in front of the television. By the time children reach school age, they have watched over 25,000 commercials. By the time most of us graduate from high school, we will have spent 50 percent more time watching television than in the classroom or having quality experiences with our families and parents.

Dennis Waitley, in *10 Seeds of Greatness*, asks, "If a 60-second commercial, by repeated viewing, can sell us a product, then isn't it possible for a 60-minute soap opera or 'smut.com,' by repeated viewing, to sell us a lifestyle?" We are being sold a lifestyle through television, movies and literature in many quarters that is contrary to how God designed us to live.[2]

Studies by a Stanford University research team have revealed that "what we watch" affects our imaginations, learning and behavior patterns. By "repeated viewing" and "repeated verbalizing," we shape our future and determine our destiny.

Here is a more excellent way: "Finally, brothers, whatever is true, whatever is noble, whatever is right, whatever is pure, whatever is lovely, whatever is admirable—if anything is excellent or praiseworthy—think about such things" (Philippians 4:8).

Caught Between Two Worlds   DAY 41

We are caught between two worlds: the world that is and the world that is to come. The world system is permeated with evil, rebels against God (James 4:4) and is destined for judgment (2 Peter 3:10). The world that is to come is described in Scripture as "a new heaven and a new earth, the home of righteousness" (v. 13).

We know that "our citizenship is in heaven. And we eagerly await a Savior from there, the Lord Jesus Christ, who, by the power that enables him to bring everything under his control, will transform our lowly bodies so that they will be like his glorious body" (Philippians 3:20, 21).

We need an eternal perspective in a temporal world. One of the most detrimental teachings of our times is that if we exercise enough faith we can have heaven on earth.

But Paul tells us, "We wait eagerly for our adoption as sons, the redemption of our bodies . . . we wait for it patiently" (Romans 8:23, 25). The promise of full redemption will be fulfilled when Jesus returns and establishes the kingdom of God on the earth. Currently, we enjoy the down payment of our eternal inheritance but not its fullness.

While we live in this present world, we are sealed with the Holy Spirit, "who is a deposit guaranteeing our inheritance" (Ephesians 1:13, 14). A deposit guarantees that the full inheritance of eternal life is yet to come.

The tension of being caught between two worlds is resolved when we do two things: First, make every day count, and second, fill each day with hope knowing that heaven is our ultimate destination.

Lord, Teach Us to Pray

Oct. 14th

What aspect of Jesus' life and ministry do you think would impress you most? We would all be captivated by His miracles. Feeding 5,000 with a sack lunch was quite a feat! Israel was filled with Jesus' miracles by the time His ministry ended. I'm also confident we would be captivated by His teaching, "Never [a] man spake like this man" (John 7:46, KJV), the Temple guards remarked. We would be stirred by His compassion, unconditional love and acceptance of every person.

But I am convinced that we would be most impressed by His prayer life. This is why the disciples said, "Lord, teach us to pray" (Luke 11:1).

He maintained the habit of prayer. He prayed early in the morning (Mark 1:35), in the hills in the evening (6:46), in solitary places (Luke 5:16), all night (6:12), in private (9:18), and in the Garden of Gethsemane (22:41-44). Christ modeled a pattern of prayer. The Lord's Prayer (Matthew 6:9-13) is more than just a pattern for prayer; it is a pattern for life. The way we pray determines how we live.

This, then, is how we should pray, Jesus instructed:

> Our Father in heaven,
> hallowed be your name,
> your kingdom come, your will be done
> on earth as it is in heaven.
> Give us today our daily bread.
> Forgive us our debts,
> as we also have forgiven our debtors.
> And lead us not into temptation,
> but deliver us from the evil one.

Make it your habit to pray the Lord's Prayer every day. You will discover its incredible power as its principles and promises become woven into the fabric of your soul. The Lord's Prayer will change you and change the world around you. We've all heard the adage, "Practice what you preach." In the same way, let us practice what we pray.

The ABCs of Faith

The watchword of the Christian life is *by faith*. "We live by faith, not by sight" (2 Corinthians 5:7). Faith is a relationship with God. Here are the ABCs of faith:

Faith acknowledges Jesus as Lord. Faith begins when you intellectually believe that Jesus is who He claimed to be—the Son of God, the Messiah and Lord. "If you confess with your mouth, 'Jesus is Lord,' and believe in your heart that God raised him from the dead, you will be saved" (Romans 10:9).

We make a mistake when we downplay the intellectual side of faith. Faith is not blind. It is highly rational. Faith is based on the historical and factual evidence of Jesus Christ, the risen Lord.

A person has to come to terms with the claims of Jesus. Faith, then, begins with a revelation of Jesus as the Son of God.

C.S. Lewis, the noted Oxford scholar, became a Christian through his intellectual investigation of the claims of Jesus. After his research, he concluded that Jesus either had to be a liar of epidemic proportions, a lunatic running around claiming to be the Messiah, or Lord. Lewis put his faith in Jesus and became a great influence for Christ, writing such classics as *The Screwtape Letters* and *Mere Christianity.*

Faith believes in Jesus as Savior. Emotionally, we trust Him to save us from sin and to give us eternal life. "For it is with your heart that you believe and are justified [that means, declared righteous before God, pardoned of all sins], and it is with your mouth that you confess and are saved. As the Scripture says, " 'Anyone who trusts in him will never be put to shame' " (Romans 10:10, 11).

Trust is emotional as well as intellectual. Peace comes to the human heart when we totally trust Christ not only to save us, but to keep us through every situation of life.

Faith commits everything to Jesus in full devotion. First the mind, then the emotions; and finally, the human will submits to Christ as Lord. The fruit of faith is obedience to the will of God. Jesus said, "If you love me, you will obey what I command" (John 14:15).

Faith starts with a revelation of Christ and results in a revolution as we seek to imitate Christ in every area of our lives. "This is how we know we are in him: Whoever claims to live in him must walk as Jesus did" (1 John 2:5, 6). WWJD? It's more than jewelry; it's a way of life. Faith is a revolution in a person's life bringing the total person to conformity to the image of Christ.

The Forgiveness Factor DAY 44

Someone hurt you and you cannot forget it. You did nothing to deserve the hurt, yet it lodges deep within your heart, slowly sabotaging your joy. You want to resolve it. But how?

We have heard that time heals all things—but experience and rationale quickly reveal this isn't always the case. In fact, the longer we harbor our hurts and unresolved conflicts, the worse the situation becomes.

The Jewish philosopher Hannah Arendt, in *The Human Condition*, said that the only power capable of stopping the stream of painful memories is the "faculty of forgiveness." But forgiveness seems virtually impossible at times.

How can we express forgiveness to those who have hurt us? We are to love, "forgiving each other, just as in Christ God forgave you" (Ephesians 4:32). Here we find two important steps in the forgiveness process.

First, *forgiveness toward others begins by experiencing forgiveness from God*. The cross of Christ is God's forgiveness for the sin of the whole world. He died for our sins; therefore, we stand forgiven. To *forgive* means "to cancel the debt." The result is that we are pardoned by God on the basis of what Christ has done.

We are forgiven! Consider this incredible truth: "God was in Christ reconciling the world to Himself, not counting their trespasses against them" (2 Corinthians 5:19, *NASB*). To be reconciled means to restore a broken relationship. We are reconciled to God through His forgiveness expressed at Calvary.

If God has so freely forgiven us, should we not forgive others even as He has forgiven us? When we come to see ourselves as forgiven people, we will be more likely to freely forgive others.

Second, *to truly forgive is to forgive just as God has forgiven us*. Focus on the words "just as." Here is our pattern. We forgive exactly the way God forgives. He forgives freely, joyfully, without reservation, without favoritism, and without limit. There is no limit to God's forgiveness. He never tires of forgiving. We have all been forgiven once for all in the Cross. All we must do is accept it by faith as a free gift. Just as God generously forgives us, we are to forgive each other.

When we forgive, we are free!

The Power of the Blessing

When you hear the word *blessing*, what comes to your mind? We say the blessing over a meal or pray that God will bless others. The Hebrew word *bless* (*barak*), occurs 330 times in the Bible and means "to kneel, to honor, to bless." The New Testament Greek verb, *eulogeo*, means "to speak well of," and is used in reference to praising God, as well as the blessings God bestows upon us.

Parents and grandparents are to bestow the blessing of the Lord on their children and grandchildren. To bless other persons means to honor and praise them and to seek their highest good (Hebrews 11:20, 21).

Did you know that one-third of the 5 million touch receptors in your body are centered in your hands? A study done by UCLA shows that a person needs 8 to 10 meaningful touches each day to maintain emotional and physical health. Dr. Dolores Krieger, professor of nursing at New York University, has made numerous studies on the physical benefits from the laying on of hands. Inside our bodies is hemoglobin, the pigment of the red blood cells, which carries oxygen to other tissues. Dr. Krieger has found that, during the act of the laying on of hands, hemoglobin levels in our bloodstream rise in both the giver and the recipient. Increased levels of hemoglobin mean more oxygen to body tissues, which aids in the regeneration process when someone is ill.

The blessing of the Lord is to be spoken. Remember, the word *blessing* means "honor." The greatest gift we can give others is praise, which builds their confidence, self-esteem and dignity. The blessing contains a prophetic element. Blessings help shape our destiny.

Receive the blessing today: "The Lord bless you and keep you; the Lord make his face shine upon you and be gracious to you; the Lord turn his face toward you and give you peace" (Numbers 6:24-26).

oct 18

Nevertheless

Every day we choose to live by fear or by faith. Fear is a feeling of alarm, anxiety, dread or terror. Fear has a profound negative effect on us. Fear stifles creativity, immobilizes action, hinders prayer, damages relationships, paralyzes decision making and jeopardizes health. Fear is a reaction to a real or perceived threat to our security.

Faith is an action independent of circumstances. Fear is based on what is happening around us. Faith is based on what is happening within us. Fear says, "What if?" Faith says, "Nevertheless!" We can define faith as the *nevertheless* principle.

Faith gives an unflinching hope in times of despair. Our world is filled with hopeless people. We all face apparent hopeless situations at one time or another in our lives. But in Christ nothing is hopeless. *Hope* is "a confident expectation based on certain fundamental truths and actions." It is the most fundamental truth in the faithfulness of God.

Faith is unreserved commitment in times of disloyalty. Jesus faced the crisis of the cross with commitment (Matthew 26:39). No sooner did He finish praying than the disciples deserted Him. This spiritual commitment stood firm to do the will of God—"nevertheless."

Faith means unfailing faith in times of failure. When Simon Peter first met Jesus, he had spent all night fishing. He and his buddies caught nothing. It was a time of failure. Jesus told them to throw their nets in once again. Although Peter was exhausted and probably wanted to go home, he said, "Nevertheless at Your word I will let down the net" (Luke 5:5, *NKJV*). A great catch of fish was the result. Sure he had failed on his own, but he said the faith word, *nevertheless!*

You may be at a point of failure in your life, business, marriage or relationships, but Jesus can enable you to move from failure to fulfillment as you trust Him.

Add this powerful word to your vocabulary, *nevertheless.* When tempted to fall into fear and say, "What if?," stand up in faith and say, "Nevertheless!"

The Law of the Harvest   DAY 47

Everywhere we look, we discover laws that govern the universe. These laws are fixed, absolute and predictable. We toss an object into the air, it falls to the ground, and we call it the law of gravity. We board a plane, it rises into the clouds, and we call it the law of aerodynamics.

We have a built-in sense of "oughtness," an inner voice distinguishing right from wrong, and we call it the law of conscience. God has established laws to govern our universe ranging from matter to men, from planets to people, and from atoms to attitudes.

These are the laws of the kingdom of God. When we keep them, life works for us. When we break them, life works against us. God's rule is eternally established. We don't break the laws of God, they break us! Or better yet, they make us as we keep them.

Just as God has established physical laws, He has established spiritual laws. These too are fixed, absolute and predictable. The Bible is the law of God.

One of the most interesting of all spiritual laws is the law of the harvest. This law applies to every area of life spiritually, socially, financially and physically. "Do not be deceived: God cannot be mocked. A man reaps what he sows" (Galatians 6:7).

We reap what we sow. It works both positively and negatively. I once read the statement that some people sow their wild oats six days of the week, attend church on Sunday and pray for a crop failure. But the crop always comes up.

Tomorrow we will continue our thoughts on the law of the harvest. Today, let us consider carefully that we get out of life exactly what we put in it. If we don't like the return, let's reconsider the investment.

Sowing and Reaping   DAY 48

Oct 26

If you don't like what you're getting out of your life, then change what you are putting into it. The law of sowing and reaping determines the quality of our lives.

Yesterday, we learned that we reap what we sow. Today let's look at three more principles of the law of the harvest.

We reap the same kind that we sow. Genesis tells us that all things produce after their own kind. If you plant corn you get a harvest of corn, not wheat. But the issue for us is whether we sow to the flesh or to the Spirit. I ran across some startling statistics recently concerning child abuse in America. Did you know that one out of every 10 children will be sexually abused this year? That one out of every four girls and one out of every seven boys will be sexually abused before 18 years of age. This is the product of a nation sowing to the flesh and reaping a corrupt harvest.

We reap in a different season than we sow. There is a time to sow and a time to reap. This is certainly evident in child-rearing. Proverbs 22:6

says, "Train up a child in the way he should go, and when he is old he will not depart from it" (*NKJV*). The raising and harvesting of godly children follows a diligent season of spiritual training.

We reap if we persevere. I am firmly convinced that most of us give up too soon in our life's pursuits. The majority of divorces in this country happen during the first five years of marriage. Giving up too soon!

James J. Corbett, former heavyweight boxing champion, when asked what advice he would give to young aspiring fighters, said: "Fight one more round! When your arms are so tired that you can hardly lift your hands, fight one more round. When your nose is bleeding and your eyes are black and you are so tired that you wish your opponent would crack you on the jaw and put you to sleep, fight one more round, remembering that the man who always fights one more round is never whipped."

Put the law of the harvest to work in your life and reap an abundant harvest.

What Fools These Mortals Be   DAY 49

"What fools these mortals be," wrote Shakespeare. How foolish we are when God is not the center of our lives and we make the self central.

The foolishness of sin was illustrated recently when a couple in York, Pennsylvania, named their newborn daughter, "Atheist Evolution." George, the father, said that the name was their reaction to the popularity of Biblical names. He said, "There's so many people named Christian or Christina. This is just one person named Atheist. What the heck's the difference?"[3]

David describes the foolishness of sin:

> The fool says in his heart, "There is no God." They are corrupt, their deeds are vile; there is no one who does good. The Lord looks down from heaven on the sons of men to see if there are any who understand, any who seek God. All have turned aside, they have together become corrupt; there is no one who does good, not even one. Will evildoers never learn—those who devour my people as men eat bread and who do not call on the Lord? There they are, overwhelmed with dread, for God is present in the company of the righteous (Psalm 14:1-5).

The Bible uses the term *fool* to refer to a person who is morally and spiritually deficient. When we are out of fellowship with God—going our own way, making our own choices, legislating our own morality, and fashioning our own gods—we become utterly foolish.

In the midst of such foolishness, God speaks a word of hope: "Be still, and know that I am God" (46:10). Let us worship Him, trust Him, and obey Him, for He alone is God.

Why Are You So Fearful?　　　　　DAY 50

The question is one worth asking. We all battle fear. Fear is a feeling of dread, alarm, panic and anxiety. Fear ranges from mild anxiety to panic attacks. The psychiatric association has categorized a variety of phobias, such as acrophobia, claustrophobia and agoraphobia.

Where does fear come from? Research indicates that we are born with only two fears—the fear of falling and the fear of loud noises. All other fears are learned responses.

Jesus put His finger on the root cause of fear. One night the disciples were caught in a furious squall on the sea. But Jesus was fast asleep. They awoke Him and shouted anxiously, "Teacher, don't you care if we drown?" (Mark 4:38).

Jesus got up, rebuked the sea: "Quiet! Be still!" Then the storm subsided. He said to His disciples, "Why are you so afraid? Do you still have no faith?" (vv. 39, 40).

The root cause of fear is insecurity. They doubted His love. They had been with Him for several years, seen His miracles, listened to His teachings and experienced His provision. Still, they had no faith.

Sure, they had a measure of faith—as we all do. But they hadn't developed deep roots of faith in the soil of His love. So, they were fearful. And so are we.

Somewhere along the line, if we are going to conquer fear, we will have to settle two basic questions of faith: Does God exist? Does God care about me? Listen to Hebrews 11:6: "And without faith it is impossible to please God, because anyone who comes to him must believe that he exists and that he rewards those who earnestly seek him."

Peter encourages us to drown our fears in the sea of God's care: "Cast all your anxiety on him because he cares for you" (1 Peter 5:7). We can set our fearful hearts at rest in His presence when we truly know and rely on the love God has for us.

Real Christians   DAY 51

When you hear the word *Christian*, what comes to your mind? Today the word is used so lightly and in such varied contexts that we are prone to ask, "Will the real Christians please stand up?"

The word *Christian* comes from two words: *Christ* and *man*. A man living in Christ and Christ living in a person creates a dynamic relationship. Adolf Deissmann, a German theologian, suggests that the word *Christian* means "slave of Christ" in the same way that the word *Caesarean* means "slave of Caesar."

What is a Christian? *Letter to Diognetus*, which dates to the second century A.D., describes early Christians:

> Christians are not differentiated from other people by country, language or custom. They live in both Greek and foreign cities, wherever chance has put them. They follow local customs in clothing, food, and the other aspects of life. But at the same time, they demonstrate to us the unusual form of their own citizenship. They live in their own native lands, but as aliens. . . . Every foreign country is to them as their native country, and every native land as a foreign country.
>
> They marry and have children just like everyone else, but they do not kill unwanted babies. They offer a shared table, but not a shared bed. They are passing their days on earth, but are citizens of heaven. They obey the appointed laws and go beyond the law in their own lives.
>
> They love everyone, but are persecuted by all. They are put to death and gain life. They are poor yet make many rich. They are dishonored and yet gain glory through dishonor. Their names are blackened and yet they are cleared. They are mocked and bless in return. They are treated outrageously and behave respectfully to others. When they do good, they are punished as evildoers; when punished, they rejoice as if being given new life.

From Stress to Strength

Stress has become public enemy number one to our happiness and our health. Stress-related health problems such as ulcers, high blood pressure and heart attacks cost the American economy $200 billion a year in absenteeism, insurance claims and medical costs.

Stress is a state of mental, emotional and physical tension. When we get stressed out, we lose our enthusiasm and our motivation. Life comes to a grinding halt. We can barely muster enough energy to get out of bed in the morning and go to work. Stress overload leaves us fatigued, feeling like we're running on empty. We lose our desire and passion for life. How do you go from stress to strength?

1. *Refocus your energy on your goals.* Sit down and write out your plan of action. Get your life back on track. Quit being driven by the tyranny of the urgent and get back to doing what is important. The apostle Paul says, "Make the most of every opportunity because the days are evil" (see Ephesians 5:16). Stop floundering and start focusing!

2. *Replenish your spiritual and emotional resources.* Don't allow yourself to run on empty too long. Take a mini-vacation. Go to church. Read a good motivational book. You have to feed your mind and heart just as you do your body. Inner renewal is the antidote to burnout.

3. *Renew your hope.* I once read that hope is the confident expectation based on certain fundamental truths and actions. Those fundamental truths and actions are the promises of God. Take time to find promises of God in Scripture that relate to the important situation, decisions and opportunities you are facing. Remember, "with God all things are possible" (Matthew 19:26).

Believe God's promise today and move from stress to strength: " 'For I know the plans I have for you,' declares the Lord, 'plans to prosper you and not to harm you, plans to give you hope and a future' " (Jeremiah 29:11).

The Power of Patience

DAY 53

I heard a story about an Englishman who visited the United States years ago to see what made Americans tick. He made three different visits. After his first visit he concluded that we are driven by a compulsion for wealth. After his second visit he concluded that we are driven by a compulsion for power. After his third visit he concluded that we are driven by a compulsion for speed.

He was right. We live in the fast lane. We are somewhat like the hurried businessman who came dashing out of the office building, hailed a cab and began to shout, "Go man! Go! Go!" The driver looked around rather confused and asked, "Where?" The businessman replied, "Anywhere, man, anywhere! I've got business everywhere!"

But then Jesus confronts our fast-lane living: "In your patience possess ye your souls" (Luke 21:19, KJV). Somewhere along the line we've got to come to terms with the value of patience. One man did and said, "I got out of the rat race. The rats won!"

But what does Jesus mean when He says, "In your patience possess ye your souls"? He means that patience is the power of self-control. The problem so many of us face is a lack of self-control. Circumstances control us. People control us. Environmental conditions control us. We seem to be pulled to and fro by a whole host of external forces and the whole time we are never in control of ourselves.

We explode in anger without explanation. We say harsh words to the people we love and say, "I'm sorry. I don't know what made me say that." We awake in the middle of the night filled with worry, tension and anxiety regarding some situation, conflict or decision. It all spells lack of self-control. Patience means that our motivation is internal, that our inner strength is greater than external stress, and that we are in control of our thoughts, feelings, attitudes and actions.

The Patience Principle DAY 54

Let's continue our thoughts from yesterday on Christ's message, "In your patience possess ye your souls" (Luke 21:19, KJV). While I tend to enjoy modern English translations of the Bible, I like the way this verse reads in the Old English. It has a punch to it.

Patience is the power of perseverance. The context of Jesus' statement was the persecution His followers would later receive for their circumstances. He was telling them that without patience they would be unable to persevere, endure and stand firm under that pressure.

Patience is the ability to endure, to stand firm, to continue stead-fastly in the face of opposition, adversity or difficulty. We cannot always change the outward circumstances, but we can always change our inward attitude. *Patience* is that inward attitude that enables us to stand, and having done all to stand.

Patience also is the power of consistency. Inconsistency is a problem that defeats many people. We make all sorts of new resolutions and are filled with a variety of good intentions, but when it comes to following through, it is another story. Starting the race is no problem. Establishing a consistent pace that will carry us across the finish line is the real issue. We've all heard the prayer, "Lord, give me patience, and I want it right now!" We want everything "right now" but fail to realize that reaching our goals involves a time process.

The word *wait* is almost extinct from our vocabulary. Patience is that ability to wait for the fulfillment of our dreams. My mother used to remind me of the old adages, "Fools rush in where angels fear to tread," and "Rome wasn't built in a day." Sure, they were just adages, but I got the point.

The next time you find yourself hurried, uptight, in the middle of the rat race, remember Christ's words, "In your patience possess ye your souls."

Living With Passion   DAY 55

Thomas Carlyle, the Scottish essayist and historian, said, "For every person who can handle prosperity there are a hundred who can handle adversity." That statement might strike you as odd. He is saying that it is easier to handle adversity than prosperity.

Horace, the Roman lyric poet, said, "Adversity has the effect of eliciting talents which, in prosperous circumstances, would have lain dormant." I once read that Christians are like tea bags—you never know what they're made of until you put them in hot water.

This is not to say that we need to pray for adversity. Life will see to that on its own. But we need to beware of the spiritual and moral danger we face when times are good—the danger of becoming spiritually lax. This was the case of Lot in Sodom (Genesis 19:16), Israel in Canaan (Amos 6:1), and the church at Laodicea (Revelation 3:15-17).

God calls us to keep our spiritual fervor and to stay alert to the times in which we live. Paul tells us, "Never be lacking in zeal, but keep your spiritual fervor, serving the Lord" (Romans 12:11). His challenge to Timothy is appropriate for us: "Fan into flame the gift of God, which is in you" (2 Timothy 1:6).

We see the zeal of Jesus throughout the Gospels. He was consumed with the zeal of the Lord (John 2:17), His food was to do the Father's will (4:34). He said that we are to work while it is day, for the night is coming when no man can work (9:4). He felt passionate about His Father's business (Luke 2:49), to preach the gospel (4:43), and to finish His work (John 4:34).

Rise above the mundane, the mediocre and the monotonous. Never lose your zeal! Keep your spiritual fervor! Serve the Lord with passion!

I Shall Not Be Moved DAY 56

Our world is caught up in a whirlwind of change. People long for stability. Here are five steps to living an unshakable life: "Be on your guard; stand firm in the faith; be men of courage; be strong. Do everything in love" (1 Corinthians 16:13, 14).

1. *Be on your guard.* This is a military term that means "to stay awake at one's post of duty; to be alert to any oncoming attack of an enemy." We need to be on our guard against the spirit of secularism that erodes our faith and values. Like Samson, we too can get lulled to sleep in the lap of Delilah if we are not on guard.

2. *Be firm in your convictions.* As America slides down the slippery slope of moral decay, we are called to be the salt of the earth and the light of the world, reflecting the character of Christ.

3. *Be courageous.* Webster defines *courage* as "that quality of mind or spirit enabling one to meet danger or opposition with fearlessness, calmness and firmness; bravery." The Holy Spirit is our source of courage. A Sunday school teacher dropped into a shoe store one day and courageously witnessed to a young shoe clerk. That young clerk eventually accepted Christ. His name was Dwight L. Moody. He went on to evangelize America and Europe. The teacher's name was Edward Kimball, a person of courageous faith.

4. *Be strong.* Don't allow yourself to become spiritually weak. Keep yourself strong through the Word of God, prayer, fellowship and active ministry. Paul challenges us, "Finally, be strong in the Lord and in his mighty power" (Ephesians 6:10).

5. *Do everything in love.* Always show unconditional love to everyone. Remember to find your joy in God's love. "Keep yourselves in God's love" (Jude 21).

Winning Over Worry   DAY 57

One of the most destructive of all human emotions is worry. In many respects it is much like the deadly python, which squeezes the life from its victim by constriction. We've all been touched by its painful effects.

By definition, *worry* is "an anxious, troubled or fearful state of mind." It means to be disturbed or distressed and to feel undue care and anxiety.

One psychiatrist referred to worry as the most subtle and destructive of all human diseases. From a more humorous standpoint, worry is today's mouse eating tomorrow's cheese.

Enough talk about the problem . . . what's the solution? I once received a card that said, "There is a secret to living without frustration and worry: Try to avoid becoming personally involved in your own life!" Well, we know that solution won't work, so let's consider these:

- Worry is an exercise in futility. There are no benefits of worry. There are no returns on your investment of time when you waste it by worrying.
- Worry won't pay the bills.
- Worry won't secure a job promotion.
- Worry won't retrieve rebellious children.
- Worry won't mend broken relationships.
- Worry won't solve marital conflicts.

Corrie ten Boom said, "Worry is a cycle of inefficient thoughts whirling around a center of fear." *Inefficient* is the key word here. It produces no desired results. Why is worry so futile? Because 90 percent of the things we worry about will never happen, and the other 10 percent . . . we will end up handling.

Justice Oliver Wendell Holmes was once in a despondent, worrisome mood. During that period he found a note on his desk from his wife. It said: "Dear Oliver, you have lived a long time and have seen many troubles—most of which have never happened."

Take the words of Jesus to heart: "Therefore, I tell you, do not worry. . . . But seek first [God's] kingdom and his righteousness, and all these things will be given to you as well" (Matthew 6:25, 33).

The Untroubled Heart   DAY 58

"Let not your heart be troubled," Jesus tells us (John 14:1, KJV). Worry is the number one troublemaker of the heart. Let's continue our thoughts from yesterday on how to conquer worry. Worry is a luxury no one can afford. The negative effects of worry are devastating.

The Anglo-Saxon word from which we get our word *worry* means "to choke." Some medical doctors have stated that such factors as financial disaster, frustration, tension, apprehension, loneliness, grief, long-held resentment, and habitual worry are precipitory causes of arthritis.

One study conducted of 176 American executives with an average age of 44 showed that one-half suffered either high blood pressure, heart disease or ulcers. In every case, worry was a prominent factor.

The antidote to worry is a meaningful faith. The psalmist David says, "Be still before the Lord and wait patiently for him; do not fret" (Psalm 37:7). That's the antidote for worry. Here is Jesus' counsel to seek an untroubled heart:

> Therefore I tell you, do not worry about your life, what you will eat or drink; or about your body, what you will wear. Is not life more important than food, and the body more important than clothes? Look at the birds of the air; they do not sow or reap or store away in barns, and yet your heavenly Father feeds them. Are you not much more valuable than they? Who of you by worrying can add a single hour to his life? And why do you worry about clothes? See how the lilies of the field grow. They do not labor or spin. Yet I tell you that not even Solomon in all his splendor was dressed like one of these. If that is how God clothes the grass of the field, which is here today

and tomorrow is thrown into the fire, will he not much more clothe you, O you of little faith? So do not worry, saying, "What shall we eat?" or "What shall we drink?" or "What shall we wear?" For the pagans run after all these things, and your heavenly Father knows that you need them. But seek first his kingdom and his righteousness, and all these things will be given to you as well. Therefore do not worry about tomorrow, for tomorrow will worry about itself. Each day has enough trouble of its own (Matthew 6:25-34).

Financial Peace   DAY 59

People worry about everything—from paying bills to sending their children to college, to the future of Social Security, to insuring they have sufficient retirement. The Bible is rich with insights for achieving financial peace.

1. *Consecrate your finances.* Holy consecration means to "offer your bodies as living sacrifices, holy and pleasing to God" (Romans 12:1). Your wealth is an extension of yourself. Your income is derived from an investment of your time, hard work and creativity. Giving financially to the cause of Christ is an expression of the consecration of one's self to God as a living sacrifice. The Macedonia believers "gave themselves first to the Lord," before they gave their finances (see 2 Corinthians 8:1-5).

2. *Celebrate God's financial blessings.* When the Israelites possessed the land of promise, they were taught by Moses to enjoy its abundance by giving thanks to God. He cautioned them not to take their prosperity for granted nor to assume they had made themselves prosperous. "But remember the Lord your God, for it is he who gives you the ability to produce wealth, and so confirms his covenant" (Deuteronomy 8:18).

3. *Conserve your financial resources.* The average American family spends 115 percent of his or her net annual income. Living above one's means produces financial stress. Make your money last. Stretch a dollar as far as it will go. Avoid the trap of consumerism that spends with no end in sight. While we are not to hoard wealth (James 5:1-4), we are to save and invest properly (Matthew 25:19-21). Consistent saving and investing is fundamental to success.

4. *Comprehend the power of money.* Learn all you can about money and the power of wealth. Money has the ability to multiply itself if invested properly. Money is a powerful resource. Did you know that if you save $5.50 a day from the time you are 21 to 41, invested at 9 percent, it will be worth $1 million when you reach age 65? Also, think of what you can accomplish for the kingdom of God with your money. Money is a temporary resource that can produce an eternal reward when given for the gospel.

Today, take the words of Proverbs to heart: "Honor the Lord with your wealth" (3:9).

Manage time? In response, consider the following steps:

1. *Discover your personal "time robbers" and seek to eliminate them.*
2. *Plan your daily activities.* Write them out and monitor the schedule at the end of each day. Keep track of your accomplishments each day.
3. *Prioritize appointments, events and opportunities.* Remember to focus on the important instead of the urgent.
4. *Avoid the trap of being busy.* Avoid cluttering your schedule. Seek to accomplish each day only what is feasible. Time management consultants say that 80 percent of the results are produced by 20 percent of the effort. This means that the other 80 percent of our efforts contribute to only 20 percent of the results. Learn to say no to things that will only waste energy but produce no results.

Time is our most precious resource. It can't be saved, only used. So, use it wisely.

Honor the Lord With Your Wealth   DAY 60

W hen Jesus said, "Seek first the kingdom of God" (Matthew 6:33, *NKJV*), He was talking about having the right attitude toward material possessions. Stop and ask, "How can I use my money for the glory of God?" The act of giving produces a harvest of persons into the kingdom of God.

Let's continue from yesterday with more principles of Biblical financial management.

Be content financially. To be *content* means "not inclined to complain or desire something else; satisfied; submissive to circumstances; freedom from worry or unsatisfied desires." The difference between those who are contented and those who are discontented is not how much stuff they have, but whether or not they enjoy what they have. Contentment does not mean to maintain the status quo, to settle for second best, or to turn down opportunities to better yourself or your lifestyle. Such ideas of contentment are far from the Biblical concept.

To the contrary, believers are called to press on, to rise up to their potential, and to accomplish great things for God. We keep our ambitions in check as we learn to be content regardless of our financial position. Paul said, "I have learned to be content whatever the circumstances" (Philippians 4:11).

Finally, *contribute your financial resources.* Parents seek to instill one basic value in their children as early as possible—SHARE. We want our children to share their toys, and by so doing, to learn to share throughout their lives. Our heavenly Father wants us to share. After Pentecost, believers were "selling their possessions and goods, [and] they gave to anyone as he had need" (Acts 2:45). God blesses those who tithe (the first tenth of one's income) and give offerings (Malachi 3:9, 10). But He is most concerned about the attitude of the giver. "God loves a cheerful giver" (2 Corinthians 9:7). We are never more like God than when we give. "For God so loved the world that he gave . . ." (John 3:16).

As we honor God, He honors us. "Honor the Lord with your wealth, with the firstfruits of all your crops; then your barns will be filled to overflowing, and your vats will brim over with new wine" (Proverbs 3:9, 10).

Be Strong in the Lord   DAY 61

It has been said, "The price of freedom is eternal vigilance." Liberty undefended is liberty lost. So it is spiritually. Just as political and national freedom has to be defended, so does spiritual freedom. "Be sober, be vigilant; because your adversary the devil walks about like a roaring lion, seeking whom he may devour. Resist him, steadfast in the faith" (1 Peter 5:8, 9, *NKJV*).

Some 2,000 years ago Jesus died for our sins. He freed the world from the power of sin. When we receive Christ as Savior, we are set free from the penalty and power of Satan. Yet, we must maintain spiritual vigilance if we are to live in that freedom. Spiritual freedom can be lost, just as political freedom can. "It is for freedom that Christ has set us free" (Galatians 5:1).

The greatest war facing us today is not the threat of an external enemy with nuclear weapons. It is an enemy within our borders, the Enemy of sin and spiritual darkness.

The casualties of this war are great: an epidemic of abortions, violence in schools, moral decay, the pandemic of AIDS, outlawing prayer in public places, the removal of the Ten Commandments from our institutions, substance abuse, the breakdown of the family, secular values and moral relativism, corruption of the arts, debased television programs, political scandals.

As believers, we are called to take up arms in this spiritual war. One of the most poignant pictures of the Christian life is the portrait of a soldier who is armed for battle and dressed for victory (see Ephesians 6:10-18). Paul's masterpiece passage on the armor of God begins with one challenge, "Be strong in the Lord and in his mighty power" (v. 10).

What does it mean to be strong spiritually? It means to have the courage to face a new challenge. Three times God told Joshua, "Be strong and courageous" (1:6, 7, 9). What a challenge to take the place of Moses. Joshua felt he was in over his head. But God was with him and that made all the difference. Whatever God has called you to do, be courageous—the Lord is with you!

Strength for the Day   DAY 62

Let's continue our reflections on the challenge to "be strong in the Lord" (Ephesians 6:10). To be strong means . . .

Obedience to God's commands. Toward the end of his life, David challenged Solomon: "I am about to go the way of all the earth. . . . So be strong, show yourself a man, and observe what the Lord your God requires: Walk in his ways, and keep his decrees and commands . . . so that you may prosper in all you do and wherever you go" (1 Kings 2:2, 3). Power and obedience go hand in hand.

Maturity in the faith. I read that "Bibles that are falling apart usually belong to people who are not." Let's be honest. No person can ever grow spiritually beyond the quality of his or her own walk with God. We need to grow deep roots so that when the storms of life rage, we can "withstand . . . and having done all, to stand!" (Ephesians 6:13, *NKJV*).

Resiliency against life's pressures. It's easy to complain when times are tough. Mark Twain once said, "Don't complain about your problems. Eighty percent of the people won't care. The other 20 percent will think you deserve them." Christians in China, when faced with Communist persecution, had a slogan: "Christians are like nails. The harder you hit us, the deeper we go."

Dependency on God's power. The first step to gaining strength is to realize your weakness. Here are 10 words that will change your life: "I can do all things through Christ who strengthens me" (Philippians 4:13, *NKJV*). It literally reads, ". . . who pours His strength in me."

We are to be strong "in the Lord." The phrase "in the Lord" means in and through our vital union with Jesus. Just as the vine pours life and strength into the branches, Jesus pours His power into our hearts (John 15:1-10). The branch has only one responsibility—to stay connected to the vine! Through prayer, Bible reading, praise and fellowship with believers, we stay connected to Christ, the Vine. He pours His resurrection power in us so that we can overcome every problem, every temptation and every disappointment. So, *be strong in the Lord!*

When Hope Fades   DAY 63

Orison Marden (1848-1924), editor for *Success* magazine, said, "There is no medicine like hope, no incentives so great, and no tonics so powerful as the expectation of something better tomorrow."

What a tragedy to lose hope. In America today, the third leading cause of death among teenagers is suicide. Our urban centers are steeped in an endless cycle of violence and poverty. Eighty percent of children in some inner cities are born to unwed mothers. Overall, the rate is 30 percent. Some 17.6 million Americans suffer from depression—costing an estimated $23.8 billion in lost work and productivity and $12.4 billion in treatment costs.

If you were an artist and decided to paint a picture to best portray the meaning of hope, what would you paint? Years ago an artist named Watts titled one of his paintings, "Hope." It showed a woman sitting on a world that had treated her most unfairly. Her eyes are bandaged, preventing her from seeing her way ahead. In her hands she holds a harp; all the strings except one are broken. Triumphantly she strikes that last string, and from it, a beautiful melody lifts from the harp over her world and fills her dark night with stars.

In the midst of a broken world, God gives us a harp with a string called *hope*. Here is God's invitation to reawaken your hopes: "Call to me and I will answer you and tell you great and unsearchable things you do not know" (Jeremiah 33:3).

"Call to me." Prayer is communication with our Creator. When we bother God with our problems, our problems will bother us less because we know God will work everything out for our good.

"I will answer you." God promises to hear and to respond to our prayers. Start expecting God to answer. Start observing His hand at work in your life, and stop taking all the good things for granted or thinking they are coincidences.

"Great and unsearchable things." If you are hopeless, search the Scriptures for passages of hope. God will speak to you and show you His plan and promises for your life. Situations are never hopeless because with God, all things are possible.

If It's to Be, It's Up to Me   DAY 64

I believe Zig Ziglar coined the expression, "If it's to be—it's up to me." I like it because it empowers us to take charge of our lives instead of sitting around waiting for life to happen on its own. You've got to get up and make it happen.

The psalmist said, "The steps of a good man are ordered by the Lord" (37:23, *NKJV*). But I contend that we have to take some steps on our own for the Lord to have something to direct.

A man came to America many years ago from Europe. After being processed at Ellis Island, he went into a cafeteria in New York City to get something to eat. He sat down at an empty table and waited for someone to take his order. Of course, nobody ever did.

Finally, a man with a tray full of food sat down opposite him and told him how things worked. "Start at the end," he said, "and just go along and pick out what you want. At the other end they'll tell you how much you have to pay for it."

"I soon learned that's how everything works in America," the man said. "Life is a cafeteria. You can get anything you want as long as you're willing to pay the price. You can even get success. But you'll never get it if you wait for someone to bring it to you. You have to get up and get it yourself."

Paul adds a valuable thought on this point: "Whatever you do, work at it with all your heart, as working for the Lord, not for men" (Colossians 3:23).

Remember, "If it's to be—it's up to me."

Stay Hungry   DAY 65

I watched a television interview with Arnold Schwarzeneggar, conducted by Barbara Walters. He won the "Mr. Universe" title eight consecutive times and went on to a successful acting career and became the governor of California. She asked him, "Do you have a philosophy of life?"

He replied, "Stay hungry."

Jesus said, "Blessed are those who hunger and thirst for righteousness, for they will be filled" (Matthew 5:6). *Want power* comes before *will power* in the equation of success.

One day a young man came to Socrates desiring to be tutored by the great philosopher. "I want to acquire knowledge," he told Socrates. Socrates told him to meet him the next day down by the lake. When the young man arrived the next day, Socrates led him out into the lake.

Then suddenly, Socrates grabbed him by the head and plunged him under the water. He held him down until the young man thought he would drown. Finally, he let him up. He sprang out of the water, gasping for air. After catching his breath, he demanded angrily, "Why did you do that? I could have drowned!"

Socrates asked, "What did you want more than anything else when I held you under the water?" The young man replied, "I wanted air!"

Socrates said, "When you want knowledge as much as you wanted air, you will get it."

Guard against apathy and keep the fire burning. "Never be lacking in zeal, but keep your spiritual fervor, serving the Lord" (Romans 12:11).

Quality Control   DAY 66

I am a big believer in quality control. While we can't always control the quantity, we can always control the quality.

Some people are control freaks, thinking they can control everything. Sadly, they only drive themselves and everyone around them crazy in the process.

There are so many things in life we can't control. We can't control other people or even circumstances, for the most part. But there are some things you *can* control. Denis Waitley, in *10 Seeds of Greatness*, gives seven *C*'s of control:

1. We control the *clock*—the way we use our time and organize our schedule.

2. We control our *concepts*—how we think and our attitudes toward life.

3. We control our *contacts*—the people we spend time with and those who influence us.

4. We control our *communication*—what we say or don't say, and how well we listen and understand others.

5. We control our *commitments*—the ways we invest our time, energy and money.

6. We control our *causes*—the spiritual and community service endeavors that add meaning to our lives.

7. We control our *concerns*—those things we tend to worry about.[4]

Here's an axiom I live by: *Control the things you can control, and leave the rest to God.* Or, in the words of Paul, "Do not be anxious about anything, but in everything, by prayer and petition, with thanksgiving, present your requests to God. And the peace of God, which transcends all understanding, will guard your hearts and your minds in Christ Jesus" (Philippians 4:6, 7).

What the Cross Nailed Down   DAY 67

O ne of the most important questions of faith being asked today is, "What relevance does a man dying on a cross in the first century have to do with us in the 21st century?"

In reality, it has everything to do with us because only the Cross answers the deepest longing and need within every person—the need to be reconciled to God.

At the bottom of the well of all human suffering is our estrangement from God. Augustine wrote, "Our hearts were made for Thee, O God, and they shall not rest until they rest in Thee."

Goethe noted, "All human longing is really the longing for God." Because of sin, there is an uncrossable chasm between God and man. The Cross is the place where God and humanity meet and are reconciled.

- At the Cross . . . He was wounded for our transgressions.
- At the Cross . . . He was bruised for our iniquities.
- At the Cross . . . by His stripes we are healed.
- At the Cross . . . God made Him who knew no sin to be sin for us.
- At the Cross . . . we become the righteousness of God in Christ.
- At the Cross . . . where sin increased, grace increased all the more.
- At the Cross . . . old things pass away.
- At the Cross . . . all things become new.

At Calvary, the record of our sins—past, present and future—was nailed to the cross, never again to be remembered against us. When we accept Jesus Christ as our personal Savior and Lord, it means death for us. We die with Him, our old life of sin dies with Him, and we come forth from the grave with Him to walk in newness of life.

"I have been crucified with Christ and I no longer live, but Christ lives in me. The life I live in the body, I live by faith in the Son of God, who loved me and gave Himself for me" (Galatians 2:20).

The Empty Tomb Still Speaks

In Moscow's Red Square stands a mausoleum containing the remains of Lenin in a crystal casket. Written upon it are these words: "For he was the greatest leader of all people of all time; he was the lord of the new humanity; he was the savior of the world."

How distinctively different from that epitaph are the words of Jesus Christ: "I am the resurrection and the life" (John 11:25).

This world has witnessed many great leaders, statesmen and prophets, but only one who could say, "I am the resurrection and the life." Of world leaders we say, "He was." But Christ says, "I Am."

When we visit the tombs of men, regardless of their station or prominence in this life, we read the words "Here lies so-and-so." But at the tomb of Jesus, we still hear the words of the angelic announcement, "He is not here; he has risen!" (Luke 24:6). What does the empty tomb say to us in the 21st century?

First, *the empty tomb offers us life.* What is life? Shakespeare wrote, "Life is a tale, told by an idiot, full of sound and fury, signifying nothing." Is life measured merely by the breathing of the lungs and the beating of the heart?

Isn't there more to life than the physical, material and temporal? The empty tomb of Christ tells us there is more: "In him was life, and that life was the light of men" (John 1:4). Abundant life is found on a spiritual plane as we live in fellowship with God through faith in Jesus.

Furthermore, *the empty tomb guarantees life after death.* Daily we are reminded of our finiteness: "It is appointed unto men once to die, but after this the judgment" (Hebrews 9:27, KJV). In Christ we face death with the assurance of eternal life in the presence of God. "To be absent from the body [is] to be present with the Lord" (2 Corinthians 5:8, *NKJV*). As believers, we look down at the grave in victory and declare, "Where, O death, is your sting? Where, O grave, is your victory?" (See 1 Corinthians 15:55).

Finally, *the empty tomb calls for a response of faith.* One leaves the site of Christ's resurrection with either faith or unbelief—no room for indecision. The risen Lord says, "Follow Me."

The empty tomb confronts us with the question of faith. What do we really believe? When Thomas met the risen Lord, he declared, "My Lord and my God!" (John 20:28).

Because He Lives

It is imperative to remember that the resurrection of Jesus is not simply an experience of personal faith, but it is an event rooted in historical reality.

There were the eyewitnesses. The women at the tomb, Peter and John, the chief priests and elders, and the Roman authorities all saw the empty tomb. Furthermore, Christ appeared to the apostles and to over 500 people who were eyewitnesses of His resurrection (see 1 Corinthians 15:5-7). He ate with His disciples, and they touched the places where the nails were driven in His hands and feet and where the spear was thrust into His side. Acts 1:3 tells us, "After his suffering, he showed himself to these men and gave many convincing proofs that he was alive."

There was the cover-up. Why did the Sanhedrin and the Roman authorities seek to cover up the Resurrection by fabricating a story that Jesus' disciples had stolen His body? In order for them to steal His body, they would have needed to overpower a posted Roman guard. If Christ had not truly been risen, there would have been no motivation for such a cover-up story. The fact remains: "Christ the Lord is risen."

Mounting Evidence

Today let's consider two other great evidences of the resurrection of Jesus:

There is the prophetic record. Repeatedly in the Old Testament, we hear the prophecies of the Resurrection (see Psalm 16:10, 11). Jesus often alluded to the Old Testament prophecies concerning His death and resurrection. He predicted to His closest disciples His death and resurrection. After His resurrection, Jesus appeared to His disciples on the Emmaus road. During His discourse with them, He asked, "Did not the Christ have to suffer these things and then enter his glory?" (Luke 24:26). Luke adds, "And beginning with Moses and all the Prophets, he explained to them what was said in all the Scriptures concerning himself" (v. 27).

There was the seven-week interval. Why is there a mysterious seven-week interval between Christ's reported resurrection and the preaching of this message? The only reason is that for 40 days the disciples were with Him, and He taught them about the kingdom of God and prepared them for their future mission (see Acts 1:1-11).

"Because I live," Jesus promised, "you also will live!" (John 14:19). The whole meaning of Christian life is the fact that we live the resurrected life. We have come out of the tomb of spiritual death and have been given abundant and eternal life. As Paul wrote, "When you were dead in your sins . . . God made you alive with Christ. He forgave us all our sins" (Colossians 2:13).

Let us celebrate the life we enjoy in Christ, and let us trust Him to release His resurrection power in and through us in service to others.

The Evidence Is In   DAY 71

Today we will consider the final three evidences of Jesus' bodily resurrection:

There was the empty tomb. The historical fact is, Christ's tomb was empty on that Easter morning. The only item found in that tomb was Christ's burial cloth. Today, if we were to travel to Jerusalem, His tomb would still speak the ageless message, "He is not here; he has risen!" (Luke 24:6).

There was the witness of the early church. What can account for their zeal? Enthusiasm? Willingness to suffer for His name? Power? Miracles? And what about the church today? Believers worldwide celebrate His resurrection. It is the presence of the risen Lord in the midst of the church that gives us the power to witness in His name.

There is the evidence of a transformed life. What changed those frightened disciples into firebrands for God? What caused an angry, murderous Pharisee named Saul to become the great apostle Paul? What power revolutionized people like John Newton, a profane slave trader who would become a preacher of the gospel, to write the beautiful hymn, "Amazing Grace," and to become the man who caused slavery to be overthrown in England? The only power that brings about such change in the human life is the power of the risen Lord. When His resurrection power touches us, we become new creations in Him, old things pass away, and all things become new (2 Corinthians 5:17)!

The greatest evidence of the Resurrection is not the eyewitnesses,

the cover-up, the prophetic record, the seven-week interval, the empty
tomb, or the witness of the early church. The greatest evidence is in the
words of the hymn:

> I serve a risen Savior, He's in the world today;
> I know that He is living, whatever men may say.
> . . . You ask me how I know He lives?
> He lives within my heart.

Power-Packed Priorities DAY 72

A chieving success is a matter of priorities. This principle holds true if
you are pursuing personal success, success in marriage and raising
children, financial success, or spiritual success. Jesus stressed the need
of proper priorities: "But seek first his kingdom and his righteousness,
and all these things will be given to you as well" (Matthew 6:33). The
Kingdom, which means the rule of God, is to dictate our priorities.

A *priority* is defined as "a first right established on emergency or
need." *Priority living* means putting first things first.

Priorities are a matter of balance, not simply a matter of order. You
can't always list priorities in order. There are many important areas of
life. Each needs a required investment of time and energy. Seek to balance your priorities instead of wrestling with trying to figure out how
you should order them. There are seven priorities that matter most in
life.

First, *your walk with God*. The greatest commandment is to love
the Lord with all your heart, mind and strength (Deuteronomy 6:5).
Make spiritual growth a priority in your life. Jesus said, "Blessed are
those who hunger and thirst for righteousness, for they will be filled"
(Matthew 5:6). Early Christians set a new tradition of worshiping. They
set aside the first day of the week to celebrate the resurrection of Jesus
(see 1 Corinthians 16:2). The first day, Sunday, also sets the tone for the
week that God comes first in our lives.

Second, *family commitment*. George Burns said, "Happiness is having a large, loving, caring, close-knit family in another city." Family living can be tough, but there is nothing more important in your life than
your family.

First Things First   DAY 73

Let's continue today looking at the seven priorities of a well-ordered life from our devotion yesterday:

Third, *time management*. Time is our most precious commodity. The way we manage our time has more to do with our level of success in life than any other single factor. We offer seminars on time management to help us handle stress and become more productive. We talk about spending quality time at home to counteract the breakdown of the family. We even measure distance in terms of time. Stick to the important tasks and devote yourself to the important people in your life.

Fourth, *financial investments*. I once read: "You write your autobiography in your checkbook." Solomon said, "Honor the Lord with your wealth" (Proverbs 3:9). Jesus said, "Where your treasure is, there your heart will be also" (Matthew 6:21). Give generously, save consistently, and spend wisely.

Fifth, *gift utilization*. "Each one should use whatever gift he has received to serve others" (1 Peter 4:10). Find a place of service and use your gifts for the glory of God.

Sixth, *significant relationships*. Friendships and family are vital to life. Jesus told His disciples, "I have called you friends" (John 15:15). Every person needs three relationships: a person to mentor you, a person to mentor, and a person to encourage you. Your friendships will either make you or break you. Choose your friends well.

Seventh, *personal development*. Look out for yourself. That's not being selfish, it's being smart. Look out for your spiritual, mental, educational, recreational and social development. Take time to do things in life you like to do. Set some goals just for you, and you will discover a whole new world of personal fulfillment.

Look Up   DAY 74

In 1666, a rumor spread through England that the world would end that year. The conclusion was drawn from certain Biblical students relating the mark of the Beast to that particular year. As the rumor spread, more and more people, commoner to royalty alike, lived under a sense of impending disaster.

During the summer of 1666, a violent storm arose in western England as Sir Matthew Hale presided as judge in his courtroom. A lawyer present that day wrote:

> All of a sudden the courtroom grew completely dark, though it was still midday. Then the entire courtroom seemed to shake as peals of thunder shook the walls, and bright flashes of lightning illuminated the room. People inside the courtroom were overcome with fear and, as if by common consent, each fell to his knees and prayed for mercy, believing that the 'terrible day of the Lord' had arrived.

The lawyer noticed, however, that Judge Hale sat unmoved by the storm. He continued to take notes of the trial as though nothing out of the ordinary had happened. The lawyer concluded that Judge Hale's heart was "so stayed on God, that no surprise, however sudden, could discompose him."

When Jesus tells us to "look up!" (see Luke 21:28), He doesn't mean that we are to live passively, waiting for His return. Rather, He commissions us to fulfill the mission He gave us to make disciples of all nations. We are not to face world conditions, however bleak they may be, with our faces downcast, but rather at all times, in every way, we are to look up!

When we think of the end of the age, how do we respond? The end of this present age will come with the return of Jesus Christ. When He comes, He will establish the kingdom of God as a living reality on the earth. The New Testament gives over 300 prophecies of Christ's return. These prophecies are a source of hope, not a prediction of doom. In light of world events, we are told, "Look up and lift up your heads, because your redemption draws near" (v. 28, *NKJV*).

When He Returns
DAY 75

The second coming of Christ is the ultimate hope for the world. The question arises, Why will Jesus come again?

Christ will return to rapture the people of God. Before the Great Tribulation period and the emergence of the Antichrist kingdom, Christ will snatch His people from the earth. In the words of the great apostle, we will be "caught up together . . . in the clouds to meet the Lord in the air" (1 Thessalonians 4:16-18).

Christ will return to rule the world. At the end of the Tribulation period, which will last seven years according to Daniel 9:24-27, Christ will return in triumphant glory at the Battle of Armageddon to rule as King of kings (Revelation 19:11-16).

Christ will return to remove evil. Jesus will rule the world with His people during the Millennium. Then the Millennium will end with the final destruction of Satan and the Great White Throne Judgment (20:7-15). The Millennium will be an age of unprecedented peace and prosperity under the rule of Christ (Isaiah 2:1-5).

Christ will return to restore all things. The Bible ends with a vision of a new heaven and a new earth (Revelation 21:1-7). In other words, what God started in Genesis, He completes in Revelation. The earth will return to its original condition of Paradise.

How should we then live? We need to reach the same conclusions as James Gray, who said that when he began to take the coming of Christ seriously, it made a fivefold impact on his life: "It awakened my love for God's Word, it quickened my zeal for Christ, it delivered me from worldly success, it gave me patience in suffering, and it broke the bands of covetousness and set me free to give."

Praise in the Valley   DAY 76

Life is a series of mountain peaks and valleys. While we wish life only involved the mountain peaks, we know that we must pass through the valleys as well.

Faith can turn every valley experience into a valley of praise. This is what the Old Testament King Jehoshaphat did. One day he received news that three armies in an allied coalition had set their sights on destroying Jerusalem. The account is recorded in 2 Chronicles 20.

The Spirit touched Jahaziel, and he prophesied. God gave a threefold admonition in verses 15 and 17:

1. Fear not, the battle is not yours, but God's.
2. Stand firm and see the deliverance the Lord will give you.
3. Go out and face the enemy!

He called a nationwide prayer service. Jehoshaphat told the people, "Have faith in the Lord your God and you will be upheld; have faith in his prophets and you will be successful" (v. 20). He then charged the worshipers to lead the army into battle, and they sang, "Give thanks to the Lord, for his love endures forever" (v. 21). God miraculously defeated the allied coalition on behalf of Judah: "As they began to sing and praise, the Lord set ambushes against the men of Ammon and Moab and Mount Seir who were invading Judah, and they were defeated" (v. 22).

After the battle, it took the Israeli army three days to collect all the plunder left by the enemy on the battlefield. Then they gathered in the valley and praised the Lord. They named the valley *Beracah*, which means "the valley of praise."

The lesson is profound: We can turn every valley into a valley of praise and see what great things God will do for us. Follow the battle strategy: Fear not, the battle is not yours, but God's! Stand firm and see the deliverance the Lord will give you! Go out and face the enemy!

Whatever valley you find yourself in today, turn it into the Valley of Beracah—the Valley of Praise.

Searching for the Good Life   DAY 77

The cry of this age is, "I want a life—not just a lifestyle!" Jesus came into the world to give us life. *Sin* is the great enemy of life. Sin means alienation from God and, consequently, all that is truly life. "The wages of sin is death, but the gift of God is eternal life" (Romans 6:23). Eternal life is more than simply going to heaven when you die. *Eternal life* means the highest quality of life today! What did Jesus teach about life?

Life is freedom. Often, in midlife crisis a person will say, "I'm tired of doing what everybody wants me to. I want to make my own decisions and live my own life." Life is something we live. It is active as we pursue our own course. Christ frees us from the rule of the self so that we can live for Him. Jesus taught that to be alive means to be free from perishing (see John 3:16) and free from judgment (see 5:24).

Life is direction. After suffering a setback, a loss of someone we love, or the loss of a job, we say, "It is time to move on with my life." Life has the idea of moving forward, or going somewhere. Christ gives us eternal purpose.

In whose footsteps do you walk? To follow the crowd is often to follow a path of destruction. Many people flounder without direction—in their personal life, in their marriage and family, in their career. God wants us to live with goals that make life count.

What Is Life? DAY 78

Life is an adventure. Jesus says, "He who loses his life will find eternal life" (see John 12:25). To lose yourself in the will of God is the greatest adventure of all. Self-preservation is the first law of natural law, but self-denial is the first law of spiritual law. Christ wants to take us on an adventure. Now to be sure, life has its routine. But there can be more when you abandon yourself to the will of God and the challenges and opportunities He brings your way.

Life is purpose. We talk about wanting to accomplish something with our lives. Life is active, not passive. Only when each day has meaning do we feel we are truly alive. Be about the business of living, not just maintaining a lifestyle.

Jesus was a joyful person. To be happy means to be satisfied, content and fulfilled. What good is life if you're not happy? God wants us to enjoy life and enjoy the good things of life. When Christ is truly Lord of our lives, we can't wait for each day to begin so that we can work, play and love in the presence of God. We face each day declaring, "This is the day the Lord has made; let us rejoice and be glad in it" (Psalm 118:24).

"How can I have this life?" you may ask.

"In him was life" (John 1:4). The key phrase is "in Him." To be in Christ means more than simply accepting Christ, believing in Christ, acknowledging Christ or confessing Christ; it means to be intimately acquainted with Christ, inseparably bound to Him in loving devotion and faithful commitment.

This is the great dividing line of humanity—in Christ or outside Christ. Every attitude, value, belief, philosophy of life, and behavior is either in Christ or outside Christ. To be in Christ is to be in life. To be outside Christ is to be outside of life, as E. Stanley Jones observes.

When you trust Christ as your Savior, you are instantaneously placed "in Christ," by the power of God. Christ is in you, and you are in Him.

Functional Failures

Success is largely determined by the way we handle failure. When Thomas Edison invented the light bulb, he tried over 2,000 experiments before he got it to work. A young reporter asked him how he felt after failing so many times. He said, "I never failed once. I invented the light bulb. It just happened to be a 2,000-step process." Now that's a positive perspective on failure!

We need to understand that failure provides a unique opportunity for personal growth. Failure is often the chisel God uses to sculpt us into great men and women for His honor. Failure is never final. The prophet Micah declared: "Do not gloat over me, my enemy! Though I have fallen, I will rise" (7:8).

How do you get back up when you fail?

1. *Experience forgiveness.* Only God's grace can ease the effects of a moral or spiritual failure. King David connected with God's forgiveness after his adultery with Bathsheba and prayed, "Create in me a pure heart, O God, and renew a steadfast spirit within me" (Psalm 51:10).

2. *Face life with courage and confidence.* Failure has a way of lowering our confidence and weakening our courage. We grow tired and second-guess ourselves. Yet, God encourages us. "Have I not commanded you? Do not be discouraged. Do not be afraid. Be strong and very courageous, for I am with you wherever you go" (see Joshua 1:9). If you have failures, get up and face life knowing that your God is with you every step of the way.

3. *Get back in the race.* Life is a race, and we have to run it with perseverance. Get up when you fall down and run the race so as to win the prize!

Get a Grip!

Oscar Wilde came to America for a visit in 1882. When asked by the customs agent if he had anything to declare, he boasted, "Only my genius." Fifteen years later, alone and broken in prison, he reflected on his life of waste and excess. He wrote: "I have been a spendthrift of my genius. . . . I forgot that every little action of the common day makes or unmakes character."

The Bible records the tragic epics of those who failed to get a grip on their desires:

- Cain failed to discipline his anger and murdered his brother.
- Esau failed to discipline his appetite and sold his birthright.
- Lot failed to discipline the lust of his eyes and coveted the plains of Sodom.
- Samson failed to discipline his passions and lost his power.
- King Saul failed to discipline his quest for power and lost his throne.
- King David failed to discipline his lustful desires and was unfaithful to God.
- Judas failed to discipline his self-interests and betrayed Christ with a kiss.
- Pilate failed to discipline his political aspirations and washed his hands of Jesus, even though he knew Jesus was innocent.
- The disciples failed to discipline their fears and deserted Jesus at His trial.

The Book of Judges chronicles a dark period of Israeli history. It was a time marked by spiritual decline and social degradation brought on by the lack of discipline. The writer simply says: "Everyone did as he saw fit" (21:25). No law. No accountability to God or others. No moral boundaries. No absolutes. As a result, chaos reigned.

Life is not a matter of what we *feel*; it's a matter of what we *will*. Transcend your feelings, impulses and desires by the power of your will. "For to me, to live is Christ and to die is gain" (Philippians 1:21).

When Olympic gymnast Kerri Strug was asked by her coach, Bela Karolyi, if she could do the vault that helped earn the U.S. women a gold medal in team competition, she said, "Yes, I will, I will, I will."

Fret Not Thyself   DAY 81

The psalmist gives us timely wisdom we all need to take to heart: "Fret not thyself" (37:1, KJV). Here is the prescription for a worry-free life.

Let's be honest: It's not what we're eating, but what's eating us that causes most our problems. Mark Twain said, "I have been through some terrible things in my life, some of which actually happened."

Worry is an anxious, troubled or fearful state of mind. Someone has said that worry is thinking with our emotions. Worriers experience the phenomenon of the "racing mind," characterized by an endless stream of anxious thoughts.

Worry causes increased muscle tension, eating disorders, anxiety and depression, which leads to more serious health problems. Chronic worriers often suffer from low self-esteem.

The Greek word for *worry* means "to be divided or inwardly distracted." The worried mind is a divided mind—a mind torn between faith and fear. James tells us, "A double-minded man is unstable in all his ways" (1:8, KJV). Double-mindedness occurs when we vacillate between faith and fear.

Worry chokes out our hopes, dreams and aspirations, leaving us trapped in a prison of fear. Here is a beatitude worth remembering: *Blessed is the man who is too busy to worry during the day, and too sleepy to worry at night.*

So, if we can't worry, what can we do? "Humble yourselves, therefore, under God's mighty hand, that he may lift you up in due time. Cast all your anxiety on him because he cares for you" (1 Peter 5:6, 7).

When Fear Knocks, Let Faith Answer — DAY 82

The sign read: "Fear knocked at the door. Faith answered, and there was no one there." John the apostle said, "This is the victory that has overcome the world, even our faith" (1 John 5:4).

Fear haunts us with an endless list of what ifs: What if you fail? What if your business goes under? What if you can't finish what you started? What if you get sick? What if your marriage fails? What if . . . ?

When fear knocks on the door of your heart, let faith answer by saying, "I can do all things through Christ who strengthens me" (Philippians 4:13, NKJV).

Fear is simply **F**alse **E**xpectations **A**ppearing **R**eal. President

Roosevelt said so wisely in his 1933 Inaugural Address, in the wake of the Great Depression, "There is nothing to fear but fear itself."

My friend Dr. John Haggai says in his excellent book, *How to Win Over Worry*: "'Died of worry' could be written factually on many tombstones."

A French soldier in World War I used to carry this note to help him overcome his fears and worries:

> Of two things, one is certain: Either you are at the front, or you are behind the lines. If you are at the front, of two things, one is certain: Either you are exposed to danger, or you are in a safe place. If you are exposed to danger, of two things, one is certain: Either you are wounded, or you are not wounded. If you are wounded, of two things, one is certain: Either you recover, or you die. If you recover, there is no need to worry. If you die, you cannot worry. So, why worry?

When fear knocks, let faith answer—you will find no one there!

Victims or Victors? DAY 83

Viktor Frankl, survivor of Hitler's death camp, said, "The last and greatest of all human freedoms is the ability to choose one's own attitude in any given set of circumstances." He found meaning even in suffering and survived such horrible conditions.

When you learn to live by your choices instead of your feelings, you will be a victor instead of a victim. Victim psychology is an epidemic in America today. To be sure, there are real victims of our times—victims of crime, discrimination and injustice.

Victimization, however, is an attitude that shrinks back from taking responsibility. The victim cries, "It's not my fault." The victim demands, "The world owes me a living." Today we have no-fault divorces, no-fault auto insurance, and now no-fault moral choices.

What happens to you is not your fault. But how you respond to life's circumstances and challenges is your responsibility. You make the choice—victim or victor. Which will it be?

- The victim says, "I can't"; the victor says, "I can do all things through Christ who gives me strength."

- The victim says, "It's not my fault!"; the victor says, "I am responsible for my actions."
- The victim says, "We never did it that way before"; the victor says, "Nothing ventured, nothing gained."
- The victim lives in fear; the victor walks by faith.
- The victim sees problems; the victor sees opportunities.
- The victim strikes back; the victor turns the other cheek.
- The victim harbors resentment; the victor forgives even as God has forgiven him.
- The victim gives up; the victor presses on.
- The victim explains why it can't be done; the victor believes it can be done.
- The victim offers excuses; the victor sets an example.
- The victim is reactive; the victor is proactive.
- The victim says, "With man, this is impossible"; the victor says, "With God, all things are possible!"
- The victim says, "The odds are against us"; the victor says, "If God be for us, who can be against us?"

Overcoming Overwhelming Odds   DAY 84

I've always been inspired by the life of Booker T. Washington. He grew up in a time of cruel discrimination. As a boy, he would stand outside the schoolhouse and gaze through the windows, wanting more than anything else to get an education. He was deprived of the simple privilege of going to school. But nothing could keep him from his dream. When he grew up, he had the opportunity to complete his education.

Washington was a victor when it would have been easy to be a victim and give up. He said, "Success is not measured by what one achieves in life but rather by the obstacles one overcomes in the achievement of that success." He refused to be a victim of discrimination. He chose rather to be a victor.

There's a thought-provoking line in *Gone With the Wind*: "Ain't nothin' from the outside can lick any of us." It's what is on the inside that defeats us—attitudes of fear, pessimism and negativism.

Helen Keller was a victor. Although blind and deaf, she refused to play the role of a victim. She shows us how to rise above victimization in her poem "They Took Away."

> They took away what should have been my eyes;
> But I remembered Milton's Paradise.
> They took away what should have been my ears;
> Beethoven came and wiped away my tears.
> They took away what should have been my tongue;
> But I talked with God when I was young.
> He would not let them take away my soul;
> Possessing that I possessed the whole.

One of the greatest titles given to the people of God in Scripture is the title *overcomer*. God promises, "He who overcomes will inherit all this, and I will be his God and he will be my son" (Revelation 21:7).

Join the procession of overcomers today: "But thanks be to God, who always leads us in triumphal procession in Christ and through us spreads everywhere the fragrance of the knowledge of him" (2 Corinthians 2:14).

A Made-Up Mind DAY 85

There's a statement in the Gospel of Luke about Jesus that inspires me: "Jesus resolutely set out for Jerusalem" (9:51). The word *resolutely* literally means "He set His face like a flint." He was steadfast in His purpose.

Jerusalem, for Jesus, meant rejection and, eventually, death. Even His own disciples tried to prevent Him from going to Jerusalem. They knew the risk He was taking. Still, He *resolutely* set out for Jerusalem to do the will of God.

The question is, What have you resolutely set out to accomplish with such determination that you cannot be dissuaded?

Remember, *it's not what you feel, it's what you will* that brings success. Don't allow your emotions to rule your life. Make decisions based on what you will, not on what you feel. We put too much emphasis on what we feel and not enough on what we will.

I'm sure Noah didn't feel like building an ark and being the laughingstock of the community; but he obeyed God, built the ark, and saved his family.

I'm sure Abraham didn't feel like taking Isaac to Moriah, but he arose early in the morning and set out to the place God showed him and discovered that God will provide.

I'm sure Moses didn't feel like going to Egypt and confronting Pharaoh, but he went in obedience and led Israel out of Egypt into the promises of God.

I'm sure Deborah didn't feel like leading Israel as a prophetess and judge in a society dominated by male leadership, but she took the challenge and led her nation to victory.

I'm sure David didn't feel like facing Goliath alone in battle; but he took his sling, along with five smooth stones, and declared, "I come to you in the name of the Lord of Hosts" (1 Samuel 17:45, *NKJV*).

I'm sure Mary, the mother of Jesus, didn't feel like being chosen for the Virgin Birth. (Can you image trying to explain that to your fiancé, family and friends?) Yet, she said to the angel, "I am the Lord's servant. May it be to me as you have said" (Luke 1:38).

I'm sure Jesus didn't feel like going to Calvary; but "for the joy set before him [He] endured the cross" and redeemed the world (Hebrews 12:2).

I'm sure the apostle Paul didn't feel like preaching the gospel at the cost of rejection, imprisonment, and eventually a martyr's death; but he declared, "I have fought a good fight, I have finished the race, I have kept the faith" (2 Timothy 4:7).

The Path of Least Resistance   DAY 86

If you were to visit Boston and study the road system, you might conclude that there was no master design to the roads. They wind around with no rhyme or reason. That's because the first roads were constructed along cow paths.

Cows take the path of least resistance. When cows walk up a hill, they don't say, "Here's a hill. Let's navigate the best path possible." No, they simply follow the path of least resistance, stepping around the next rock or steep grade. When they return to the same area, they simply follow the previous course, eventually beating down the grass and forming a path.

Stay off the path of least resistance! Don't take the easy road. Count the cost. Pay the price. Persevere until you reach your goals. Paul writes, "Endure hardship as a good soldier of Jesus Christ" (2 Timothy 2:3, *NKJV*).

Success requires us to go beyond the initial excitement of a project and finish what we start. Enthusiasm must be tempered with determination for dreams to become reality. The main difference between success and failure lies in the ability to finish what you start. The world is filled with starters but lacking in finishers. Live in such a way that you, too, can say, "I have finished the race" (4:7).

Keep Playing　DAY 87

Ignacy Paderewski was a famous concert pianist and prime minister. A mother bought tickets to a Paderewski performance to encourage her young son's progress on the piano. Arriving at the concert, they found that their tickets were near the front of the stage. They eyed the majestic Steinway waiting on stage. While the mother was talking to a friend, her son slipped away in the crowd.

When the concert began, the spotlights came on. The audience became quiet. Suddenly everyone noticed the little boy sitting at the piano innocently picking out, "Twinkle, Twinkle, Little Star."

The mother was horrified. Then the master appeared on stage. "Don't quit—keep playing," he said to the boy. Leaning over him, Paderewski reached down his left hand and started playing a bass part. Then, with his right hand, he added a running obbligato. Together, Paderewski and the little boy thrilled the crowd.

Success comes when we take the little we have and give it to God. He makes up the difference and says, "Don't quit—keep playing."

"Be steadfast, immovable, always abounding in the work of the Lord, knowing that your labor is not in vain in the Lord" (1 Corinthians 15:58).

Count the Cost　DAY 88

The fine art of finishing begins with counting the cost before you embark on a project, an endeavor, or even a relationship. You need to count the cost. Jesus said:

"Suppose one of you wants to build a tower. Will he not first sit down and estimate the cost to see if he has enough money to complete it? For if he lays the foundation and is not able to finish it, everyone who sees it will ridicule him, saying, 'This fellow began to build and was not able to finish'" (Luke 14:28-30).

Having built two houses myself, I know firsthand the wisdom of Jesus' words. If you have ever built a house, you, too, know the necessity of counting the cost. About halfway through the project, you ask yourself, "What in the world ever possessed me to build my own house?"

The only sure way to finish construction on time and within budget is to count the cost. So it is with life. Before launching a project, seeking a college degree, entering the ministry, starting a new business, changing careers, moving to another city, getting married or having children—count the cost. Make sure you have what it takes to finish what you start.

An advertisement for an automobile-brake business read: "If you can't stop, don't start." Good advice for driving; great advice for life.

Here's how to count the cost:

1. Remember, things usually take longer and cost more than you originally planned.

2. Decide up front the emotional, spiritual and physical investment you will need to make so that you don't run out of resources halfway through.

3. Map out your strategy one step at a time so that you can pace yourself in the achievement of your goals.

Then, "set your face like a flint" (see Isaiah 50:7) and go for it!

Transcend! DAY 89

If I were to choose one word to describe the power of faith, it would be *transcendence*. To *transcend* means "to rise above; to be above and beyond in excellence and degree."

We transcend fear when we trust God with our problems. We transcend insults when we turn the other cheek. We transcend depression when we rejoice in the Lord always. We transcend selfishness when we consider others better than ourselves. We transcend negativism when we give thanks in all circumstances.

Isaiah the prophet said, "They that wait upon the Lord shall renew their strength; they shall mount up with wings as eagles" (40:31, KJV). What a portrait of transcendence. You can rise above life and soar on the wings of an eagle. You don't have to allow people and circumstances to get you down.

Mother Teresa poignantly describes the transcendent life in her poem, "Anyway":

People are often unreasonable, illogical and self-centered;
Forgive them anyway.
If you are kind, people may accuse you of selfish, ulterior motives
Be kind anyway.
If you are successful, you will win some false friends and some true enemies;
Succeed anyway.
If you are honest and frank, people may cheat you;
Be honest anyway.
What you spend years building, someone could destroy overnight;
Build anyway.
If you find serenity and happiness, they may be jealous;
Be happy anyway.
The good you do today, people will often forget tomorrow;
Do good anyway.
Give the world the best you have, and it may never be enough;
Give the world the best you have anyway.
You see in the final analysis, it is between you and God;
It was never between you and them anyway.

Inspiration Plus Perspiration   DAY 90

The achievement of any goal is mainly the result of hard work. William Temple, archbishop of Canterbury, said, "When I pray, coincidences happen, and when I do not, they don't."

Stephen Leacock said, "I am a great believer in luck, and I find the harder I work, the more luck I have." As a high school senior, I wrote a paper on the life and work of American novelist William Faulkner. When asked what part inspiration played in his success, he said, "My work is 2 percent inspiration and 98 percent perspiration."

Your life is God's gift to you; what you do with your life is your gift to God. God has endowed every person with gifts, talents and abilities, both naturally and spiritually. But God gives those gifts and abilities in their raw, undeveloped form. It's up to us to develop the gifts and then use them for His glory.

There's only one supreme task in life: *To leave the world a little better off than when you arrived.* If you don't make the world a better place, there isn't much reason for being here, is there?

Jesus challenges us to do something significant with our lives.

"To whom much is given . . . much will be required" (Luke 12:48). We all fit into that category—to whom much is given. When you stop and think about it, we've all been given much. It's up to each one of us to take what we've been given and produce something with it.

God gives us the inspiration. We give the perspiration. And the result is a life for His glory.

God Is Watching   DAY 91

There's an interesting story about Adam and Eve in Genesis. When God created Adam, He commissioned him to give names to all the animals. In fact, God "brought them to the man to see what he would name them" (2:19). Man, not God, gave names to all the animals. (I suppose that's why some animals have a strange name.)

I find it fascinating that God watched to see what Adam would name them. I get the feeling that God still watches to see what each one of us will do with what He has given us.

I once read that we are God-created, but self-molded. God expects us to take charge of our lives and to produce something with what He has given us.

Someone has aptly stated: "Control your thoughts—thoughts become words, words become actions, actions become habits, habits become character, character becomes destiny."

Theodore Roosevelt said, "If you're not actively pursuing the person you want to be, then you're pursuing the person you don't want to be."

God is watching to see what you will do today with what He has given you. Don't get distracted by what He has given others. That is the seed of discontentment. What gifts and opportunities do you have? Seize them today and make the most of every opportunity.

"Each one should use whatever gift he has received to serve others, faithfully administering God's grace in its various forms" (1 Peter 4:10).

Fan the Flame   DAY 92

Everybody has goals. But only people who can motivate themselves through tough times ever reach their goals. As the old adage goes, "The road to hell is paved with good intentions."

Ask God to give you new motivation if you feel burned out. I have discovered prayer to be an incredibly inspiring and motivating experience. When I pray, my thoughts are clearer, my attitude is more positive, my outlook is more hopeful, my concern for others is deeper, and my resolve to press on toward my goals is stronger.

A man driving through the Midwest came to a run-down gas station in the middle of nowhere. The sign read: "Last stop for gas for 100 miles." So he stopped to fill up his car.

The owner was a rough, rugged old-timer. As the man paid the owner, he noticed a big pot of black coffee brewing behind the counter. The sign read: "World-Famous Chicory Coffee."

He turned to leave when the old-timer said, "Wait. Won't you try a cup of my world-famous chicory coffee?"

"Thanks, but not today," replied the traveler.

"Come on, try a cup."

"No, thank you."

At that, the old-timer pulled out a gun, pointed it at the man and demanded, "I said try a cup of my world-famous chicory coffee!"

So, he took a cup, drank it and nearly choked, it was so strong.

Then, the old-timer handed him the gun and said, "Now, hold the gun on me while I drink a cup!"

The point of the story is, don't wait until someone holds a gun on you before you get motivated. Keep yourself fired up! "Fan into flame the gift of God, which is in you" (2 Timothy 1:6).

Live Life

Ours is the age of television, DVDs and the Internet. Sometimes we find ourselves watching life more than living it. We can get caught in the trap of living life vicariously through watching television, movies, or surfing the Net. But don't settle for watching life—live it!

I've identified three reasons we escape from life into the world of visual stimulation.

First, we get caught in the trap of the paralysis of analysis. We spend so much time analyzing situations and opportunities that we never act.

Second, we procrastinate because we're afraid of failure. But the only people who never fail are those who never try anything. If you try, you will fail. That's OK. Rebounding from failure is fundamental to success. Try to live by two resolutions:

Resolution #1: I promise to make my fair share of mistakes.

Resolution #2: I promise to keep on trying until I reach my goals.

Mark Twain is attributed to have said, "Twenty years from now you will be more disappointed by the things that you didn't do than by the ones you did do. So, throw off the bowlines. Sail away from the safe harbor. Catch the trade winds in your sails. Explore. Dream. Discover."

Finally, we fail to live life because we aim for perfection. "Life is not a spelling bee!" Harold Kushner says. When you make one mistake in a spelling bee, you're out of the game. It's all-or-nothing.

Life is more like a baseball season—long and drawn out. You don't have to win all the games to have a winning season. Just win a few more games than you lose, and you'll have a winning season. So it is with life.

Jesus said, "I have come that they might have life, and that they might have it more abundantly" (John 10:10, KJV). So, don't get caught sitting on the couch watching life on a big-screen TV—get out of the house and live it!

We're Counting on You

Thousands of fans in Camden Yards baseball stadium stood to their feet on September 6, 1995, to honor one man, Cal Ripken Jr.

Exuberant fans cheered for 20 minutes, stopping the game to salute the Baltimore Orioles shortstop.

Why? Other players had better statistics. Five other Orioles held higher batting averages that year; three hit more home runs.

The fans cheered Cal because he set the new record for most consecutive games played, which was 2,131. They cheered his faithfulness. He was dependable. They knew they could count on Cal.

Did you know that people are counting on you? You need to succeed, not only for yourself, but also for those who are depending on you.

That's a lot of pressure, you may be thinking. Sure it is, but we need that pressure. That's what keeps us going. If people weren't counting on us, we would never reach our potential.

Take a minute and think about the people who are counting on you. Write their names on a list. There are probably more people than you realize. Begin every day by telling yourself, "Today, God, my family and my friends are counting on me. And I'm not going to let them down."

Faithfulness starts with the little things of life. A popular book says, "Don't sweat the small stuff." But there is some small stuff you need to sweat if you expect to get ahead. Jesus said, "You have been faithful with a few things; I will put you in charge of many things" (Matthew 25:23).

You can't be perfect, but you can be faithful, and that's all God expects.

Use What You Have   DAY 95

After 23 years with the IRS, Anne Sheiber retired from her job in 1944. During her years of service, she had never earned more than $4,000 a year and never received a promotion, despite having a law degree and leading her office in turning up underpayments and underreporting.

When she retired, she took her savings of $5,000 and invested it in the stock market. Some 50 years later, in January 1995, Anne died at the "young" age of 101. By that time her $5,000 investment had grown to $22 million in stocks. She made all her investment decisions reviewing *The Wall Street Journal* daily, and her portfolio included such blue-chip stocks as Coca-Cola and Paramount Studios. She willed all her stock holdings to Yeshiva University in New York—a university that had never even heard of her.

You don't need more to be successful—more talent, more money, more opportunity, more faith, more confidence—you just need to use what you have.

Jesus needed only five loaves and two fish to feed a multitude. And He said that you could move a mountain with just a mustard seed of faith. Scripture says, "Be content with what you have, because God has said, 'Never will I leave you; never will I forsake you' " (Hebrews 13:5).

Jesus has the miracle power, but the young boy had the bread and fish. It wasn't much, certainly not enough to feed 5,000 people.

Because he submitted to Jesus, the miracle of multiplication took place. Give yourself, your talent and your resources to Jesus in faith. Seek to do His will, and watch Him multiply your efforts.

Do You Want to Change the World? DAY 96

When Apple Computer fell on difficult times, Apple's young chairman, Steve Jobs, traveled from Silicon Valley to New York City. His purpose was to convince Pepsico's John Sculley to move West and revitalize the struggling company.

As the two men overlooked the Manhattan skyline from Sculley's penthouse office, the Pepsi executive started to decline Jobs' offer. "Financially," Sculley said, "you'd have to give me a million-dollar salary, a million-dollar bonus and a million-dollar severance."

Stunned, Jobs agreed, that is, if Sculley would move to California. But Sculley would only commit to being a consultant from New York. At that, Steve issued him a challenge: "Do you want to spend the rest of your life selling sugared water, or do you want to change the world?"

In his autobiography *Odyssey*, Sculley admits Jobs' challenge "knocked the wind out of me." He said that he had become so caught up in his comfort zone that an opportunity to change the world nearly passed him by. Instead, he reevaluated his life and went to Apple.

You need to commit yourself to a cause greater than yourself.

Set goals that will stretch you beyond your comfort zone. The only way to step up to the next level is to be challenged. You need an environment that challenges you to move upward and onward in life.

Jesus calls us to be world changers: "Go into all the world and make disciples of all nations" (see Matthew 28:19; Mark 16:15). Eleanor Roosevelt said, "It is better to light a candle than to curse the darkness."

We change the world—one person at a time—as we share the good news of Christ's love, forgiveness and hope in a world of darkness.

More Blessed to Give   DAY 97

Psychologist Alfred Adler, who coined the term *inferiority complex*, noted that all human failure is attributed to the inability to grasp the fact that "it is more blessed to give than to receive" (Acts 20:35).

As a young man, John D. Rockefeller Sr. demonstrated strength and determination in his goals. By age 33, he earned his first million dollars. By age 43, he controlled the largest company in the world. At age 53, he was the richest man in the world and the world's only billionaire.

He then contracted a rare disease. His hair fell out, his eyebrows and eyelashes disappeared, and he was shrunken like a mummy. While his weekly income was $1 million, his diet consisted of milk and crackers. He was so anxious that he maintained bodyguards. Unable even to sleep, he lost all joy for living.

The medical doctors predicted he would not live another year. The newspaper wrote his obituary in advance. During those sleepless nights, he began to take stock of himself. He realized that he could not take any of his money with him into the next world.

He made a new resolution and began giving his money to hospitals, medical research, and mission work. He helped the poor and needy by establishing the Rockefeller Foundation, whose funding led to the discovery of penicillin as well as cures for malaria, tuberculosis and diphtheria.

He began to sleep again. The symptoms began to disappear. He became happy again. Instead of dying at 54 as predicted, he lived to be 98. He was faithful with what God gave him.

Acts 20:35 is true: "It is more blessed to give than to receive." The secret to a joy-filled life is giving yourself away.

Teamwork Works

Since Lombardi put teamwork into perspective: "The challenge for every organization is to build a feeling of oneness, of dependence on one another . . . because the question is usually not how well each person works but how well they work together."

An airplane is a good example of teamwork. I once read that an airplane can be defined as "millions of parts flying together in close formation."

Working for someone is demeaning; working with someone is dynamic. When Jesus selected the Twelve, He chose them "that they might be with him" (Mark 3:14). Note their relationship was *with* Him, not *for* Him.

Late in the 15th century, two young apprentice wood-carvers in France wanted to study painting. But such study would take money, and both Hans and Albrecht were poor. They decided that one would work and earn income while the other studied. Then, when the educated one became successful, he would help the other. They tossed a coin, and Albrecht won.

While Albrecht studied in Venice, Hans worked as a blacksmith. He sent money to help Albrecht complete his studies. After a year, Albrecht returned home a master painter.

However, when they met together, Albrecht couldn't help but notice Hans' hands. They were callused and bruised from the heavy labor in the blacksmith shop. His fingers could never handle a delicate painter's brush. Albrecht was moved deeply by the sacrifice of his friend.

In humble gratitude to Hans for his years of sacrifice, Albrecht Durer painted a portrait of the work-worn hands that had labored so faithfully on his behalf. He presented this painting of praying hands to his devoted friend. Since then, the famous praying hands have inspired millions.

Grow Up!

We talk about growing up, not growing down. When did anyone ever get excited about corporate downsizing? We'd rather have corporate "upsizing"! You see, growth is upward, not downward.

When someone tells me they have a problem, I reply, "You mean an opportunity." Problems are opportunities in disguise.

Turn every problem into an opportunity for personal growth and the advancement of your goals.

I refuse to listen to people talk about their problems. That's too negative. When we turn problems into opportunities, and see them in a positive light, then we are poised to do something about them.

If you like boating, fishing or water skiing, you're familiar with the name *Evinrude*. Ole Evinrude was in love and engaged to be married. He and his fiancée went out on a beautiful summer's day to row across the lake and enjoy a picnic on the other side. Just as they finished setting up the picnic, she realized they had forgotten the dessert.

So, Ole rowed the boat back across the lake. He picked up the dessert and started making the lengthy row back across. About halfway, he was exhausted. The heat and the rowing had nearly drained him. While the ice cream melted, he thought, *There's got to be a better way.*

That exasperated thought prompted him to invent the first portable outboard motor. Ole's experimentation began in 1906. By 1909, he had produced the first commercially successful outboard motor. In 1910, he was granted a patent for his invention. His company went on to dominate the market for years. He turned an obstacle into an opportunity.

Scripture teaches us to see every experience of life as an opportunity: God "works out everything in conformity with the purpose of his will" (Ephesians 1:11).

A Vision for Life   DAY 100

Charles Allen, in *Life More Abundantly,* tells the story of a beggar who sat every day on a street corner across from an artist's studio. Day after day, the artist saw him and decided to paint his portrait.

After a couple of days, he finished the portrait. Then he walked across the street to the beggar and invited him to his studio. "There's something I want you to see," he told him. Once inside the studio, the artist unveiled the portrait.

At first the beggar didn't recognize himself. "Who is it?" he kept asking. The artist just smiled and said nothing.

Then, suddenly, the man saw himself in the portrait—not as he was, in his dejected state, but as he could be.

"Is that me? Is it really me?" he asked excitedly.

"That's the man I see in you," the artist replied.

The beggar said, "If that's the man you see, then that's the man I'll be."

It is said of Jesus that in the company of sinners, He dreamed of saints. The Lord looks beyond our faults and sees our need of His grace and our potential for greatness in Him.

One day Jesus walked by a group of fishermen on the shores of the Sea of Galilee. He saw in them potential for greatness. He said, "Come, follow me . . . and I will make you fishers of men" (Matthew 4:19).

Come, follow Me. Jesus' invitation for a relationship with Him is given to everyone. He calls us into a close, personal relationship.

I will make you. You don't have to make yourself—He will make you. He will work in your life and shape your character as you follow Him.

Fishers of men. As we follow Jesus, our lives bring the influence of His grace and love to others. Our lives have eternal purpose. Go out today and go fishing—fish for others who need to know Jesus Christ.

More Than Enough   DAY 101

The Gospels record 38 miracles of Jesus. Yet, only one appears in all four Gospels. Can you guess which one it is? It's the miracle of feeding the multitude.

A little boy partnered with Jesus to feed a multitude of 5,000. The miracle required two things—the power of God and the boy's lunch. It wasn't much until he put it in the hand of Christ. Then his lunch fed a multitude.

But he had to give it. The disciples didn't chase him down and take his lunch away from him. And God is not going to force us to give.

A proverb in the Apocryphal book of Sirach says, "The gift of a grudging giver makes the eyes dim" (18:18). God does not need us to give. We need to give because the giving conforms our character to be like God. "For God so loved the world that he gave" (John 3:16). "God loves a cheerful giver" (2 Corinthians 9:7).

The little boy gave his lunch freely and joyfully. When he did, he experienced the miracle of *more than enough*. There were 12 baskets left over. I wonder if the little boy got to take the leftovers home. Now that would have been a sight—to see the look on his mother's face when she asked, "Johnny, did you eat your lunch?"

"Yes . . . but not all of it!"

Not only did he have his need met, he also helped meet the needs of so many others because he gave what he had. He put it in the hands of Jesus, and it was multiplied. The "more than enough" principle goes into operation when we partner with Jesus through giving.

Jesus said, "Freely you have received, freely give" (Matthew 10:8).

When You Get Too Caught Up . . . Look Up   DAY 102

A father sat down in his favorite recliner, exhausted after a long day at the office and fighting the traffic. He started to read the paper when his 4-year-old son said, "Daddy, let's play." Thinking fast of what he could do to occupy his son, he noticed an ad with a picture of the earth taking up a full page in the paper.

"Let's play a game," he told his son. He took a pair of scissors and cut up the earth like a jigsaw puzzle. "Now take some tape and put the world together." He knew it would take him at least half an hour, but his boy was back with the picture complete in only five minutes.

"How did you do that so fast?" he asked.

The boy turned the page over. "There's a picture of a man on the back. When I put the man together, the whole world came together."

The only way to get your private world together is to put your relationship to God first and foremost. When your relationship to God is in order, your whole world will come together.

Paul writes, "Set your hearts on things above . . . set your minds on things above, not on earthly things" (Colossians 3:1, 2). Now, he doesn't mean that we are to only be occupied with spiritual things. We don't have to escape to a monastery to experience God.

You may be thinking of the adage, "Some people are so heavenly-minded, they are of no earthly good." But remember, the One who was the most heavenly-minded did the most earthly good. We can also be so earthly-minded that we are of no heavenly good.

Since we are in Christ, our values have changed. We no longer live by the values of a world that is passing away. We live by eternal values—by the kingdom of God. We value forgiveness more than revenge, giving more than receiving, and the timeless more than the temporary.

Don't get so caught up that you forget to look up. Put first things first, and everything else will fall into place.

What Matters Most · DAY 103

Johann Wolfgang von Goethe (1749-1832), German poet, dramatist and novelist, said, "Things which matter most must never be at the mercy of things which matter least." When you feel anxious about something, pause and ask, "Will this make any difference in light of eternity?"

Consider the story of Mary and Martha (Luke 10:38-42). Martha invited Jesus to their home for dinner, but she had no time for Him. She was too busy. Jesus did not take issue with her organization, hard work, or type A personality. I mean, without her, there would be no dinner.

"Martha," Jesus said, "you are worried and upset about many things, but only one thing is needed. Mary has chosen what is better" (vv. 41, 42).

Martha had three issues that kept her from experiencing the power of His presence—even while she was fixing dinner.

First, *she was distracted.* The word means "to draw away, to be over-preoccupied with something, and to be encumbered." In 1 Corinthians 7:35, Paul uses the word in a negative form to mean "undivided devotion to the Lord."

Second, *Martha was worried,* which actually means "to draw in different directions or to divide the mind." In Matthew 6:25 the word is translated "Take no thought" (KJV). Don't allow your mind to be conquered by anxious thoughts.

Finally, *Martha was upset, or troubled, about many things.* But only one thing really mattered, and Mary knew it. She sat at Jesus' feet and hung onto every word He spoke. Jesus was not rewarding laziness; Mary was not a lazy person. She was seizing a rare and unique opportunity to spend time with Jesus.

In a world filled with worries, distractions and responsibilities, we would do well to seize those moments of inspiration when we feel the presence of God. As you go about your daily routines and activities, be mindful of the nearness of God and practice His presence.

The Greatest Desire   DAY 104

We spend our lives trying to get what we want. But the greatest desire is a relationship with Jesus: "[For my determined purpose is] that I may know Him [that I may progressively become more deeply and intimately acquainted with Him, perceiving and recognizing and understanding the wonders of His Person more strongly and more clearly]" (Philippians 3:10, *Amp.*).

I want to know Him as . . .

- Adam's covering of atonement
- Abel's sacrifice of praise
- Noah's ark of safety
- Abraham's ram in the thicket
- Isaac's well of supply
- Jacob's ladder to heaven
- Moses' cloud of glory
- Joshua's commander in chief
- Samuel's anointing
- David's shepherd
- Solomon's wisdom
- The Hebrew children's fourth man in the fire
- Isaiah's Wonderful Counselor and Prince of Peace
- Malachi's Sun of Righteousness
- John the Baptist's Lamb of God
- Simon Peter's Messiah
- The Revelator's King of kings and Lord of lords!

As you go about the day, may your deepest desire be, *I want to know Christ!*

Go to the Ant

"**G**o to the ant, you sluggard; consider its ways and be wise!" (Proverbs 6:6). Ants can teach us a lot about life if we will learn their ways. The word *sluggard* appears 14 times in Proverbs as a caution against unproductive living, which leads to poverty.

Here's a profile on ants: Ants are the most successful of all social insects in the sense that they hold their own under the most adverse circumstances. They live in communities as colony makers. Colonies consist of up to 20 million ants headed by a queen who bears male and female offspring. There are an estimated 1 quadrillion (1 x 10 to the 15th power) ants alive at any one time (I'm not sure who counts all these ants).

Not all ants are the same. Army ants defend the colony as well as work. They have an armor-like covering and stronger jaws than other ants. Harvester ants feed on seeds and gather seeds for seasons of dryness. Gatherers and herders gather plant liquids. Fungus-growing ants (leaf-cutters) cut green leaves on which they grow fungi for food.

Bulldog ants, which live in Australia, are extremely large (about 3/4 inch in size) and are feared because of their aggressiveness and the painfulness of their sting. Carpenter ants are industrious collectors of honeydew and are destroyers of food. Desert ants live in dry regions of North America and have an elaborate system for storing supplies.

Who is welcome in an ant colony? Other ants and several thousand other kinds of insects are welcomed. Tomorrow, we will learn why God tells us to emulate ants.

So, our thought for the day is, *act like an ant!*

Act Like an Ant

What does God want us to learn from the work habits of the ant? The Book of Proverbs admonishes us to act like an ant if we want to succeed.

Ants are self-motivated. The ant has "no commander, no overseer or ruler, yet it stores its provisions in summer and gathers its food at harvest" (6:7, 8). They are self-motivated, in spite of the fact that they have no commander to direct them, no overseer to inspect their work, and no ruler to prod them on. *Motivation* means "the art of producing incentive, drive and desire." We, like ants, need to keep ourselves motivated.

The story is told of a stonecutter in the Middle Ages who was working on a Gothic cathedral. He had spent days and weeks hewing out the features of a small figure to be placed on the top of the cathedral—not one of the prominent gargoyles that would sit atop the corners of the roof, but a smaller statue, which would be tucked away in an obscure nook.

Finally an onlooker said: "That's going to be a beautiful little statue, but tell me, why are you working so hard on it when you know that once it is up, no one will see it?" The stonecutter replied, "God will see it."

We do our best when we are motivated to bring honor to God in all we do. "Whatever you do, work at it with all your heart, as working for the Lord, not for men" (Colossians 3:23).

Goals for Greatness   DAY 107

Let's continue our lessons from the ant. We learned first that ants are self-motivated.

Ants are also goal-oriented. The ant "stores its provisions in summer and gathers its food at harvest" (Proverbs 6:8). Ants prepare for the future. They look ahead. Their daily routines fit in with a larger master plan.

Human nature is purposeful and goal-oriented. God endowed us with creative power to plan, dream and envision. The danger we face is shortsighted living. "Where there is no vision, the people perish" (29:18, KJV). Take the long-range view on things, and you will go far in life.

Ants go beyond their limitations. "Ants are creatures of little strength, yet they store up their food in the summer" (30:25). The key word is *yet*; it means "in spite of." What kind of limitations are you facing? Do you remember what Jesus said to His disciples when they faced insurmountable odds? He told them, "If you have faith as a grain of a mustard seed, you can speak to the mountain, and it will move" (see Matthew 17:20). In other words, go beyond your limitations.

There are three kinds of people in the world: the wills, the won'ts and the can'ts. The wills accomplish everything. The won'ts oppose everything. The can'ts fail at everything.

People who transcend their limitations have shaped history. Cervantes stuttered but became a gifted public speaker. Theodore Roosevelt was a sickly child. The doctors said he would never fully mature, but he became president of the United States. Franklin D. Roosevelt was crippled by paralysis. Milton was blind, yet out of his blindness, he wrote *Paradise Lost, Paradise Regained.* Thomas Edison was nearly deaf when he invented the phonograph at the age of 30. Beethoven was deaf when he composed the Ninth Symphony. Robert Louis Stevenson became an invalid due to hemorrhaging in the lungs; yet, out of his illness, he wrote the classics *Treasure Island* and *Dr. Jekyll and Mr. Hyde.*

"Go to the ant . . . consider its ways and be wise!" (Proverbs 6:6).

Spiritual Warfare   DAY 108

Someone asked me recently if I thought spiritual warfare was real. I responded, "Absolutely!" The man went on to describe the pressures he was facing and a cloud of oppression that seemed to be hanging over his family.

We all face spiritual battles. Sure, there are the natural problems and pressures of life, but there are also spiritual forces of evil that attack us. The fight is on! "Our struggle is not against flesh and blood, but against the rulers, the authorities, against the powers of this dark world and against the spiritual forces of evil in the heavenly realms" (Ephesians 6:12). Note carefully the phrase "spiritual forces of evil." We live in a spiritual world, as well as a natural world.

So, how can we wage spiritual warfare and win?

Tap into the power of prayer. Get a prayer partner and pray in agreement as Jesus taught (see Matthew 18:19). To pray in agreement actually means to sound together as a symphony. No one goes into battle alone. The greater the size of the army, the more certain the victory. You make a serious mistake when you try to fight spiritual battles alone. You need a battle partner—someone to watch your back; someone to get in the foxhole with you and fight to the finish.

When Paul ends his description of the spiritual armor we are to wear, he says, "Pray in the Spirit" (Ephesians 6:18). That means to pray as the Holy Spirit enables us to pray. "Resist the devil, and he will flee from you," says the apostle James (4:7). And how are we to do that? "Come near to God and He will come near to you" (v. 8).

Keep yourself in shape spiritually. "Be strong in the Lord" (Ephesians 6:10). We get attacked at our point of weakness. I am a great believer of physical exercise and healthy nutrition, but I believe even more strongly in staying in shape spiritually through prayer, Bible reading, and fellowship with other believers.

Fight the Good Fight DAY 109

We are told to "fight the good fight of faith, lay hold on eternal life" (1 Timothy 6:12, *NKJV*). We are in a spiritual war. We fight against sinful allurements, the world system, and spiritual forces the Bible calls demons or evil spirits.

Let's consider three additional steps to spiritual victory from our devotion yesterday.

Get on the offensive. Fight against the Enemy. Don't be passive. Actively attack your problems and struggles with the will to win. What goals can you set to fight this battle? What steps can you take to gain the victory over your problems?

Close any door of opportunity for the Evil One. Paul tells us, "Do not give the devil a foothold" (Ephesians 4:27). The King James Version reads, "Neither give place to the devil."

What is a door of opportunity for Satan to wreak havoc in our lives? Unforgiveness is a door, as well as unconfessed sin, resentment toward others, and dabbling with the occult through astrology, consulting psychics, and tarot cards—all of which have become popular in our times. Renounce anything in your life that is an open door for spiritual attack.

Maintain a spirit of praise. When Job was attacked, he worshiped God (see Job 1:20-22). Praise is a weapon against temptation, doubt, fear, depression and hopelessness. "May the praise of God be in their mouths and a double-edged sword in their hands" (Psalm 149:6). Praise brings joy, and joy is our source of strength.

So, persevere in the fight. The season of attack will pass, and the victory will be yours.

What Winners Never Say — DAY 110

Words are very powerful. Jesus said, "Simply let your 'Yes' be 'Yes,' and your 'No,' 'No'; anything beyond this comes from the evil one" (Matthew 5:37). Say what you mean, and mean what you say. Keep your communications clear and concise.

The way we communicate has a great deal to do with our level of success. We can talk ourselves into faith or fear, victory or defeat, hope or disillusionment.

Here are five things winners never say:

I can't. The confident person says, "I can, and I will." Paul said, "I can do all things through Christ who strengthens me" (Philippians 4:13, *NKJV*). Make that your affirmation.

I'll try. Commit yourself to your goals and settle for nothing less than doing what you set out to do.

I'll do it tomorrow. Tomorrow never comes for the person who procrastinates. We procrastinate because we are afraid of failure, or because we are perfectionists. We wait until everything is perfect before we act, and since it's never perfect, we never act. If it's worth doing, do it today, in spite of your fears.

I have a problem. No, you have an opportunity. Problems are opportunities in disguise. Stop trying to solve problems and start setting goals, and you will get somewhere in life.

It's not my fault. Even if it's not your fault, don't get in the habit of saying, "It's not my fault." Winners assume responsibility, and they don't blame others. Take charge of your attitudes, values, beliefs and behavior. Life is a matter of choice, not chance.

A prayer for today: "Set a guard over my mouth, O Lord; keep watch over the door of my lips" (Psalm 141:3).

When Christ Returns

The New Testament contains over 300 promises of Christ's return to this earth. While many viewpoints exist concerning when and how He will return, the promise of His return is certain.

Early Christians held to the belief that Christ's return was imminent. This simply means His coming is always at hand—it could happen at any moment. They lived with expectancy and preparation, "looking for the blessed hope and glorious appearing of our great God and Savior Jesus Christ" (Titus 2:13, *NKJV*).

But how does His promised return affect us?

Because Christ will return, we find peace in the sovereignty of God. History is heading toward a "new heaven and a new earth" (2 Peter 3:13). History is not cyclical, nor is it spinning out of control. It may sound trite, but God is in control of all things. While it is true that God allows human history to run its course, He also set the ultimate boundaries. If history is in the hands of God, then we are in the hands of God. So we can live at peace.

Because Christ will return, we live by Kingdom values. Jesus said, "Lay up for yourselves treasures in heaven" (Matthew 6:20, *NKJV*). Missionary David Livingstone said, "I place no value on anything I have unless it is in relationship to the kingdom of God." We should use every resource and relationship God has given us to make an eternal investment. One day we will give an account. So, get a good return on every investment of your time, talent and treasure.

Because Christ will return, we will seize every opportunity to share our faith. Some people overreact to the promise of Christ's return by becoming passive. If Jesus is coming, why try to reach the world with the gospel? The return of Christ is not for sensationalism but sensibility. His promise is to make us productive, not passive. We are not to get caught up in Rapture fever, but we must be faithful stewards.

When Christ returns, may He find us doing what He commissioned us to do. He said, "This gospel of the kingdom shall be preached in all the world for a witness unto all nations; and then shall the end come" (24:14, KJV).

A New World Order

A *U.S. News and World Report* poll found that nearly 60 percent of Americans think the world will end sometime in the future; almost a third of those think it will end within a few decades. More than 61 percent say that they believe in the second coming of Christ. Nearly half believe a literal Antichrist will arise, and 44 percent believe a Battle of Armageddon will occur.

The end of the world no longer seems a far-fetched idea. Charles B. Strozier, psychoanalyst and history professor at the City University of New York, said, "We no longer need poets to tell us it could all end with a bang, or a whimper, or in the agony of AIDS. With the looming possibility of nuclear or environmental destruction, it now takes an active imagination *not* to think about human endings."[5]

The end of this age is really the beginning of a new age when Christ returns with "power and great glory" (Matthew 24:30). How different the second coming of Christ will be from His first coming into the world that starry night in Bethlehem.

- When Christ came the first time, He was meek and lowly of heart, but He will return as Judge of all the earth.
- When Christ came the first time, He was born in a manger and was wrapped in swaddling clothes; but when He returns, He will be clothed with glory.
- When Christ came the first time, He was given a reed for a scepter; but when He returns, He will rule the nations with a rod of iron.
- When Christ came the first time, He wore a crown of thorns; but when He returns, He will be crowned with many crowns.
- When Christ came the first time, He was rejected, mocked and crucified; but when He returns, every knee will bow before Him and every tongue confess that Jesus Christ is Lord to the glory of God the Father (Philippians 2:10, 11).

The Revelator heard the voices of the hosts of heaven shouting of Messiah's return: "The kingdom of the world has become the kingdom of our Lord and of his Christ, and he will reign for ever and ever" (Revelation 11:15).

Are We Alone in the Universe? DAY 113

A mericans have a growing obsession with life on other planets. We all wonder if we are alone in the universe. Several facts exist.

First, no other planet in our solar system can sustain life as we know it. Earth has a unique canopy over it, which provides the delicate atmospheric balance of 78 percent nitrogen, 20 percent oxygen, and 2 percent other gases. If the oxygen content were raised to 32 percent, the planet would burst into flames. Earth also has the right climate, allowing for water to exist in a liquid form, which is fundamental to the existence of life.

In addition, Earth is placed in precisely the needed proximity to the sun at 92,800,000 miles. If Earth were 3 million miles closer, it would be too hot to sustain life, and if it were 3 million miles farther away, everything would freeze. Whatever we might speculate about life on other planets, one thing is for sure: The existence of life here on Earth is more than a coincidence. Genesis 1:1 states, "In the beginning God created the heavens and the earth." God planned from the beginning of time to do something special on this planet.

Second, science has been unable to verify life on other planets or, for that matter, discover a planet known to have the climate necessary for life. However, two planets have been discovered that are temperate enough to allow water to exist in liquid form. The first planet orbits the star 47 Ursae Majoris, 200 trillion miles (34 light-years) from Earth in the Big Dipper, and is two and a half times the mass of Jupiter. The second planet (though some scientists consider it to be a brown dwarf star) circles the star 70 Virginis in the constellation Virgo, and is also 200 trillion miles away and is more than six times the mass of Jupiter.

We will continue our investigation of life on other planets tomorrow. For now, let us reflect on God, the source of life. "In him we live and move and have our being" (Acts 17:28). God is the source and center of our existence. "Every good and perfect gift is from above" (James 1:17).

Let us join the hosts of heaven and declare, "You are worthy, our Lord and God, to receive glory and honor and power, for you created all things, and by your will they were created and have their being" (Revelation 4:11).

Aliens and Angels

Are we alone in the universe? We can't help but wonder. Among the planets revolving around sun-like stars in our own galaxy—the Milky Way, 100 billion stars strong—is there life out there somewhere? Scientists are eagerly awaiting the results from the Infrared Space Observatory (ISO), a newly orbiting European satellite that can detect the faint heat from distant planets.

In 1997, a new infrared camera was installed on the Hubble space telescope, which could take a picture of at least one of the newly discovered worlds. By 2010, NASA hopes to launch "Planet Finder," a telescope with 3- to 6-foot mirrors spread out over 300 feet, orbiting Jupiter, where the solar-system dust begins to thin out.

We really don't need a telescope or satellite to answer the question. The Bible tells us that we are not alone in the universe. Whether or not intelligent life exists on other planets, no one knows, and the Bible offers us no answers. But, make no mistake about it, we are not alone in the universe, nor on Earth.

The Bible tells us that there are angels in the world. The word *angel* means "messenger." There are 108 references to angels in the Old Testament and 165 references in the New Testament. Angels are "ministering spirits sent to serve those who will inherit salvation" (Hebrews 1:14). Angels sometimes appear in human form, so we don't recognize them. "Do not forget to entertain strangers, for by doing so some people have entertained angels without knowing it" (13:2).

God's angels watch over us. "The angel of the Lord encamps around those who fear him, and he delivers them" (Psalm 34:7).

Wherever you go today, remember: There's an angel in disguise watching over you.

Practicing God's Presence

The single greatest principle for a life of inner peace is practicing the presence of God. The psalmist declared in the midst of troubled times, "The Lord of hosts is with us; the God of Jacob is our refuge" (46:7, *NKJV*).

But isn't God everywhere? Yes, but there is a difference between the omnipresence of God and the experienced presence of God. God is everywhere, but unless we are aware of it, we will not experience His presence.

Atheism asserts that God does not exist. Agnosticism admits God exists, but says that He has not revealed Himself to us. Pantheism argues that God is the power or the life force within everything. Deism says that God exists, but He has left us to our own devices. But Scripture reveals that God exists, and His presence can be experienced.

The Bible uses the term the *presence of the Lord* to speak specifically of the experienced presence of God. "My presence will go with you, and I will give you rest," God promises (Exodus 33:14). The psalmist said of the Lord, "You will fill me with joy in your presence" (16:11). Jesus said, "For where two or three come together in my name, there I am with them" (Matthew 18:20).

Haralan Popov survived being imprisoned for his faith by practicing the presence of the Lord. He spent 13 years in a Communist prison. While in solitary confinement he wrote these inspiring words:

> I was alone for ten days. I felt so close to God in solitary confinement that I spent the time in praise and worship. Such close communion with God; I talked with Him. He comforted me. It was a spiritual feast for me. During this time, I received new strength, though my body wasted away to nothing.

> Tears of joy ran down my face. Here in the DS prison, alone and with nothing, I had everything—Christ. Stripped of everything, without any worldly distractions, I found a deep and beautiful communion with God. Joy and peace flooded my soul. My body ached with starvation, but my spirit has never been closer to God. Lying starved, alone, and too weak to move; I felt I could reach to God and be taken in His arms.

Face the challenges of life by declaring, "The Lord of Hosts is with us!"

The Word Works   DAY 116

Researcher George Barna reports that 4 out of 5 Americans believe the Bible to be the literal or inspired Word of God. In his book, *The People's Religion: American Faith in the '90s,* he observes that

"Americans revere the Bible—but, by and large, they don't read it. And because they don't read it, they have become a nation of Biblical illiterates." Furthermore, "8 in 10 Americans say they are Christians, but only 4 in 10 know that Jesus delivered the Sermon on the Mount."

In 1994 a survey of 1,200 people, ages 15 to 35, found that most of those polled could name no more than two of the Ten Commandments. And essayist Cullen Murphy said, "They weren't too happy about some of the others when they were told about them."

The Word of God is our source of authority, faith and morality.

"Let the word of Christ dwell in your richly as you teach and admonish one another with all wisdom" (Colossians 3:16). The word *dwell* means to inhabit spiritually and to infix mentally.

In 1787, a ship left Britain heading for the South Sea Islands. The trip took 10 months. After arriving, the crew spent the first six months planting fruit-bearing trees. At the end of that time, they decided to return to Britain.

A mutiny occurred. The one who chose to stay sent Captain Bligh and the small crew out to sea on a ship, hoping they would die at sea. The rest stayed on the island.

The society that developed on that island became one of the most lawless, debased societies ever developed. Every type of sin, vice and debauchery was practiced without restraint. Disease spread, killing off nearly everyone except one man—Alexander Smith, along with a few women and children.

He found a Bible among the remains. He began reading it and teaching the Ten Commandments and other portions as the law of God for their small community.

Twenty years after the mutiny occurred, a British ship returned to that very island. They found a virtual utopian society among the islanders—a society of peace, prosperity and productivity based on God's laws.

The Word works when we believe it and put it into practice.

Treasure in a Book DAY 117

At the age of 45, Jack Wurm had reached the depths of depression and despair. Having failed at business, he was walking on the California beach between job interviews. As he strolled along the beach, he noticed a half-hidden bottle in the sand. He stooped down to examine it.

Seeing a note inside, he broke it open and read, "To avoid confusion, I leave my entire estate to the lucky person who finds this bottle and to my attorney, Barry Cohen, share and share alike. Daisy Alexander. June 20, 1937." The name, Daisy Alexander, didn't mean anything to Jack Wurm, so he dismissed it as a joke. Later, however, he learned that Daisy Alexander was heiress to the vast Singer Sewing Machine fortune. If he could prove the validity of the note, he would be entitled to half of the $12 million estate.

Research revealed that Daisy Singer Alexander was an eccentric who lived in England. She often tossed bottles into the water to see where they went. She died at 82 in 1939 and left no final will. Wurm claimed the fortune, and the case began to wind its way through the long court process. An oceanographer testified that a bottle dropped in the Thames River could wash to the English Channel, then to the North Sea, through the Bering Straits, into the North Pacific and end up in either California or Mexico. The journey would take about 12 years. In actuality it took 11 and three-fourths years. Jack Wurm was awarded the fortune. He had found a treasure in a bottle.[6] So it is with the Bible. When we read it we stumble on a spiritual fortune.

We too have found a treasure; not in a bottle, but in a book—the Bible. "I rejoice in your promise like one who finds great spoil" (Psalm 119:162). Jesus said, "Man does not live on bread alone, but on every word that comes from the mouth of God" (Matthew 4:4).

Take time each day to feast on the riches of the Word of God.

Timeless Truths   DAY 118

Carl F.H. Henry, in *The Christian Mind in a Secular Society*, states emphatically that "Biblical truth, transcultural as it is, has an indispensable message for modern man."

The Bible is the timeless revelation of God and His will for us. The Bible has been translated in over 1,600 languages and dialects, the written languages of more than 97 percent of the world's population.

Let me show you just how up-to-date the Bible really is. Several years ago a Biblical archaeologist followed the Bible's directions, leading to the discovery of the famous mines of King Solomon.

An industrialist began his search for oil in the Bible. He read in Genesis: "The Lord rained upon Sodom and upon Gomorrah brimstone and fire from the Lord out of heaven.... The smoke of the country went up as the smoke of a furnace" (19:24, 28, KJV). To him, these flames meant natural gas, which indicates the presence of oil. Taking the cue from Genesis, geologists found evidence of oil, and Israel's first well was drilled in November 1953.

Someone did a study a few years ago of the *New York Times* editorial page and found 466 Bible verses, phrases and references used in 367 editorials in 262 days.[7]

The Bible is more than sacred literature, a collection of wise sayings, prophetic writings, inspired poetry, or a historical document. The Bible is the living and enduring Word of God. Take time to read it (Joshua 1:8), believe it (Romans 10:17), meditate on it (Psalm 1:2) and, above all, practice it (James 1:22). "Blessed is the one who reads the words of this prophecy, and blessed are those who hear it and take to heart what is written in it" (Revelation 1:3).

Treasure the timeless truths found in its sacred pages. "For the word of God is living and active. Sharper than any double-edged sword, it penetrates even to dividing soul and spirit, joints and marrow; it judges the thoughts and attitudes of the heart" (Hebrews 4:12).

Who Is This Jesus? DAY 119

Someone has written:

He was born in an obscure village. He worked in His father's carpenter's shop until He was 30. He then became an itinerant preacher. He never went to college. He never had a family or owned a house. He never held an office. He had no credentials but Himself. When He was only 33, the tide of public opinion turned against Him. All His friends ran away. He went through the mockery of a trial. He was nailed to a cross between two thieves.

While He was dying His executioners gambled for His clothing, the only possession He had on earth. He was laid in a borrowed grave. Nearly 20 centuries have come and gone, yet He remains the central figure of the human race. All the armies that ever marched, all the navies that ever sailed, all the parliaments that ever sat, and all the kings that ever reigned have not affected the life of man on this earth as much as that *one solitary life* (Anonymous, *One Solitary Life*).

When Colonel James Irwin of Apollo 15 was asked to explain the significance of their mission, he replied, "God walking on the earth was more than man walking on the moon."

The entire weight of the Christian faith rests on the person of Jesus. Perhaps there is no greater description of Jesus than is found in the first chapter of the Gospel of John:

> In the beginning was the Word, and the Word was with God, and the Word was God. He was with God in the beginning. Through him all things were made; without him nothing was made that has been made. In him was life, and that life was the light of men (vv. 1-4).

Jesus, the Word   DAY 120

John the apostle calls Jesus the Word of God. "In the beginning was the Word" (1:1). John is very strategic in his use of the term *the Word* to refer to Jesus in his Gospel.

This is the Greek word *logos*, from which we could translate "logic, reason or mind." A word is a vehicle to communicate an idea or a truth. Notice that John does not say that Jesus is *a* word but *the* Word. The uniqueness of Jesus' divinity is in view.

Why does John choose this word *logos* to describe Jesus? Scholar William Barclay sheds great light on John's reference to Jesus, the Word, in *The Gospel of John*. He points out that the New Testament was not written by theologians but by evangelists who wanted to communicate the person of Jesus to their world. When they began, evangelism was simple—Jews telling fellow Jews that Messiah, the Son of David, had come. But when they began to evangelize Gentiles, the message did not relate to the listeners. The Greeks had no idea what was meant by the terms *Messiah* or *Son of David.* So John used the title *Logos* to communicate Jesus in the language of both Jews and Greeks.

A word is more than a sound. It is power. A public speaker or singer can move people to joy or sadness by the power of words. One professor says, "The spoken word to the Hebrew was fearfully alive. . . . It was a unit of energy charged with power."[8] The power of words is underscored in the Old Testament. *Logos* is connected with Creation: "And God said . . ." (Genesis 1:3). The word brought the universe into existence. "The universe was formed at God's command" (Hebrews 11:3).

When Isaac blessed Jacob instead of Esau, the word was binding in its effect; it could not be taken back (see Genesis 27:37). The priestly blessing was a word that brought God's blessings. When the priests spoke the blessing, they put the name of the Lord on the people, and God promised to bless them (Numbers 6:24-27). Just think how powerful the Word of God is: "He sent forth his word and healed them" (Psalm 107:20).

Jesus is the Word and, by that, John means He is the mind behind the universe and the ultimate revelation of God. When we look at Jesus, we have looked into the face of God.

The Eternal Word   DAY 121

We continue our reflection today on Jesus, the Word of God. John the apostle has a strategic reason for calling Jesus the Word, or *Logos* (1:1). To the Greeks, Logos embraces both logic and reason. Moffatt simply translates the verse, "The Logos existed in the very beginning." The concept of Logos developed along three lines of thought, according to the research of scholar William Barclay.

Heraclitus was a Greek philosopher who, like John, lived in Ephesus during the sixth century B.C. He observed two governing principles in the universe. First, everything is in a state of change. Life itself is change. Second, there is a consistency in the midst of the change. Laws are permanent, dependable. The universe is governed by consistent cause-and-effect relationships. The seed planted always yields the same harvest. Seasons are orderly and predictable, not erratic. What is the dependable law operative in the changing universe? Heraclitus called it the Logos. *Logos* is the mind, the reason and the governing agency on which the whole creation depends. All creation depends on God for its order.

The Stoics, although pantheists, were fascinated with creation. They believed that a mind existed behind the universe. It is impossible that the cosmos just happened. The mind behind it all they called Logos, the mind of God, which controls the universe so that the chaos became the cosmos. The Logos is the most important thing in the universe. Order always implies a mind, and the order of the universe implies that a mastermind—the mind of God—created the universe. *Logos* is the power of God, which makes sense of the universe and which keeps the world going.[9]

The writer of Hebrews says of Jesus, "The Son is the radiance of God's glory and the exact representation of his being, sustaining all things by his powerful word" (1:3).

In Him Was Life   DAY 122

Philip Yancey, in *The Jesus I Never Knew*, tells of being raised in the church. But his view of Jesus was quite erroneous. He shares honestly why he is a Christian: first, because of the lack of good alternatives; second, because of Jesus.

To the *hedonist*, life is the pursuit of pleasure. He pedals the philosophy, "Eat, drink and be merry, for tomorrow we die." To the *materialist*, life is the accumulation of things. The one with the most toys wins. To the *naturalist*, life is merely a biological process. To the *evolutionist*, life is the by-product of natural selection. For them, life has no ultimate design or destiny.

But then Jesus weighs in on the subject. He tells us that life is spiritual. Jesus came into the world to give us life. Sin is the great enemy of life. Sin means alienation from God and, consequently, all that is truly life. "The wages of sin is death, but the gift of God is eternal life" (Romans 6:23). Eternal life is more than simply going to heaven when you die (although heaven is a sure promise). Eternal life means the highest possible quality of life today!

John simply, yet emphatically, says, "In him was life" (1:4). The key to being fully alive is to be in Him. Life can be found nowhere else but in Him. E. Stanley Jones explains what it means to be in Christ. To be in

Christ means to be uprooted from the soil of the self and the crowd and be planted in the soil of Christ. It means to totally surrender the self to Christ so that we become one with Him in a dynamic relationship.

We are either in Christ or outside Christ. There is no in-between area. Every attitude, value, belief, philosophy of life, and behavior is either in Christ or outside Christ. To be in Christ is to be in life. To be outside Christ is to be outside life—here and in the hereafter.

In Him was life!

He Came to His Own   DAY 123

Max Lucado said, "If there are a thousand steps between us and God, He will take all but one. He will leave the final one for us. The choice is ours." God has taken every step necessary for our eternal salvation when He sent His Son into the world. He has left one step for each of us—to believe in His Son.

Faith in Jesus is the ultimate choice. God reveals Himself to every person through the wonders of creation and the human conscience, but most clearly through Jesus, who is "the image of the invisible God" (Colossians 1:15).

We, then, exercise the freedom of choice and believe in Jesus Christ. We must take the leap of faith. Faith is the ultimate act of freedom. You are free to believe in Christ. When you do, you will experience the greatest freedom of all.

Our salvation is purely the work of God. We cannot save ourselves from our sins. Christianity is the story of God searching for us. Religion is the story of man searching for God. John the apostle writes: "He came to His own" (John 1:11, *NKJV*). His coming for us says something about who God is and who we are in relation to Him.

He came. He is the seeking Savior. "For the Son of Man came to seek and to save what was lost," said Jesus (Luke 19:10). We aren't searching for God—God is searching for us. We don't "find the Lord," as we sometimes say—He finds us. Jesus is like the jewel dealer in His parable who searched intently for the pearl of great price. When he found it, he sold everything to possess the pearl. You are the pearl of great price. He sought you and paid for your salvation by His sacrifice on the cross.

He came to His own. "We are his people," sings the psalmist, "the sheep of his pasture" (100:3). But, we are wayward children. "All we like sheep have gone astray; we have turned, every one, to his own way" (Isaiah 53:6, *NKJV*). Here comes the amazing part of the story: "The Lord has laid on Him the iniquity of us all" (v. 6).

Here, then, is the good news of Christianity: You don't have to find God through meditation, good deeds, or New Ageism. You have a Savior who searches for you and will not give up His pursuit until He has found you.

Rejecting Jesus DAY 124

One of the most troubling statements in Scripture is John 1:11: "He came to that which was his own, but his own did not receive him." What could be worse than being rejected by your own family?

Why do people reject Jesus? If you are still trying to make up your mind about Jesus, I pray that the next few days of our journey together will clear up your doubts so that you can believe and give Him your life.

Some say, "I don't need a Savior." They are content with their scientific, objective view of reality and don't need the "crutch" of religion. Like Karl Marx, they believe religion is a crutch. While preaching, Billy Graham quoted Marx and said, "I agree. Religion is a crutch. But who's not limping?" They deny the existence of God or of moral absolutes. For them, sin is a myth based on the illusion of religion. Or, they believe that their eternal state will depend on whether or not their good works outweigh their evil deeds.

Humanists believe man is basically good, not evil. So who needs a Savior? Instead of redemption, humanity needs a new environment that will bring out our innate goodness. We aren't sinners, says the humanist, we are good people corrupted by a bad environment. Our problem is external, not internal; social, not spiritual. But the Bible teaches, "All have sinned and fall short of the glory of God" (Romans 3:23).

Now for the good news: Just as all have sinned, all "are justified freely by his grace through the redemption that came by Christ Jesus" (v. 24). "The wages of sin is death," writes Paul, "but the gift of God is eternal life in Christ Jesus our Lord" (6:23).

Some people reject Jesus because they can't look past the failures of those who claim to be His followers. I'll admit that this is a big hurdle, but we can jump it.

True, there are those who manipulate the gospel for their own gain. Jesus said charlatans would come promoting false miracles and turning ministry into a sideshow. But they do not represent Jesus.

We need to get our faith focused properly and look past the manipulators and hypocrites. "Let us fix our eyes on Jesus, the author and perfecter of our faith" (Hebrews 12:2).

Let's Get Historical   DAY 125

There is no denying the fact that Jesus actually lived. The impact of His life continues to transform the world as the kingdom of God conquers the kingdoms of this world.

Flavius Josephus was a guerrilla commander in the war against Rome between A.D. 66 and 70. After that, he turned historian and wrote to restore the dignity of Jews in the eyes of Romans. He writes about the Herods, Caiphas the high priest, John the Baptist, and James "the brother of Jesus, so-called Christ"—all names that are familiar to us in the New Testament. He writes an extensive piece on Jesus himself:

> And there arose about this time (that is, Pilate's time, A.D. 26-36) Jesus, a wise man, if indeed one should call him a man; for he was the performer of astonishing deeds, a teacher of those who are happy to receive the truth. He won over many Jews, and also many Greeks. He was the Christ (or Messiah). In response, to a charge presented by the leading men among us, Pilate condemned him to the cross but those who had loved him at first did not give up; for he appeared to them on the third day alive again, as the

holy prophets had foretold, and had said many other wonderful things about him. And still to this day the race of Christians, named after him, has not died out (Antiquities 18:3.3).[10]

As you go about your day, join the company of the redeemed and tell others "wonderful things about Him." As the psalmist proclaimed, "Let the redeemed of the Lord say so!" (107:2).

Getting Past Yourself   DAY 126

You have to get past yourself in order to follow Jesus. Some people shy away from becoming a Christian, or if they do, they don't tell anyone because they have such deep feelings of spiritual inadequacy and guilt. "I'm not good enough to follow Jesus," they tell themselves.

I meet a lot of people like that. Their guilt and sense of being unworthy of the grace of God keeps them from Christ. But Jesus said that He did not come into this world to call the righteous, but sinners (Matthew 9:13). There is only one condition to come to Jesus—you have to be a sinner. If you can admit that, you can be free. Only a sinner needs a Savior.

Frederick the Great once toured a prison in Berlin. As he walked along the rows of cells, the prisoners fell to their knees beseeching him to free them. They all proclaimed their innocence, except for one man who remained silent. Frederick had the silent man brought to him. He asked, "Why are you here?"

The man answered, "Robbery."

Frederick asked, "Are you guilty?"

The man paused, hung his head and answered, "Yes, Sire, I am. I'm guilty and deserve the punishment I'm receiving."

Immediately, Frederick the Great ordered that the man be released and granted a full pardon. The man thanked him and then asked why he was granting him his freedom.

Frederick said, "You are a guilty man. I will not have you in this prison corrupting these fine, innocent people who occupy it."

Here is the good news: "If we confess our sins, he is faithful and just and will forgive us our sins and purify us from all unrighteousness" (1 John 1:9).

Making a Masterpiece out of a Mess DAY 127

Some people believe they have made such a mess of their lives that they could never be a follower of Jesus. They feel unqualified for service in the kingdom of God. But He is in the business of making masterpieces out of messes. Just read the Gospels and see the kind of characters Jesus called to be His disciples. You and I have a lot in common with that motley crew of fishermen, tax collectors and zealots.

"Follow me," says Jesus, "and I will make you . . ." (Matthew 4:19). We follow, He makes. He can make a masterpiece out of the mess of your life if you will give it all to Him and trust Him to do the work.

Some years ago in Scotland, a couple of men spent the day fishing. That evening, they sat in a local inn having dinner. One of them got carried away describing the size of one of the fish he caught. As he flung his hands, he hit the cup of tea the waitress was about to put on the table. The teacup was dashed against the wall, creating an ugly brown stain.

The fisherman began apologizing, when a customer at another table jumped up and said, "Don't worry about it." He pulled a pen from his pocket and began to sketch around the ugly stain. Soon there appeared a beautiful royal stag with his antlers spread. The artist was Sir Edwin Landseer, England's foremost painter of animals.

Jesus is the Master of human messes.

Fully Alive DAY 128

"The glory of God is a human being who is fully alive," noted Ireneus, an early-church leader. Jesus saves us so that we can live for Him. "This is to my Father's glory, that you bear much fruit, showing yourselves to be my disciples" (John 15:8).

Jesus used the allegory of the vine and the branches to teach about living productive lives. In the Old Testament, Israel is portrayed as the vineyard of the Lord. Jesus says that He is the true Vine, the only source of life, into which we have been grafted.

The first step in bearing spiritual fruit is the pruning process. "I am the true vine and my Father is the gardener. He cuts off every branch in me that bears no fruit, while every branch that does bear fruit he prunes so that it will be even more fruitful" (vv. 1, 2).

There are two kinds of branches: fruitful and unfruitful. The wood of the Palestinian vine is not useful for a good fire because it is too soft. When the Jews brought their portion of wood to be used in the Temple, they were forbidden to bring the wood of the vine. It was gathered in a bonfire, then burned up as useless. Lifeless branches are cut off so that they don't use up the nourishment that needs to go to the fruitful branches.

Then, the branches that are fruitful are pruned so they can bear more fruit. Gardeners in Israel prune back the branches for the first three years so that the branches are not allowed to bear fruit until after three years of growth. Premature fruit is not quality fruit.

God prunes us, or cleans us, so that we can bear more fruit. His pruning work comes through adversity, circumstances, conviction, and the Word of God. God does the work. He's the Gardener.

A prayer for today: "Father, prune the dead, lifeless areas of my life today so that I may bear fruit for You."

Abiding in the Vine   DAY 129

Let's continue our reflections on the vine and the branches. Jesus said, "Remain in me, and I will remain in you. No branch can bear fruit by itself; it must remain in the vine. Neither can you bear fruit unless you remain in me" (John 15:4).

The word *remain*, or *abide*, is used 11 times in the allegory of the vine (see vv. 1-17). To remain in Jesus means to persevere because there is the danger of falling away from our faith.

Remaining in the Vine describes a personal closeness and dependency on Him. "Apart from me you can do nothing" (v. 5). Apart from Him you can do nothing, but through Him you can do all things (see Philippians 4:13). We move from nothing to all things by simply remaining in Christ.

We remain in Him in four ways:

1. *Remain in His Word*: "If you remain in me and my words remain in you . . ." (John 15:7).

2. *Remain in prayer*: "Ask whatever you wish, and it will be given you" (v. 7).

3. *Remain in love*: "As the Father has loved me, so have I loved you. Now remain in my love" (v. 9).

4. *Remain in Him through obedience*: "If you obey my commands, you will remain in my love, just as I have obeyed my Father's commands and remain in his love" (v. 10).

So, let me ask you, What is the only thing necessary for the branch to bear fruit? Stay attached to the Vine. The life, strength and nourishment flow naturally from the vine to the branch. The strength of Christ flows into our lives as we remain in Him.

The Only Debt You Should Owe   DAY 130

We hear a lot today about getting out of debt. It used to be vogue to have debt. We were advised to build credit through having debt. Paul says, "Let no debt remain outstanding, except the continuing debt to love one another" (Romans 13:8).

Let's look at the first part of this principle: "Let no debt remain outstanding," or literally, "Do not keep on owing anyone anything." Paul does not say that it is wrong to borrow money. He says not to let the debt remain unpaid.

Nowhere does the Scripture forbid the responsible use of debt. Jesus taught us to lend to those who want to borrow: "Do not turn away from the one who wants to borrow from you" (Matthew 5:42).

When it comes to debt, the Bible forbids four things: (1) not paying one's debts in a timely manner; (2) failure to pay a debt altogether, which is stealing; (3) signing a contract we can't fulfill; and (4) charging high interest (see Exodus 22:25-27; Nehemiah 5:1-11). Even Jesus advised the use of banks to earn interest on investments (Matthew 25:27).

However, to stay in debt continually is a poor testimony. Debt should be used responsibly and paid on time. Avoid high interest and penalties, which is poor stewardship. Be aware of the difference between consumer debt and asset-building debt, such as a home mortgage.

"Always show good faith," my mother taught us. My parents had large medical bills and had to pay them slowly over years. But they always gave generously and never hid from creditors.

While all debts need to be paid, there is one that we can never pay off, and it is good to feel the obligation of this debt—the debt to love one another.

A Debt of Love   DAY 131

"Let no debt remain outstanding, except the continuing debt to love one another" (Romans 13:8). Let's consider this debt of love that we are to never retire.

The Greek word used here for *love* is *agape*, which is the unconditional love of God. *Agape* means "devotion, commitment, compassion and care." Agape functions on command. True love feels a sense of obligation.

To whom do we owe? We owe God our duty (see Luke 17:10). We owe a debt of love to those who have gone before us and have paved the way of faith for us (see Hebrews 12:1). We owe those who defend our freedom, our parents and family, our friends, mentors who have shaped our lives, and the list goes on of significant people.

Paul the apostle makes an amazing statement next: "Love is the fulfillment of the law" (Romans 13:10). Now get this, all the commandments are summed up in this one rule: "Love your neighbor as yourself" (v. 9). You see, "love does no harm to its neighbor" (v. 10), and that's why love is the fulfillment of the Law of God.

We tend to make the Christian life complicated. Paul was a Pharisee, a strict religious leader who prided himself on trying to keep as many laws as he could. He enjoyed thinking up new laws and regulations for people to keep. There he met Jesus. Love set him free from his sins and from himself. We try to keep rules because we think we can save ourselves. Jesus sets us free and gives us one rule: Love.

"Love God and do as you please," said Augustine. For if you make every decision based on love for God and love for others, you will always be in the center of God's will.

Love Always Protects

True love is not fickle; you can count on it. It's not here today and gone tomorrow. Love remains faithful through thick and thin. "It always protects, always trusts, always hopes, always perseveres" (1 Corinthians 13:7).

We live in an insecure world. The spread of terrorism has increased our fears and insecurities at an exponential rate. On a more personal level, we live in times of economic instability, which threatens our sense of financial security. Many live in unstable homes on the verge of breaking up. Nothing makes us more insecure than when a family falls apart.

God gives us His love to counter our insecurities. Love will protect us and keep us safe. We are to be agents of God's love, providing a shelter of spiritual protection for others.

Love always *protects*. The Greek word means "to hide by covering" or "to protect or preserve by covering." "Love covers over a multitude of sins" (1 Peter 4:8). This doesn't mean that we are to cover over criminal activity or that we are not to hold people responsible for their moral choices. Love demands accountability.

Love protects a person's dignity when he or she falls. Noah's sons covered his shame after he sinned (Genesis 9:20-23). We, too, should hide the sins of those we are commissioned to help as we seek to restore them. Another translation reads, "[Love] bears all things" (1 Corinthians 13:7, *NKJV*). While love is tolerant of the sins of others, it does not "delight in evil but rejoices with the truth" (v. 6). Love does not destroy the fallen by broadcasting their sins to the world.

Surrender your worries to the heavenly Father whose love will always protect you. Then become an ambassador of His love to others.

You Can Count on Love

Love always trusts (1 Corinthians 13:7). Love sees the best in others, believes the best about others, and seeks to cultivate the best in them. Now, don't be naïve, gullible, or close your eyes to pretense or deception. The *Moffatt* translation reads, "[Love] is always eager to believe the best." It's easy to think the worst, to fall prey to gossip about someone, but love keeps the faith.

Can you imagine how much better our relationships would be if we were eager to believe the best? "But I've been hurt," you may object. I'm sure you have, but don't allow the injustices or insults of others to make you cynical. You are an agent of God's love, and love is always eager to believe the best in others. Everyone needs a second chance sometime in life.

Karl Downs was a Methodist preacher in Oakland, California, who died of a heart attack when he was still quite young. Several years before he died, Karl was asked by the juvenile court to take responsibility for a young man who was always getting into trouble.

Karl Downs accepted the responsibility and became a father to this young man. While you may not know who Karl Downs is, you probably know who the young boy is—Jackie Robinson. But there would probably have never been a Jackie Robinson if there hadn't been a Karl Downs.

Love is always eager to believe the best.

Optimistic Love   DAY 134

The older I get, the more I am drawn to positive people, and the more I avoid negative people. Positive people dream dreams, build enterprises, and make the world a better place to live.

Love is optimistic. "[Love] always hopes" (1 Corinthians 13:7). Love looks forward. I don't mean fantasy thinking that ignores reality. But love can stare adversity in the face and believe that a better day is ahead. Love refuses to accept failure as final. Love believes that ultimately the grace of God will conquer. "Where sin increased, grace increased all the more" (Romans 5:20).

Here is a powerful blessing I want you to receive by faith today: "May the God of hope fill you with all joy and peace as you trust in him, so that you may overflow with hope" (15:13).

Paul also says, "[Love] always perseveres" (1 Corinthians 13:7). Love goes the distance. Love never fails, never gives up, and never gives out. Love persevered all the way to the cross for you and for me. Love prayed in the Garden of Gethsemane, "Father . . . not my will, but yours be done" (Luke 22:42). Love wore the crown of thorns. Love died on a cross for the sins of the world. Love shouted from the cross in victory, "It is finished" (John 19:30).

Show Up and Stick With It | DAY 135

The two greatest keys to success in any endeavor are (1) *Show up*, and (2) *Stick with it*! I am a great believer in the power of perseverance. When you know you are on the right path, pursuing the right goals, stick to your plan. Never give up. Never say, "I quit." Take those words out of your vocabulary. Perseverance declares confidently, "I press on toward the mark" (Philippians 3:14, KJV). Finish what you start. Don't stop short of your goals.

After being expelled from college, Duke Rudman drifted in and out of jobs in Texas oil fields. As he gained experience, he dreamed of independent oil exploration. Whenever he would get a few thousand dollars together, he leased drilling equipment and sank a well. He drilled 29 wells in two years and came up dry every time. At age 40, he remained unsuccessful. He began studying land formations, shale types, and other aspects of geology to improve his chances. He leased his 30th tract of land, and this time, a large oil reservoir was discovered.

Still, 75 percent of the wells he drilled are dry. After some 60 years of drilling for oil, he says that he believes he has failed more than anyone in the business. But he struck oil enough times to earn $220 million. "There were days I wanted to quit," says Rudman, "but I'd just push the thought away and get back to work."

You, too, can succeed in every endeavor of life when you have a clear vision of where you want to go and how you plan to get there. Stick to your plan. Eventually, you, too, will strike oil. So, push back every negative thought and get back to work.

Take Jesus' counsel to heart: "No one who puts his hand to the plow and looks back is fit for service in the kingdom of God" (Luke 9:62).

When Life Settles Down, I'll Pray DAY 136

Today everyone is busy. In fact, being busy has almost become an American virtue. But God has not called us to be busy—He has called us to be productive. Fruitfulness, not "busy-ness," glorifies God. When we are busy, we tend to say, "When life settles down, I'll pray." But prayer is not an inconvenience.

Jesus' commitment to prayer is seen in Mark 1:35-39:

> Very early in the morning, while it was still dark, Jesus got up, left the house and went off to a solitary place, where he prayed. Simon and his companions went to look for him, and when they found him, they exclaimed: "Everyone is looking for you!" Jesus replied, "Let us go somewhere else—to the nearby villages—so I can preach there also. That is why I have come." So he traveled throughout Galilee, preaching in their synagogues and driving out demons.

People pressured Jesus with constant demands on His time, but He pulled away. So must we.

Oswald Chambers, in his classic devotional *My Utmost for His Highest,* puts the issue in perspective for us:

> Remember, no one has time to pray. We have to take time from other things that are valuable to understand how necessary prayer is. The things that act like thorns and stings in our personal lives will go away instantly when we pray; we won't feel the smart any more, because we have God's point of view about them. Prayer means that we get into union with God's view of other people.

Prayer can often appear to be the most useless and fruitless experience. As Oswald Chambers noted:

> Prayer to us is not practical, it is stupid, and until we do see that prayer is stupid, that is, stupid from the ordinary, natural, common-sense point of view, we will never pray. It is absurd to think that God is going to alter things in answer to prayer. But that is what Jesus says He will do. It sounds stupid, but it is a stupidity based on His redemption. The reason that our prayers are not answered is that we are not stupid enough to believe what Jesus says.

Treasuring Time   DAY 137

Every day, God gives us the gift of time—24 hours, 1,440 minutes, or 86,400 seconds. Time is a unique commodity. You can spend it, you can waste it, but you can't save it. Time passes quickly. It waits for no one.

Use your time wisely. Invest it in what is important and refuse to be driven by the urgent. Workaholics do not get more done than others; they just burn out faster. Don't work harder; work smarter through wise planning.

Moses prayed, "Teach us to number our days aright, that we may gain a heart of wisdom" (Psalm 90:12). Paul teaches us to "[make] the most of every opportunity, because the days are evil" (Ephesians 5:16).

The great enemy to using our time wisely is procrastination. The word *procrastination* comes from two Latin words: *pros*, meaning "forward," and *cras*, meaning "tomorrow." Some people take Mark Twain's humor seriously: "Never put off until tomorrow what you can put off until the day after tomorrow."

Moses asked Pharaoh when he wanted God to stop the plague of frogs that had come upon Egypt. Pharaoh replied, "Tomorrow" (Exodus 8:10).

Tomorrow? He might as well have said, "Give me one more night with the frogs!"

The word is not *tomorrow*—the word is *today*!

No Other Foundation   DAY 138

Some people think Jesus was a figment of the imaginations of early Christians. Now that is amazing, given the fact that over one-third of the world's population is Christian, and the number of believers is growing at an exponential rate!

The historical evidence for Jesus is undeniable. Let me give you just one example among the many historical records that exist to this day.

Tacitus was a great Roman historian. In the year A.D. 115, he wrote a careful record of major events under each emperor on an annual basis. He wrote an interesting account concerning the year A.D. 64, the year of the great fire that engulfed the city of Rome. He concurs with the prevailing view of the people that Nero was responsible for the fire because he wanted to rebuild the city for his own renown. Here is the record of Tacitus about Jesus of Nazareth:

> To dispel the rumor, Nero substituted as culprits and treated with the most extreme punishments, some people, popularly known as Christians, whose disgraceful activities were notorious. The originator of the name, Christ, had been executed when Tiberius was emperor by order of the procurator Pontius Pilate. But the deadly cult, though checked for a time, was now breaking out again not only in Judea, the birthplace of this evil, but even throughout Rome (Annal 15.44).

It's obvious that Tacitus was no friend of Christianity, but he did get his history right. He records that Christ was born in Judea and lived in the reign of Tiberius (A.D. 14-37), was executed by Pilate (who governed the province in A.D. 26-36), and had an influential following of disciples.[11]

Our faith is not based on fiction, but on historical fact. "For no one can lay any foundation other than the one already laid, which is Jesus Christ" (1 Corinthians 3:11). As the hymn proclaims, "On Christ, the solid Rock, I stand; all other ground is sinking sand!"

Receiving Jesus   DAY 139

Let me share with you today the greatest promise in Scripture: "Yet to all who received him, to those who believed in his name, he gave the right to become children of God—children . . . born of God" (John 1:12, 13).

Do you truly know who Jesus is? There were those who saw Him, yet they never recognized Him as the Messiah, the Son of God. But Peter truly recognized Him when he exclaimed, "You are the Christ, the Son of the living God!" (Matthew 16:16).

When we recognize Him as the Son of God, we will receive Him. Jesus never coerced followers; He only gave an invitation to believe in Him. He comes knocking on the door of every human heart, but we have to open the door to Him and receive Him as a guest.

I heard the story about a young girl whose parents were atheists. They never talked to her about God or took her to church. When she was about 5 years old, her father snapped. He took a gun and shot his wife and then killed himself before her eyes.

She went to live with another family who were Christians. They took her to Sunday school for the first time. The teacher showed the kids that day a portrait of Jesus. "Does anyone know who this is?" she asked. The little girl said, "I know who that is. That is the man who held me the night my parents died."

Faith moves from recognition to reception and, finally, to a revolution. He gives us the right to become the children of God. The word *right* means the full rights of sonship. The Jews saw entrance into a family as a privilege, a gift to be received. All this happens when we believe in Jesus.

In *Mere Christianity*, C.S. Lewis says, "The Son of God became a man to enable men to become sons of God." But birth leads to growth. We *become* children of God. Someone has observed, "The conversion of a soul is the miracle of a moment, but the manufacturing of a saint takes a lifetime."

God's Masterpiece   DAY 140

God has created every person with incredible potential for a life of purpose and productivity. "We are God's workmanship, created in Christ Jesus to do good works, which God prepared in advance for us to do" (Ephesians 2:10). The word *workmanship* literally means a poem or a work of art.

Regardless of how we feel about ourselves or how people may have put us down; regardless of our performances, failures and struggles . . . the fact remains: *We are God's workmanship*. God has a purpose for every person's life. David understood this truth and proclaimed: "I will praise You, for I am fearfully and wonderfully made" (Psalm 139:14, *NKJV*).

Jesus saw people's potential and called it forth: "Come, follow me . . . and I will make you fishers of men" (Matthew 4:18). Common, ordinary fishermen like Peter, Andrew, James and John became world-changers because they came to the understanding that they, too, were God's works of art.

We are created to do good works, which God prepared in advance for us to do. God has a plan for your life. You are not lost in the cosmos. Jesus went so far as to say that the Creator has numbered the very hairs on our heads and He knows when a single sparrow falls to the ground (Matthew 10:29-31).

God works His plan in our lives as we trust Him and as we submit to His will. He is working even when we are unaware of it. "For it is God who works in you to will and to act according to his good purpose" (Philippians 2:13).

Priceless in God's Sight   DAY 141

A well-known public speaker began his seminar by holding up a $20 bill. He asked the group, "Who wants this $20 bill?" Everyone's hand went up.

He said, "I am going to give the $20 bill to one of you, but first, let me do this." He proceeded to crumple up the $20 bill and then asked, "Who still wants it?" Still the hands went up.

"What if I do this?" he asked as he dropped it on the floor and stepped on it with his shoe, grinding it into the floor. He picked it up, crumpled and dirty, and asked, "Who still wants it?" Still the hands went up.

He said, "We have learned a valuable lesson today. No matter what I did to the money, you still wanted it because it did not decrease in value. It was still worth $20."

Many times in our lives we are dropped, crumpled, and ground into the dirt by life's experiences. We feel like we are worthless. But no matter what has happened to us, nothing can change our value in the sight of God. Dirty or clean, crumpled or neatly pressed, you and I are priceless, especially to those who love us. Most importantly, we are priceless to God. Our worth is not measured by what we do, but by who we are.

We are created in the image of God and endowed by our Creator with incredible potential. Even though that image has been marred by sin and failure, God's grace restores the image of God in us. This is what Paul has in mind when he says, "For whom [God] foreknew He also predestined to be conformed to the image of His Son" (Romans 8:29, *NKJV*).

You are priceless in God's sight. You are redeemed by His grace. You are filled with His power. So go out today and live up to the greatness God has placed within you for His glory.

After They Prayed

I have always believed that prayer is the most important of all spiritual disciplines, and yet, the most difficult to master. It is easy to grow weary in well doing when it comes to prayer.

I know from personal experience that prayer is the secret to getting things done in the spiritual realm. As Paul Billheimer wrote in his classic book on prayer *Destined for the Throne*: "Prayer is where the action is."

Success in life and ministry ultimately rests on prayer. As was true of the early church, so it is true for us: "After they prayed, the place where they were meeting was shaken, and they were all filled with the Holy Spirit and spoke the word of God boldly" (Acts 4:31).

The key is "after they prayed." It is only after we pray that we see the spiritual results of ministry as the kingdom of God advances, reaching the lost, empowering believers, and working miracles.

We are all dependent on others praying for us. One of the greatest gifts we can give is the gift of intercessory prayer. As Paul sat in prison penning the words of the Ephesian letter, he asked for prayer:

> And pray in the Spirit on all occasions with all kinds of prayers and requests. With this in mind, be alert and always keep on praying for all the saints. *Pray also for me*, that whenever I open my mouth, words may be given me so that I will fearlessly make known the mystery of the gospel, for which I am an ambassador in chains. Pray that I may declare it fearlessly, as I should (6:18-20, emphasis added).

Who is counting on your prayers today? Pause now and bring them before the Lord, seeking His mercy and grace to help them in their time of need.

Claiming Your Inheritance

When Joshua prepared to lead the people of Israel into the Promised Land, God gave him a promise and a prescription for claiming their inheritance: "I will give you every place where you set your foot, as I promised Moses" (Joshua 1:3).

First, "The Lord said to Joshua" (v. 1). God speaks to each of us personally. Up to this point, the Lord had primarily spoken to Joshua through Moses, but now He spoke to him directly. Every believer is a priest before God and has access to the Father. We are a part of the universal priesthood of believers and can come boldly to the throne of grace and receive grace and mercy to help us in the time of need (Hebrews 4:16).

We don't need any human mediator or the intervention of religion to hear from God. He will speak to us in the secret place of our hearts if we will tune into His voice through prayer, meditation, and the reading of Scripture.

Second, God said, "I will give you every place where you set your foot, as I promised Moses" (Joshua 1:3). Here's a formula: *Divine promise plus human responsibility equals success.* The fulfillment of the promise was based on Joshua's faithfulness to the prescription: namely, to set his foot on the new land. God gave the land, but the people had to possess it. Even so we, by faith, claim the promises of God. We have to "set our foot" on the promise in order to possess it. God looks for active faith, not passive faith.

I have always cherished the promise of Psalm 37:23: "The steps of a good man are ordered by the Lord" (KJV). The *NIV* reads: "If the Lord delights in a man's way, he makes his steps firm." The point is, we have to take steps before God guides. We have to give God something to guide.

Sometimes we are too easily discouraged and intimidated by life's challenges. We, too, develop the grasshopper syndrome of the Israelites, which kept them from invading the land the first time and led to 40 years in the desert. When they saw the giants in Canaan, they said, "We are like grasshoppers in their eyes" (see Numbers 13:33). Passive living keeps us from claiming the promises of God.

Adequate Faith   DAY 144

A minister was on the verge of burnout due to the demands of the ministry. He went to a psychiatrist for help. After explaining his symptoms, the psychiatrist asked him, "Do you have faith in God?"

The minister replied, "Sure, I do."

"Well, why don't you use it?" asked the psychiatrist.

Do we have an adequate faith to meet the demands of life? Real faith is more than religious observance or a mere intellectual acceptance of a creed. Real faith is a relationship with the living God by which we are deeply aware of His presence with us and His power in us that equips us to handle life on its own terms.

- Faith is Job suffering yet declaring, "Though He slay me, yet will I trust Him" (13:15, *NKJV*).
- Faith is David singing, "Yea, though I walk through the valley of the shadow of death, I will fear no evil; for thou art with me" (Psalm 23:4, KJV).
- Faith is Jesus facing the sufferings of the cross, yet saying to His disciples, "Let not your heart be troubled, neither let it be afraid" (John 14:27, *NKJV*).
- Faith is Paul awaiting execution in prison writing, "The Lord will deliver me from every evil work and preserve me for His heavenly kingdom" (2 Timothy 4:18, *NKJV*).

Lin Xiango is a great leader for Christ in China. In 1949 when the Communists took over, they tried every attempt to destroy the church. Believers went underground. Countless Christians were imprisoned and killed for their faith.

In 1955, Lin was imprisoned for preaching the gospel of Christ. He was sentenced to 20 years' hard labor in a coal mining camp with Asian slaves. He was released on several occasions, only to be imprisoned again. In 1978, he was released from prison for the last time. Between 1955 and 1978, he spent 20 years in prison. In 1978, he started preaching again. In 1980, he had only four converts. In 1990, he baptized over 1,000 new believers.

In 1990, secret police came to one of his evening worship services. They stopped the meeting, confiscated Bibles and hymnals, destroyed his printing equipment, and threatened his members to not return. They took copies of the membership list to harass and intimidate his people. He was interrogated repeatedly. During one interrogation, he responded with confident faith to their threats: "I spent 20 years in your prisons. I fear nothing more." His faith was adequate to meet life's challenges.

Today, affirm the words of John the apostle: "Everyone born of God overcomes the world. This is the victory that has overcome the world, even our faith" (1 John 5:4).

Facing a Crisis

What do you do when you face a crisis? This is when we need to learn to pray the prayer of commitment. Turn the situation over to your heavenly Father and relinquish control and worry about the situation. When we have done everything in our power and have assumed our role of responsibility, we are to turn the rest over to God and enter into His rest.

The highest pinnacle of faith is resting in the power and providence of God to do for us what we cannot do for ourselves. By faith, we enter God's rest: "Now we who have believed enter that rest . . . for anyone who enters God's rest also rests from his own work" (Hebrews 4:3, 10). When we rest in Him, we are free from worry and the need to control.

Catherine Marshall offers this prayer of commitment. I trust that you will find a new level of peace as you turn your situations over to God in earnest and thankful prayer:

> Father, for such a long time I have pleaded before You regarding this, the deep desire of my heart: _____. Yet the more I've clamored for Your help, the more remote You have seemed.
>
> I confess my demanding spirit. I've suggested to You ways my prayer could be answered. To my shame, I've been bargaining with You. Yet I know that trying to manipulate the Lord of the universe is utter foolishness. No wonder my spirit is so sore and weary!
>
> I want to trust You, Father. My spirit knows that these verities are forever trustworthy, even when I feel nothing:
>
> - That You are there—You said, "Lo, I am with you always" (Matthew 28:20, KJV).
>
> - That You love me—You said, "I have loved thee with an everlasting love" (Jeremiah 31:3, KJV).
>
> - That You alone know what is best for me—for in You, Lord, "are hid all the treasures of wisdom and knowledge" (Colossians 2:3, KJV).

Perhaps all along, You have been waiting for me to give up all self-effort. At last, I want You in my life even more than I want _____. So now, by an act of my will, I relinquish this desire to You. I will accept Your will, whatever that may be. Thank You for counting this act of my will as a decision of the real person, even when my emotions protest. I ask You to hold me true to this decision. To You, Lord God, who alone are worthy, I bend the knee with thanksgiving, believing that this, too, will work together for the good. Amen.[12]

When Praise Becomes Prayer DAY 146

While many forms of prayer exist, the greatest is praise. Have you ever thought of praise as a form of prayer? Paul connects the two: "Rejoice always, pray without ceasing" (1 Thessalonians 5:16, 17, *NKJV*). Prayer and praise travel hand in hand.

G.K. Chesterton was once asked what was the greatest lesson he had ever learned in life. He answered, "The greatest lesson I have learned is to take things with gratitude and not take them for granted." He also wrote, "You say grace before meals. All right. But I say grace before the concert and the opera, and grace before the play and pantomime, and grace before I open a book, and grace before sketching, painting, swimming, walking, playing, and grace before I dip the pen in the ink."

Praise is the secret of perpetual joy. The apostle Paul prayed we would be "joyfully giving thanks" (Colossians 1:11, 12). Notice how he connects joy and thanksgiving.

Sometimes we complain about how bad we have it. A woman dealing with many problems came to me for counseling. For the first 10 minutes I listened attentively as she went through a litany of everything that was wrong in her life. Then, she stopped abruptly after listening to herself and said, "Listen to me. I sound just like a country and western song!"

One night the Biblical scholar Matthew Henry was robbed. When he got home he was still trembling with fear. Yet, he gained peace as he prayed. This is the prayer he offered and wrote in his journal: "Father, I thank You, first, because I was never robbed before. Second, I thank You because although they took my purse, they did not take my life.

Third, I thank You because although they took everything I had, it was not very much. Fourth, I thank You because it was I who was robbed and not I who robbed."

Practicing His Presence   DAY 147

A successful businessman told me, "What means more to me than anything in the world is peace of mind." The single greatest principle for a life of inner peace is practicing the presence of God. The psalmist declared in the midst of troubled times, "The Lord of Hosts is with us; the God of Jacob is our refuge" (46:11, *NKJV*).

But isn't God everywhere? Yes. But there is a difference between the omnipresence of God and the experienced presence of God. God is everywhere, but unless we are aware of it, we will not experience His presence.

Atheism asserts that God does not exist. *Agnosticism* admits God exists, but says that He has not revealed Himself to us. *Pantheism* argues that God is the power or the life-force within everything. *Deism* says that God exists, but He has left us to our own devices. But Scripture reveals that God exists, and His presence can be experienced.

The Bible uses the term *the presence of the Lord* to speak specifically of the experienced presence of God. "My Presence will go with you, and I will give you rest," God promises (Exodus 33:14). The psalmist said of the Lord, "You will fill me with joy in your presence" (16:11). Jesus said, "For where two or three come together in my name, there am I with them" (Matthew 18:20).

Today, face every challenge with the assurance that God is with you.

Prayer on the Mountain   DAY 148

Sir Edwin Arnold, author of *The Light of Asia*, when speaking to the students at Harvard College, said, "In 1776 you conquered your fathers. In 1861 you conquered your brothers. Now the next great victory is to conquer yourselves."

We all face a spiritual battle within ourselves. We battle between the desires of the sin nature and the desire to walk worthy of the Lord and to please Him in every way. In the Old Testament there is an example of this inner battle portrayed in the conflict between Israel and the Amalekites. Amalek was the grandson of Esau, who lived down south in the region of Petra. The ancient conflict between Jacob and Esau lived on in the war of the Amalekites against Israel when they tried to pass through the land of Amalek on their way to the Promised Land. Spiritual battles are won behind the scene on the mountain of prayer. That's where we find Moses as Joshua leads the troops in battle against Amalek (read Exodus 17:8-15). While Joshua fights in the valley, Moses prays on the mountain. Prayer and action go hand in hand. We have to be willing to be part of the answer to our prayers.

Moses took Aaron and Hur with him to the mountain to pray. (The Jewish historian Josephus says that Hur was Miriam's husband.) This scene in the mountain reveals the power of prayer.

We, like the Israelite soldiers on the battlefield, are engrossed in the challenges and conflicts of life. We are oblivious to those who pray for us as Moses prayed for them. I don't think most of them even knew Moses was praying for them, or realized that it was his prayer that enabled them to win the battle.

Consider the faithfulness of Moses. Prayer can be tiring to both the mind and the body. I like the fact that Moses got tired. It lets me know that when I feel the same way, I am not a failure in prayer. If Moses got tired praying, there's hope for you and me. Aaron and Hur gave him a rock to sit on when his knees got tired and his hands dropped. (Some comfort!)

Faith brings miracles. This poignant lesson is brought home to us in this story. Earlier in Moses' life, he would have never dreamed of trying to win a battle by prayer. He would have been the first to garnish the sword and enter the fight, as he did in his youth when he killed an Egyptian soldier. Now he had learned to wield a more powerful weapon—prayer. The shepherd's rod that was lifted up to God would have earlier been a weapon to strike an enemy in his youth. Only when we mature spiritually do we discover the power of prayer.

So, when you are going through a valley of difficulty, take time to go up on the mountain to pray.

We Believe, Therefore, We Speak DAY 149

I have been reflecting lately on the incredible power of faith. Faith is a wonderful gift God has given us, but it does not benefit us until we release it. Think about Jesus' words: "Have faith in God. Whatever things you ask when you pray, believe that you receive them, and you will have them" (Mark 11:22, 24, *NKJV*).

Unbelief has been called the mother of all sin. Paul tells us, "Whatever is not from faith is sin" (Romans 14:23, *NKJV*). Jesus said that when the Holy Spirit comes, He will convict the world of sin, righteousness and judgment and adds, "of sin, because they believe not on me" (John 16:8, 9, KJV).

We need to eliminate doubt and unbelief from our hearts. We need to eliminate negative words from our speech. Guard your heart and your mouth not to say such statements as "I can't do it," "I don't believe it will happen," or "I'll believe it when I see it."

Faith is located in two places: the heart and the mouth. "If you confess with your *mouth*, 'Jesus is Lord,' and believe in your *heart* that God raised him from the dead, you will be saved" (Romans 10:9).

God calls us to be agents of faith. If you believe something in your heart, you need to confess it verbally. "We also believe and therefore speak" (2 Corinthians 4:13). We are out of God's will and we limit His work in our lives when we speak words of doubt and unbelief. If we are not careful, we can also dampen the dreams of others by negative words of doubt. Christians are commissioned by Jesus to be agents of faith, hope and love. These are the three eternal virtues that change the world. "Now these three remain: faith, hope and love. But the greatest of these is love" (1 Corinthians 13:13).

Make a new resolution today to grow in your faith through a steady diet of reading and studying the Scripture. "Faith comes by hearing, and hearing by the Word of God" (Romans 10:17, *NKJV*). Harness the power of words to declare words of faith that can move mountains.

Healing Prayer DAY 150

When illness strikes, prayer is an instinctive response for everyone. Prayer to God, or to some higher power, to save a life or to perform healing is practiced in non-empirical societies as well. More importantly, the history of the people of God is marked by the healing power of God in response to prayer.

We might think in our day of technology and miracle drugs that scientifically trained physicians would scorn prayer as a means of healing, but think again. According to 133 physicians polled by *MD Magazine*, 92 of them (69 percent) openly admitted to praying for their patients.

Dr. Randolph Byrd demonstrated in his research that hospitalized heart patients had fewer medical problems when others prayed for their recovery. Byrd divided 393 patients, randomly selected, into two groups. Five to seven born-again Christians were given the first names and diagnoses of the people in one group and were asked to pray for their healing. The other group received no such prayers. The results of the "prayed for" group were astounding: they required fewer drugs and less mechanical support for breathing, and had fewer episodes of congestive heart failure, pneumonia, and cardiac arrest.

Researchers in London, England, conducted prayer experiments on 32 incurably ill patients who suffered ailments ranging from rheumatoid arthritis and spinal disease to scleroderma (disease causing hardening of skin and organs). Prayer groups of Christians and Quakers volunteered to pray for half of the 32 patients at least 15 minutes a day for six months. They were given only the patients' first names and description of disease. The results were significant: Five of the 16 patients who were prayed for showed marked improvement in their conditions six months later. In the group receiving no prayer, all except one had no improvement or became worse.

Here is the principle and promise of God's Word for today: "Confess your sins to each other and pray for each other so that you may be healed. The prayer of a righteous man is powerful and effective" (James 5:16).

Prayer Doesn't Heal—God Does   DAY 151

In his book *Healing Words: The Power of Prayer and the Practice of Medicine*, Dr. Larry Dossey, former chief of staff at Medical City Dallas Hospital, cites more than 130 studies that verify the healing power of prayer. Unfortunately, he, along with others, fails to understand the power of prayer as being, in actuality, the power of God. Some have explained these findings in terms of prayer releasing cosmic healing energies. Prayer doesn't heal—God does.

As Christians, we do not put our trust in prayer, we put our trust in God. He is the Great Physician. Prayer is a relationship of communion with the God of healing. The Old Testament records 30 cases of divine healing, while the New Testament records 38 cases. One fifth of the Gospels deals with Jesus healing the sick.

Prayer should be our first option, not our last resort. It's like the story of the ship caught in a storm at sea. As the storm raged, the captain realized his ship was sinking fast. He called out, "Does anyone know how to pray?" One man stepped forward. "Aye, Captain, I know how to pray." "Good," said the captain, "you pray while the rest of us put on our life jackets—we're one short."

James tells us in no uncertain terms, "The prayer of faith shall save the sick" (5:15, KJV). The word for *save* (Greek, *sozo*) means "to save, to mend, to make well, to restore, to cure, to soothe, and to cleanse." James also uses another Greek word for healing, *iaomai*, meaning "to cure or to heal" (see v. 16). Of all we know about healing, one fact is certain: Jesus is the Great Physician, and the prayer of faith will save the sick.

Seeing the Big Picture DAY 152

I'm sure you've heard the adage, "Don't miss the forest for the trees." Or, today we might be more prone to say, "Don't sweat the small stuff."

E. Stanley Jones said, "Often the church announces great things but deals with the little."

Several years ago, the game Trivial Pursuit was the craze. If we are not careful, we can get bogged down in trivial pursuits, spiritually speaking, and miss the greater matters of faith and ministry. By the way, didn't Jesus say something about us doing "greater works"? (see John 14:12, *NKJV*).

The legalists of Jesus' day had these problems—traditionalism, small-mindedness, tunnel vision. "Woe to you," Jesus confronted them.

"You hypocrites! You shut the kingdom of heaven in men's faces. . . . You blind guides! You strain out a gnat but swallow a camel" (Matthew 23:13, 24).

Why did He say such things? Because they "neglected the more important matters of the law—justice, mercy and faithfulness" (v. 23).

Have you ever noticed that many of the issues discussed and debated among Christians make little difference in light of eternity? We waste words in our pulpits answering questions people aren't asking. We prefer to debate the signs of our Lord's return, rather than confront the inevitable spiritual burden we should feel over those not ready for His coming. We gladly give our resources to send missionaries to foreign fields, yet feel uncomfortable around people of a different ethnicity from our own.

We sit silent on moral issues, leaving it up to CNN, C-SPAN and FOX News Network to confront moral issues. Are we, like the Pharisees, straining out gnats and swallowing camels?

Jesus' disciples struggled with small-mindedness. "Open your eyes," was His cure for their trivial concerns. "Look at the fields! They are ripe for harvest" (John 4:35). They were concerned about Him talking to a Samaritan woman and crossing ethnic boundaries; He was focused on bringing lost humanity into the kingdom of God.

In the Old Testament we read, "Asher remained on the coast and stayed in his coves" (Judges 5:17). He was "cove-minded" instead of being "sea-minded." The endless adventures of the sea lay before him, but he was content to stay by the cove.

Stop looking at the cove—the small, personal and trivial issues that concern only us. Look at the sea. Keep your sight focused on the big picture of the greater matters of the kingdom of God.

Real Revival

When you hear the word *revival*, what comes to mind? *Revival* means a coming back to life again. It is used to describe a spiritual awakening, a restoration of spiritual passion, a renewal of faith, and a returning to God. A revival is more than emotionalism or exuberance.

One of the most common misconceptions about revival is that revival is only needed by those who have fallen away from God. While this is certainly part of the process, revival is for every person. We all need seasons of renewal when the rain of the Holy Spirit is poured out in a fresh measure.

I point this out because the word *revival* has almost taken on a negative connotation. Think of revival as a time of spiritual renewal in which we are drawn and captivated more fully into following Jesus Christ as Lord.

Throughout the Bible we hear prayers for revival. David prayed, "Create in me a pure heart, O God, and renew a steadfast spirit within me. . . . Restore to me the joy of your salvation" (Psalm 51:10, 12). The psalmist prays with desperation for God to intervene in his times: "Will you not revive us again, that your people may rejoice in you?" (85:6).

God promises to send revival when we seek Him. "For I will pour water on the thirsty land, and streams on the dry ground; I will pour out my Spirit on your offspring, and my blessing on your descendants" (Isaiah 44:3). The aftermath of true revival is a deeper sense of joy that comes from the presence of God. "The joy of the Lord is your strength" (Nehemiah 8:10).

Ask God today to visit your heart and your home with a renewed passion for the things of God so that you can set your heart on things above and not on earthly things.

When Revival Comes   DAY 154

Peter said that we can have "times of refreshing . . . from the presence of the Lord" (Acts 3:19, *NKJV*). When revival comes to the church, the kingdom of God comes to the world. John Stormer, in *The Death of a Nation*, notes that the amazing thing about the major revivals throughout church history is their long-term effect on society. The following is a testimony from John Wesley's era:

> Soon the traveling evangelists had to move on to the next town. When they did, men and women on fire for the Savior who had given them a new life started Bible classes and prayer groups. On their own, they started to preach judgment for sinners and the love of the Savior to all who would listen.

They attacked decay and decadence in government, business and the church. Even though less than two and a half percent of the population was converted during Wesley's 50-year ministry, the face of England was changed. As that handful became the "salt of the earth," the slave trade was stopped. Four out of five taverns were closed for lack of business. Prison and penal reforms were instituted. The dangerous conditions under which children worked in factories were improved—and corruption in government declined.

What does it take to have revival? The noted preacher R.A. Torrey said that only three ingredients are necessary for revival. First, God's people get thoroughly right with God. Second, God's people bind themselves together in a prayer group until God opens the heavens and comes down. Third, God's people put themselves at God's disposal for Him to use in winning others to Christ.

Let us take time today to ask God for real revival in our times, believing that times of refreshing will come to us and to our world.

Renewing Our Consecration   DAY 155

The height of our spiritual leadership depends on the depth of our consecration to God. To *consecrate* means "to dedicate, to devote and to set apart" for God's purpose. The Hebrew word *consecrate* can mean "renew," speaking of times of renewed consecration.

Leviticus 14 provides an order for an anointing service for those needing physical cleansing and consecration, which represents a life that has been spiritually cleansed and consecrated to the Lord. The oil is a symbol of the presence and power of the Holy Spirit.

> The priest is to put some of the oil remaining in his palm on the lobe of the right ear of the one to be cleansed, on the thumb of his right hand and on the big toe of his right foot, on top of the blood of the guilt offering. The rest of the oil in his palm the priest shall put on the head of the one to be cleansed and make atonement for him before the Lord (vv. 17, 18).

The anointing of the ear represents spiritual receptivity. We need to tune our hearts to hear God's voice and to obey Him. Young Samuel answered the voice of God saying, "Speak, for your servant is listening" (1 Samuel 3:10). Jesus says, "If anyone hears my voice and opens the door, I will come in" (Revelation 3:20). Also, our spiritual ears need to be tuned in to the cry of the world as was Jesus (see Matthew 9:36).

The anointing of the hand represents active ministry. The laying on of hands is the act of ministry, imparting grace and blessing to others (see James 5:15). The Holy Spirit anoints us with power for Kingdom service. We are to be diligent in everything we put our hands to (see Ecclesiastes 9:10).

The Anointed Life   DAY 156

Yesterday we looked at the significance of the anointing service for the Old Testament priests. They had their right ear and right hand anointed with oil. This represents the Holy Spirit giving us spiritual sensitivity to God's voice and empowerment for ministry.

The anointing of the feet represents our walk, lifestyle, and direction of ministry. If our feet are truly consecrated, we will take steps of faith and progress. We are to walk in the footsteps of Abraham's faith (Romans 4:12). God expects us to trust Him for "great and mighty things" (Jeremiah 33:3, NKJV). Peter had to take the step of faith over the side of the boat if he wanted to walk on water.

We also need to walk, which means to govern our lives, in a Christlike way. The old English word walk means "lifestyle." Christianity is not just a way of believing; it is a way of living.

We need anointed feet that carry the good news of Jesus to others. "How beautiful on the mountains are the feet of those who bring good news" (Isaiah 52:7). Christ washed the feet of His disciples to show that they were to walk in humility. They saw their feet as consecrated and walked in the way of Christ because He had washed their feet.

Then, the anointing of the head represents submission to God and a life of service to others in love. "Submit yourselves, then, to God" (James 4:7). "Submit to one another out of reverence for Christ" (Ephesians 5:21).

Pray this prayer of consecration:

Heavenly Father, I once again consecrate myself to You to be set apart for Your sacred service. Give me the fresh anointing of the Holy Spirit on my ears to hear Your voice, on my hands to be active in ministry to others, on my feet to walk in faith and to carry the good news of Jesus wherever I go, and on my head to live in joyful submission to You. Lord, give me new joy and power as I follow You with all my heart. Amen.

Anticipating Autumn   DAY 157

I am writing this devotion in autumn. Fall is a season of new beginnings. Summer is over. Vacations draw to a close. Kids prepare to go back to school. The hot summer air begins to give way to the brisk morning air of autumn.

For some, fall simply means getting back to the grind. Others anticipate new opportunities. Life is largely a matter of what you anticipate. Autumn is a time for embracing a new season of wonderful opportunities. Opportunity has a way of seeking out people of anticipation.

The word *anticipation* means the art of foreseeing or foretasting. Anticipation is the antidote for stagnation. It is easy to let life degenerate into boredom and monotony. Life indeed has its routines that give stability and consistency. But we don't have to allow boredom to set in. Break out of your stagnation by anticipating new things and preparing yourself for them.

Anticipation also brings excitement to life. Some people just settle for what life brings. They wait for the serendipitous to happen. When it doesn't, they get disappointed with life and envy the joy, passion and excitement of others. If something would just come along for them, they would be happy.

Life seldom happens on its own. You have to make it happen. Create passion in your life. Exciting things will happen for you when you face life with anticipation. What you see is what you get. If you expect life to be routine, it will be. If you expect more, you'll get it.

Life doesn't happen accidentally or passively. Life is what we make happen. Life is something we live, not passively experience. Life is a verb!

Finally, anticipation is the essence of faith. "Faith is being sure of what we hope for and certain of what we do not see" (Hebrews 11:1). Jesus said, "All things are possible to him who believes" (Mark 9:23, *NKJV*). Your level of faith and anticipation will bring incredible blessings your way and make the impossible possible.

Raise your level of expectation. If you expect life to be boring, monotonous and routine, it will be. But if you expect to get more out of life than the status quo, you can and you will.

A Simple Plan   DAY 158

Someone once asked me to give them a simple plan for spiritual growth. I told them to do three things. Let me share them with you. First, *stay in the flow of God's grace.* You have to receive before you can give. Giving is the result of first having received something so that you can give. You minister to others only out of the level of grace and blessing you have received. "Let your conversation be always full of grace . . . so that you may know how to answer everyone" (Colossians 4:6).

We get burned out when we try to give more than we receive. Just like your car will stop running if you don't fill it up with gas, you will stop running if you don't fill up spiritually. Stay full of grace. "Day after day, in the temple courts and from house to house, they never stopped teaching and proclaiming the good news that Jesus is the Christ" (Acts 5:42).

Second, *make close Christian friends.* Jesus said, "I no longer call you servants, I call you friends" (see John 15:14, 15). Jesus sent His disciples out to minister in groups of two so that they could help each other face life's opportunities and disappointments. Christianity is community. The early church leader Augustine said, "He cannot have God for his father who does not have the church as his mother."

Finally, *make an investment of yourself through service.* Dietrich Bonhoeffer said, "The church is only the church when it lives for others." When you invest your time, talents and treasure in the kingdom of God, you will feel a surge of energy and enthusiasm about your walk with God. Peter exhorts us, "Each one should use whatever gift he has received to serve others, faithfully administering God's grace in its various forms" (1 Peter 4:10).

You will experience great joy knowing you are making an eternal investment with your life and leaving a lasting legacy of faith for generations to come.

WWJD?

A disciple is a student of Jesus. To be more specific, a disciple is a follower, learner and imitator of Jesus. Jesus' call to every person is, "Follow Me." We follow Jesus through a personal relationship so that we can learn from Him how to walk with God and how to love others as He loves us. Paul writes: "Follow my example, as I follow the example of Christ" (1 Corinthians 11:1).

The ultimate goal of learning is doing. A disciple aims to imitate Jesus in all areas of his or her life. Thomas à Kempis' classic, *The Imitation of Christ*, touches on this magnificent truth.

Paul says, "Be imitators of God" (Ephesians 5:1). Young people are taught to ask, WWJD—*What would Jesus do?* This is the essential question for the serious disciple of Jesus. Jesus said, "I have set you an example that you should do as I have done for you" (John 13:15). Imitating the example of Jesus is the highest ethic of the Christian life.

When we imitate Jesus, others see "Christ in [us], the hope of glory" (Colossians 1:27). They don't see Him perfectly in us, because we are less than perfect. But they can see glimpses of His grace and power. Even the Sanhedrin was moved by the courage of Peter and John when they testified before the court concerning the resurrection of Jesus. "They took note that these men had been with Jesus" (Acts 4:13). And people take note when we "have been with Jesus."

We "reflect like mirrors the glory of the Lord" (2 Corinthians 3:18, *Ph.*). Just as the moon reflects the light of the sun, we reflect the light of Christ. We are not the light; Christ is. However, His light shines in our hearts and reflects from our lives.

Before we take action, we need to stop and ask:
- What would Jesus do in this situation?
- How would Jesus manage money and time?
- How would Jesus respond to this crisis?
- What would Jesus do about this injustice?

- How would Jesus react to this challenge?
- How would Jesus pray about this situation?

Disciples respond to life and to others the way Jesus did. Jesus said, "A student is not above his teacher, but everyone who is fully trained will be like his teacher" (Luke 6:40). A disciple asks, "What is Christ teaching me in this experience of life? What does He want me to learn?" When you approach life this way, every event, every circumstance, every relationship becomes a learning experience to conform you to the image of Christ.

Why Excellence Matters — DAY 160

Isaac D'Israel said: "It is a wretched taste to be gratified with mediocrity when the excellent lies before us."

Excellence is the master key to success in any endeavor. *Excellence* means "the very best quality; superiority; first-rate; exceptionally good." Edwin Bliss said, "The pursuit of excellence is gratifying and healthy. The pursuit of perfection is frustrating, neurotic, and a terrible waste of time." Booker T. Washington said, "Excellence is to do a common thing in an uncommon way."

There is no room for status quo and mediocrity in the kingdom of God. God created us for excellence. Jesus deserves our excellence. The Holy Spirit empowers us for excellence. The times require excellence.

You are "fearfully and wonderfully made" by the Creator, and you are "crowned with glory and honor" with an infinite resource of potential (see Psalms 139:14; 8:4, 5). You were made for greatness.

Excellence requires us to mix hard work and diligence with the potential God has given us. Talent and ability are not enough. "Make every effort to add to your faith . . ." (2 Peter 1:5). Success doesn't come from simply making an effort but by making every effort.

As you face the opportunities before you today, do so with a commitment to excellence. "Whatever you do, work at it with all your heart, as working for the Lord, not for men" (Colossians 3:23).

A Master Plan

Do you have a mission that justifies what you do every day? We need to live with purpose. After President Ronald Reagan died, a political commentator noted that while President Reagan's policies are debated, the one thing he did right was focus on the "big ideas." His big ideas of putting America back to work after the deep recession of the '70s and of ending the Cold War were the right ideas, and he stuck to them.

We need to keep the big picture in mind and not get lost in trivial details. Your mission statement needs to begin with your spiritual commitment. Jesus gave us a master mission for life: "Go and make disciples of all nations" (Matthew 28:19). In everything we do in life—marriage, career, raising children, managing money—we are to make disciples of Jesus.

Don't drift with the tide. Get a master plan for your life. Set concrete goals and develop a workable strategy to reach them. When you build a house, you start with a master plan and then work to complete the plan, making adjustments as you go. Can you imagine the chaos that would occur by trying to build a house without a set of blueprints?

Jesus talked about the need to sit down and count the cost before we start to build to see if we have the needed resources to finish (see Luke 14:28-30).

Without a master plan, we react to one situation after another. Circumstances and emergencies plan our agenda instead of us setting our own agenda and then working the plan.

When I went to college, I went to get a doctorate, not a bachelor's degree. So, the bachelor's degree was just a step in a larger master plan. Then I got my master's degree in counseling. While it brought me a great sense of accomplishment, I was still only two-thirds of the way to the finish line. When I graduated with my doctorate, my goal was reached.

Keep your eye on the finish line with every project. Celebrate each milestone along the way, but don't stop until you finish the race. "Let us run with perseverance the race marked out for us" (Hebrews 12:1).

Quality, Not Quantity

Life won't fly on autopilot. Neither will a marriage, a career, a business or a ministry. Pay attention to details. A study revealed that businesses go bankrupt mainly because of poor service and the failure to pay attention to details.

While we need to focus on the big picture, remember that the big picture is simply a collection of details. As Solomon reminds us, "The little foxes . . . spoil the vines" (Song of Solomon 2:15, *NKJV*).

Good management means quality control. In America, we often think that bigger is better. But bigger is not always better, its just more stress. We need to focus on quality, not quantity. Control the quality of your life, work and ministry, and let God control the quantity.

Don't try to build a bigger business—build a better business, and it will grow bigger. Don't worry about making more money—focus on managing your money better, and your net worth will grow. Don't ask for more time to do a project—use the time you have in a more efficient manner. Don't chase a bigger dream—chase a better dream!

Excellence means quality control in every area of life. A commitment to quality is a mark of high self-esteem. People who care about the quality of their work care about themselves.

No one has known the power of quality any more than Antonio Stradivari, the Italian violin maker (1644-1737). He lived to be 93 years old in a time when the average life expectancy was a little over 30. He was self-taught, worked with simple tools, and worked alone, until his sons joined him in business late in his life. When Stradivari finished a violin and it passed his high standards of excellence, he signed his name on it. Today a Stradivarius violin sells for thousands of dollars, and his name is synonymous with excellence.

Role Models

Role models are vital to help us achieve our best. "As iron sharpens iron, so one man sharpens another" (Proverbs 27:17). We need iron in our relationships to test us and sharpen us. Don't surround yourself with soft people who comply with your every request. Immature people don't have enough "iron" in their lives, while mature people have true mentors and peers who sharpen them.

We need to seek out models like the young prophet Elisha sought out the seasoned man of God, Elijah. Don't expect a mentor to come looking for you. Take the initiative and seek out wise counselors and seasoned leaders.

The concept of competition is distorted in our times. Real competition means to compete against a winner so as to bring out the winner in you. We aren't trying to defeat an opponent in a triumphant sense but in an effort to reach our highest potential. We need relationships of tension to reach excellence. In the end, you are only competing against yourself—against your desires, disciplines and habits.

I run every day for exercise. When I run I am often surrounded by other runners. I don't try to run at their pace. I'm not competing against them. I am competing against my inner resolve to push myself toward the goal. However, when I get around a faster runner, it helps me push myself toward my ultimate potential.

So get some iron in your relationships, and you will be pushed toward greatness.

Examine Yourself   DAY 164

"Examine yourselves. . . . test yourselves" (2 Corinthians 13:5). When you look in the mirror, are you proud of the person you see? Plato said, "The unexamined life is not worth living." Take time to examine yourself in light of the person of Christ himself.

What is the image of Christ in us? Paul tells us clearly that "the fruit of the Spirit [that means the end result of what the Holy Spirit is doing in us] is love, joy, peace, patience, kindness, goodness, faithfulness, gentleness and self-control" (Galatians 5:22, 23).

We need to examine ourselves in light of Scripture. The Bible is the inspired, infallible and authoritative Word of God. It is a lamp to our feet and a light to our path (Psalm 119:105). The apostle James says it is a mirror by which we evaluate our attitudes, values, beliefs and lifestyle. Consistent exposure to the Bible brings a transformation of life.

Anyone who listens to the word but does not do what it says is like a man who looks at his face in a mirror and, after looking at himself, goes away and immediately forgets what he looks like. But the man who looks intently into the perfect law that gives freedom, and continues to do this, not forgetting what he has heard, but doing it—he will be blessed in what he does (James 1:23-25).

Finally, we need to evaluate ourselves in light of our best self. Ask the question: "Is this my best self?" Are you living up to your highest potential? Are you the person you want to be and who you can be?

I am sure we all are aware of our weaknesses more than we are our strengths. No one is perfect. That's not what I am talking about. We know when we are falling short of the standards and goals we have set. When we do, we need to get back on track and live up to our potential. "Live a life worthy of the calling you have received" (Ephesians 4:1).

Managing Your Mistakes — DAY 165

Here's a statement in the Bible that gives me great encouragement: "We all stumble in many ways" (James 3:2). I'm glad I'm not the only one who struggles with issues, fails at projects, and comes up short. We all do. Now, I know some people who think they are perfect, so I like to remind them that we all stumble in many ways!

The question is not whether or not you will fail, but do your failures and mistakes defeat you or develop you? Winston Churchill said, "Success is going from one failure to another without losing your enthusiasm."

Excellence does not mean perfection. "Life is not a spelling bee!" says Harold Kushner. Failure is never final with the grace of God.

Peter failed the Lord by denying Him and deserting Him. After the Resurrection, Peter gave up trying to be a disciple. He went back to his fishing business. But the risen Lord went out to the Sea of Galilee early one morning to reclaim His fallen follower (read John 21). While they were in the boats, Jesus stood on the shore and called out to them, "'Haven't you any fish?' 'No,' they answered" (v. 5).

Then came the direction they needed. Jesus said, "Throw your net on the right side of the boat" (v. 6). When they did, they caught more fish than they could contain in the nets!

What do we learn from this inspiring story? Christ gives us two directives when we make mistakes. First, *try it again.* Jesus was using fishing as a metaphor of His commission for them to be fishers of men after they failed.

Second, *fish on the right side of the boat.* Fish where the fish are biting! Don't beat your head against the wall, trying to fish in the wrong area.

One of my favorite affirmations is Micah 7:8: "Do not gloat over me, my enemy! Though I have fallen, I will rise." Make that statement right now: "Though I have fallen, I will rise!"

Keep Your Spiritual Fervor DAY 166

Jesus was the most focused and highly motivated person who ever lived. He was consumed with zeal for the house of the Lord (John 2:17). Paul challenges us: "Never be lacking in zeal, but keep your spiritual fervor, serving the Lord" (Romans 12:11).

All successful people have learned the art of self-motivation. *To motivate* means "to incite to action; to impel forward; to stir up passion." As believers, we have the Holy Spirit who motivates us. "God . . . works in you both to will and to act according to his good purpose" (Philippians 2:13).

We also need to motivate ourselves. When David hit rock bottom and no one supported him, he "encouraged himself in the Lord his God" (1 Samuel 30:6, KJV). Sometimes you just have to encourage yourself.

I heard T.D. Jakes tell his congregation, "I don't need you to make my dreams come true!" He certainly wanted their support, but he wasn't dependent on it. That was the point he was making. We certainly need others to help us and to encourage us, but at the end of the day, you and God constitute a majority. Sometimes you may have to go it alone and encourage yourself until others see your vision and lend their support. Don't give up in the lonely times. Encourage yourself in the Lord by remembering three things:

1. God is with you!
2. God is in you!
3. God is for you!

Staying Up-to-Date   DAY 167

Discard old ways of doing things that no longer work. Avoid the trap of traditions that have seen their day. The seven last words of the traditionalists are: *We never did it that way before.*

The myth that yesterday's solutions will solve today's problems is a deathblow to organizations and to relationships. We see it in stagnant marriages, unproductive businesses, and lifeless congregations. Die-hard traditionalists sit idly by, talking about the good old days while life passes them by. The only good day is today! This is the only day God has given us, so let us enjoy it and make the most of it.

Jesus taught us to get new wineskins for the new wine of God's grace (Mark 2:22). The "new wineskin" is a metaphor for a new way of doing things. He taught us to be careful that "God-in-the-box" thinking does not cause us to miss what God is doing in our times because we narrowly think, *God doesn't work that way.* Of His own generation, Jesus said, "You missed the day of God's coming to you" (see Luke 19:44). They missed out on the blessings of God because they were trapped in their traditions.

In 1968, the Swiss dominated the world market for watches, selling two out of every three watches sold. Yet within a decade, their market share plunged to a mere 7 percent, all because they clung to the assumption that electronic timepieces would never sell. They failed to modernize and lost the cutting edge of excellence.

Remember, God pours new wine into new wineskins. Get a new wineskin. Change the very way you have been doing things, and you will stay on the cutting edge.

The Big Mo   DAY 168

In athletics we call it the Big Mo. Jesus started a small movement and let it gain momentum. Today the church is the largest, fastest-growing, and most influential movement that has ever existed in the history of the world. Over a third of the world's population are devoted followers of Jesus Christ, and the movement is growing so rapidly around the world that projections are that half the world's population will be Christian within 50 years.

Many people start a project with a big bang and then fizzle out. So how do you build and keep momentum? Let me give you three steps:

1. *Start small.* Jesus started with only 12 disciples. Every great project begins small—just an idea, just a single step of faith, just a simple act. But the process toward greatness has begun.

2. *Go deep.* Develop your foundation. Grow deep roots. Strive for stability in relationships, projects, investments, ministry and business ventures. When adversity comes, you will stand firm and grow even through the hard times.

3. *Think big.* Dream big dreams. Set your sights high. Small-minded people never accomplish great things, only small things. Until you can see your dream by faith, you can't make it happen.

Jesus said the kingdom of God is like yeast that gradually works through the whole batch of dough. When it finishes its permeating effect, the whole batch is leavened (Matthew 13:33). The kingdom of God starts small but grows big.

Jesus' commission to His followers to "go into all the world and preach the good news" was an enormous vision and a huge challenge (Mark 16:15). But He was able to convince them that they were capable of reaching the whole world with the good news of His salvation. And they did!

Watch the Movie! DAY 169

W hen God guides us, He expects us to take the step of faith. "The steps of a good man are ordered by the Lord" (Psalm 37:23, *NKJV*). Many people want to know the future. But God wants us to walk by faith and to trust Him with the future. He unfolds His plan for us little by little, one step at a time.

It's like watching a movie the second time. You know what's going to happen next. The adventure is gone. I took my wife to a movie recently that I had already seen. At every suspenseful scene she would whisper, "What's going to happen next?" I told her, "Watch the movie!" We ask God in prayer, "What's going to happen next?" God says, "Watch the movie! Enjoy the adventure of your life!"

Think of the call of Abraham. God called him to leave his home and go to the unfamiliar land of Canaan. He "obeyed and went, even though he did not know where he was going" (Hebrews 11:8). He knew the general direction but had to take the first step and trust God to lead him to the next step. God only told him to leave. Just one word—*leave*.

He left even though he did not know where he was going! What an adventure he took with God. When he left, God showed him the next step—but not until he took the first step by faith. God doesn't always show us what lies around the next corner. He expects us to walk by faith and not by sight.

God's will unfolds one step at a time in a great adventure. We want a guarantee before we take the step of faith. But God is the guarantee. He doesn't give a guarantee—He is the guarantee, for His Word never fails.

"There has not failed one word of all His good promise" (1 Kings 8:56, *NKJV*).

Write Your Own Script   DAY 170

L ife is not predetermined. We determine our destiny by the choices we make. God does not have a specific will for every decision. There is no script written for your life before eternity. God's will has flexibility. You have the freedom of choice.

The apostle James tells us to make every plan based on the condition, "If it is the Lord's will . . ." (see James 4:13-17). Make plans, set goals and dream dreams, but bring it all before God and pray, "Not my will, but yours be done" (Luke 22:42).

God reserves the right to interrupt our plans with a special, definite call to do something He desires us to do. "Many are the plans in a man's heart, but it is the Lord's purpose that prevails" (Proverbs 19:21). "You are not your own; you were bought at a price" (1 Corinthians 6:19, 20).

The important thing is to be yielded. Pray this prayer: "I desire to do your will, O my God; your law is within my heart" (Psalm 40:8). We are then free from the cares of this life and free to obey the call of God.

In the late 1800s a missionary service was being held at the First Baptist Church in Richmond, Virginia. When the pledges for missions were received, the people gave generously. When the ushers counted the pledges, they found a card on which was written the word *Myself*. It was signed, "John Shuck." The card was immediately taken to the pastor, who shared it with the congregation. Young John Lewis Shuck had heard the call of God on his life and gave himself. He later became the first Southern Baptist missionary to China.

Defragging Your Life — DAY 171

Fulfillment comes when Jesus reigns as Lord over every area of our lives. Paul says the will of God or the purpose of God is "to bring all things . . . together under one Head, even Christ" (Ephesians 1:10). That begins here and now with us.

To use computer language, we need to "defrag" our lives. *Defragging* is the process of restoring fragmented files in the computer that impede its highest efficiency. We tend to live fragmented lives. We live in one area of the city, work in another, play in another, and worship in another.

The same is true personally. We get fragmented between our thinking, feeling and doing. We live Christian in one area of our lives but unchristian in another. When Christ becomes the center, we come together in complete unity and peace.

Paul put it this way: "May God himself, the God of peace, sanctify you through and through. May your whole spirit, soul and body be kept blameless" (1 Thessalonians 5:23).

You see, God wants to bring our entire self—spirit, mind and body—to a place of wholeness and peace. Bring the fragmented pieces of your life to God in prayer, and ask Him to bring all things together under the headship of Christ.

Man Proposes—God Deposes — DAY 172

Napoleon, at the height of his career, is reported to have given this cynical answer to someone who asked if God was on the side of France: "God is on the side that has the heaviest artillery." Then came the Battle of Waterloo, where Napoleon lost both the battle and the empire. Years later, in exile on the island of St. Helena, chastened and humbled, Napoleon is reported to have quoted the words of Thomas à Kempis: "Man proposes, God deposes."

The lesson from history is clear: God is sovereign. He controls the ultimate course of events. One of the difficulties we face is reconciling the sovereignty of God and free will. God is sovereign, yet He gives us the power of choice. But our choice operates within the parameters of God's ultimate will.

Did you know that you have been chosen by God? Paul tells us, "He chose us in him before the creation of the world" (Ephesians 1:4). The word *chosen* (Greek, *exelexato*) means "to pick out and select." God is the One who chooses. God's choice is inclusive, not exclusive. God wants all people to be saved and to have a relationship with Him. "The Lord . . . is not willing that any should perish but that all should come to repentance" (2 Peter 3:9, *NKJV*).

We must respond to God's calling by putting our faith in Jesus as Savior. When Jesus called the disciples, they followed Him. He gave the call, they made the choice. Max Lucado said: "If there are a thousand steps between us and God, He will take all but one. He will leave the final one for us. The choice is ours."

God has already made up His mind about you. The question is, Have you made your choice for Jesus as Lord?

Predestined!   DAY 173

Many people struggle with the concept of predestination. Yet, the Bible clearly teaches, "In love he predestined us to be adopted as his sons" (Ephesians 1:4, 5). The word means "to predetermine, to ordain in advance, or to preplan."

I had a college professor say that it means to set the boundaries beforehand. God has a purpose for Creation, and for each of us. God's choosing refers to people, while predestination refers to His purpose. He predestined the cross of Christ, the plan of salvation, our conformity to Christ's image, and even the return of Christ. "For whom He foreknew,

He also predestined to be conformed to the image of His Son" (Romans 8:29, *NKJV*).

God has given us boundaries within which we make choices, but our power of choice can never thwart His sovereign plan. Our heavenly Father "works out everything in conformity with the purpose of his will" (Ephesians 1:11). This means He has a plan and purpose for us, and He is in control. What an assurance in times of uncertainty. "But the plans of the Lord stand firm forever, the purposes of his heart through all generations" (Psalm 33:11).

God says, "My purpose will stand, and I will do all that I please. . . . What I have said, that will I bring about; what I have planned, that will I do" (Isaiah 46:10, 11). Paul reminds us, "For the Lord will carry out his sentence on earth with speed and finality" (Romans 9:28).

Giving Up Control   DAY 174

One of the best pieces of advice I have ever heard for overly anxious people who try to control everything is to resign from being God. I know this will spoil things for control freaks who often drive themselves and everyone around them crazy.

The fact of the matter is, we're not in control—God is! God "works out everything in conformity with the purpose of his will" (Ephesians 1:11). The phrase *works out* can be translated "controls." We need to distinguish between what we can and cannot control, and what we need to control, versus what we need to let run its natural course.

We cannot control people. Parents have just a few years when their children are young enough to be controlled. Then they become teenagers, and things change! We get in trouble trying to control people. "Make it your ambition to lead a quiet life, to mind your own business and to work with your hands" (1 Thessalonians 4:11). That's not a very nice thing to say, but it's solid advice. We can pray, correct, model, and encourage those we love, but we can't (nor should we) control them.

We cannot control outcomes. For every action, there is an equal and opposite reaction. We try to predict outcomes such as a political election or the price of stock. But life has a way of going its own way. When people come for counseling, I often tell them that change is risky. New issues may surface that they do not expect. Count the cost and weigh the outcomes.

We cannot control circumstances. We can, and should, make the world a better place. We are to advance the kingdom of God on earth. We are world-changers. But we fulfill our mission in the face of great tribulation. "We must through much tribulation enter into the kingdom of God" (Acts 14:22, KJV). Sure, prayer changes things when those changes are in the will of God. Miracles are real. But there are times when we cannot change the circumstances and need to surrender those things to God.

Leave the Rest to God   DAY 175

Let's continue our thoughts from yesterday on control issues. Remember this axiom: Control the things you can control, and leave the rest to God.

We need to rest in His commitment to us to work out everything in conformity to the purpose of His will. God does not cause everything, but He does work in every event for our good. We are not living out our days oblivious to our heavenly Father.

Have you ever been in a jam and needed help, and someone you trusted said, "Don't worry about it, I've got it all under control." Or, "I'll work everything out. Don't sweat the details." If you have, then you know the sense of relief that comes when those you trust tell you that they will take care of everything. That's God's message to us.

Corrie ten Boom learned this lesson. She survived Hitler's death camp but lost her family to the war. She shares this anonymous poem in her book *Tramp for the Lord*:

My life is but a weaving, between my God and me.
I do not choose the colors, He worketh steadily.
Oftimes He weaveth sorrow, and I in foolish pride,
Forget He sees the upper, and I the underside.
Not till the loom is silent, and shuttles cease to fly,
Will God unroll the canvas and explain the reason why.
The dark threads are as needful in the Weaver's skillful hand,
As the threads of gold and silver in the pattern He has planned.

Purposeful Praise

People today are asking, Does God have a plan and purpose for my life? The answer is yes! Our highest purpose is to live for the praise of God's glory: "That we . . . might be for the praise of his glory" (Ephesians 1:12).

The word *praise* appears 200 times in Scripture. *Praise* means "to commend, bless, honor and glorify God." Praise is our response of love to the love of God. "Love the Lord your God with all your heart" (Deuteronomy 6:5).

Praise is an inner attitude of reverence, humility, and gratitude to God. "The fear of the Lord is the beginning of wisdom" (Proverbs 9:10). Praise is a lifestyle that brings glory to God. "Whatever you do, do it all for the glory of God" (1 Corinthians 10:31).

The Hebrew language has 50 different words for *praise*; the most common of which is *hallal* (appearing 99 times in Scripture), meaning "to boast; to laud; to make show; to celebrate." Add the suffix *jah* (pronounced *yah*) for God's name, Yahweh, and we have the premier word for praise, *hallelujah*, which means "praise the Lord." It is only used four times in the New Testament, all in Revelation 19:1-6. It may surprise you to know that there are more references to praise in the Revelation than any other book in the Bible, except the Psalms.

Whatever you have to face today, face it with an attitude of praise. Praise brings a release of real joy, and "the joy of the Lord is your strength" (Nehemiah 8:10).

Behold . . . Reflect

We become what we worship. If we worship money, we become materialists. If we worship pleasure, we become hedonists. If we worship power, we control and manipulate others for our own ends. If we worship fame, we become gods in our own eyes. If we worship our abilities, we become humanists.

However, if we worship God in spirit and in truth, we become like Him. God made us in His image. Sin marred that image. Salvation renews the image of God in us. Worship causes us to mature in the image of our heavenly Father.

Praise brings the perfecting of character. "And we, who . . . reflect the Lord's glory, are being transformed into his likeness [image] with ever-increasing glory, which comes from the Lord, who is the Spirit" (2 Corinthians 3:18).

The word *reflect* can also be translated "behold." We reflect what we behold. David desired to worship God in the temple so that he might "behold the beauty of the Lord" (Psalm 27:4, *NKJV*).

While on a short-term mission trip, a North Carolina pastor by the name of Jack Hinton was leading a worship service at a leper colony on the island of Tobago. There was time for one more song, so he asked if anyone had a request. A woman who had her back turned away from the pulpit turned around. "It was the most hideous face I had ever seen," Hinton said. "Her nose and ears were completely gone. The disease had destroyed her lips as well. She lifted her fingerless hand in the air and asked, 'Can we sing "Count Your Many Blessings"?'"

Overcome with emotion, Hinton left the service. He was followed by a team member who said, "Jack, I guess you'll never be able to sing that song again." "Yes, I will," Jack replied, "but I'll never sing it the same way."

Are You Committed? DAY 178

When Hannibal crossed the Rubicon, he watched until the last of his troops crossed the river and then ordered the bridges to be burned. Hence, we have the phrase, "burning bridges behind you." It was his way of ensuring his troops would have no opportunity for retreat. It was a decisive moment of total commitment to a cause that had to succeed—and succeed it did.

Commitment is a lost virtue today. People talk a lot about happiness but little about commitment. There's no way to stand strong against the challenges of life without deep-settled commitments to God, to others, and to our calling. The word *commitment* means "to be dedicated to a cause, to be willing to make necessary sacrifices, to demonstrate ownership, and to fulfill one's responsibilities."

It reminds me of the story about the chicken and the pig. One morning the farmer went out to get some eggs for breakfast. When the chicken saw him coming toward the barn, she brightened up and said to the pig, "Isn't it wonderful? We get to provide breakfast for the farmer and his family."

"That's easy for you to say," the pig replied. "All you have to do is make a contribution. I have to make a *total commitment!*"

Here is a great definition of *commitment*: "We continually remember before our God and Father your work produced by faith, your labor prompted by love, and your endurance inspired by hope in our Lord Jesus Christ" (1 Thessalonians 1:3). Commitment to relationships, goals and endeavors takes work, labor and endurance that are motivated by feelings and thoughts of faith, love and hope.

Take time today to renew your commitments to God, to your family, and to the work to which God has called you.

No Excuses   DAY 179

William Glasser, in his book *Reality Therapy*, makes the statement, "Man is not irresponsible because he is ill; he is ill because he is irresponsible."

Our age has been marked the age of victimization. Victimization cries, "It's not my fault!" Victimization blames people and circumstances, denies personal responsibility, and engages in self-pity. We have no-fault auto insurance, no-fault divorces, and no-fault moral choices, according to Alan Bloom.

For example: An Oregon man who tried to kill his ex-wife was acquitted on the grounds that he suffered from "depression-suicide syndrome," whose victims deliberately commit poorly planned crimes with the unconscious desire of being caught or killed. He didn't really want to shoot his wife; he wanted the police to shoot him.

The famous "Twinkie syndrome" case involved the attorneys of the man who murdered San Francisco Mayor George Moscone. They blamed the crime on his emotional distress linked to his junk-food binges. Acquitted of murder, he was convicted on a lesser charge of manslaughter.

Pop psychology has conjured up so many new addictions that now no one can be held responsible for anything. In Los Angeles a computer hacker broke into a software system and stole an expensive security program. A social worker said it was not his fault because he was a "computer addict." He received one year in jail plus six months of treatment for this new disorder.

We used to blame the devil. Then we blamed society. Now we blame genetics. Biological determinism and "gene-mapping" promotes the belief that genetics determine behavior, so we can feel justified saying, "It's not my fault." But there is a better way to live.

Responsibility is the key to healthy and happy living. "For we must all appear before the judgment seat of Christ, that each one may receive what is due him for the things done in the body, whether good or bad" (2 Corinthians 5:10). Personal empowerment comes from excuse-free living!

Eliminating Excuses   DAY 180

Yesterday we looked at the problem of making excuses. As long as we make excuses, we fail to take charge of life, miss out on opportunities, and fall short of our potential.

Let's look at the three major excuses that keep us from reaching our potential:

1. *I didn't do it.* This excuse comes in the forms of denial, alibis or blaming others. The classic story of Adam and Eve illustrates this excuse. When they sinned, God confronted them. Adam blamed Eve and God. When God confronted Eve, she blamed the devil.

2. *It wasn't so bad.* This excuse minimizes something that is significant. We say, "It was only a little white lie." We justify our sins by providing good reasons for our actions. King Saul offered excuses for why he disobeyed God. But the prophet Samuel told Saul, "Obedience is better than sacrifice" (see 1 Samuel 15:22).

3. *Yes, but . . .* Here the admission of guilt is followed by an excuse. "I couldn't help it." "I didn't mean to do it." "It wasn't really me." We blame our mood, personality or temper. We split the personality so we can act different ways in different situations and be justified (in our minds) for doing so.

When Adam and Eve sinned, God asked them, "What have you done?" (Genesis 3:13, *CEV*). We must answer the same question. He doesn't ask, "What have others done to you?" "What privileges were you denied?" "Were you raised in a dysfunctional family?" "Have you been neglected?" "Has society treated you unfairly?" He asks, "What have *you* done?"

What are you doing *now* to take charge of life? This is the paramount question that empowers us. Victimization is a dead-end street. Victory comes when you assume responsibility and take charge of your life.

Circumcised Hearts   DAY 181

In the '70s, Coke used the slogan "It's the real thing." Today reality TV is the craze (although it's anything but real). We use the phrase "real life." But our deepest need is for *real spirituality*. God created us in His image with a need for His presence. Spirituality is often lost in the trappings of religion. People often say, "I'm spiritual but not religious."

Real spirituality is internal, not external. It is consecration, not just ceremony; love, not just law; worship, not just works; reality, not just ritual. Spirituality is a meaningful relationship with God. We hear His voice, sense His presence in everyday life, know His direction, have the assurance of forgiveness of sins and the promise of eternal life, and live with divine purpose.

Spirituality is a matter of the heart. "A man is not a Jew if he is only one outwardly, nor is circumcision merely outward and physical. No, a man is a Jew if he is one inwardly; and circumcision is circumcision of the heart, by the Spirit, not by the written code" (Romans 2:28, 29). Strong words from Rabbi Paul!

The circumcised heart is a metaphor for a real inner work of cleansing and change. Moses said, "The Lord your God will circumcise your hearts" (Deuteronomy 30:6). When we receive Christ, we are "circumcised, in the putting off of the sinful nature . . . with the circumcision done by Christ" (Colossians 2:11).

God gave circumcision as a sign of the covenant to Abraham (Genesis 17:9-14). It was an outward sign of an inward spiritual work of grace. The sin nature has been removed, and a new heart has been created.

"I will give you a new heart and put a new spirit in you" (Ezekiel 36:26). If you need a new heart, ask God to circumcise your heart from all spiritual baggage so you can love, serve and obey Him.

Move On!   DAY 182

We waste valuable time regretting the past and fretting the future. Life is right now, not yesterday and not tomorrow. *Now!* The key to getting past your past is to make the most of the moment.

Latch on to this truth: The past is resolved when the present is fulfilled.

When you are happy, you don't waste time analyzing your past. You're too busy enjoying life. It's only when life comes to a grinding halt that we get preoccupied with the past. It is time for you to stop asking "How can I get over my past?" and to start asking "How can I get on with my life?"

When the Israelites were trapped in the desert after they had been delivered from Egypt, they were in a jam. Pharaoh's army pursued them from behind. The Red Sea was in front. So, they complained to Moses, "Let's go back to Egypt!"

Moses prayed, and God answered him: "Then the Lord said to Moses, 'Why are you crying out to me? Tell the Israelites to move on'" (Exodus 14:15).

That's exactly what God says when we're stuck in the past, paralyzed by fear, resentment, failure, tragedy or disappointment: *Move on!*

Instead of asking how you can get over your past, maybe it's time to ask how you can get on with your future. When you get on with your life, you will get over the past.

Move on in faith: "All things are possible to him who believes" (Mark 9:23, *NKJV*).

Move on in confidence: "If God is for us, who can be against us?" (Romans 8:31).

Move on in courage: "I can do all things through Christ who strengthens me" (Philippians 4:13, *NKJV*).

Move on in determination: "None of these things move me" (Acts 20:24, *NKJV*).

Stop standing still. It's time to move on!

Don't Get Over It, Get On With It! DAY 183

My phone rang late one night during the Christmas season. The lady on the other end of the line was distraught. Her husband had died several months earlier. We had talked on several occasions as I tried to help her work through the grief process, but she was stuck in her grief and depression.

"How can I ever get over my loss?" she cried. "I'm so alone. I've got nothing left to live for."

Suddenly, a thought popped into my head, and I blurted out, "Don't get over it, get on with it!" My words hit her like a ton of bricks. She regained her composure. There was an awkward moment of silence. Then she asked, "What do you mean—get on with it?"

I thought to myself, *What do I mean?*

I told her that she would always love her husband, and she would always miss him. No one could take away the pain and loss she felt. "Your pain," I said, "is the measure of your love. Stop trying to get over your husband's death. There are some things in life we never get over, and this is one of them. But," I continued, "you can get on with it. Keep your pain tucked away in your heart. Treasure your memories. But get on with the business of life in spite of your pain."

And she started to get on with it. She dreamed about places to travel, career opportunities, new skills to learn, educational goals, and volunteer opportunities.

It may shock you to hear me say that there are some things you will experience that are so painful, you will never get over them. The good news is you don't have to. You can always get on with it, even when you can't get over it.

So, change your goal. Quit wasting time and energy getting over the past and get on in the present. "But one thing I do: Forgetting what is behind and straining toward what is ahead, I press on toward the goal to win the prize for which God has called me heavenward in Christ Jesus" (Philippians 3:13, 14).

It's Not What You Feel, It's What You Will DAY 184

There's a statement about Jesus that motivates me: "Jesus resolutely set out for Jerusalem" (Luke 9:51). The word *resolutely* literally means "He set His face like a flint" (see Isaiah 50:7). He was immovable in His direction and purpose. Jerusalem meant rejection and, eventually, death. His own disciples tried to prevent Him from going to Jerusalem. They knew the risk He was taking. Still, He resolutely set out for Jerusalem. He was the epitome of dedication to the will of God.

The question is, What have you resolutely set out to accomplish with your life with such determination that you cannot be dissuaded?

Remember, *it's not what you feel, it's what you will* that brings success. Don't allow your emotions to rule your life. To be successful, you will have to make choices based on what you *will*, not on what you *feel*. We put too much emphasis on what we *feel* and not enough on what we *will*.

We are millionaires in emotions. Feelings enrich our lives with joy, happiness and love. But we cannot afford to let our emotions get the best of us.

Feelings should follow choice, not vice versa. We live by *faith*, not by feelings. Jesus said, "If anyone chooses to do God's will, he will find out whether my teaching comes from God or whether I speak on my own" (John 7:17).

Submit your feelings under the power of your will. Make your emotions your servant and don't let them be your master.

When Olympic gymnast Kerri Strug was asked by her coach, Bela Karolyi, if she could do the vault that helped earn the U.S. women a gold metal in team competition, she said, "Yes, I will, I will, I will."

The Agony of Defeat DAY 185

Who among us has not felt the agony of defeat in the face of moral temptation—I mean when sin defeats us? We vowed to say no, only to say yes. We determined to stand firm, only to collapse under the pressure. We resolved to believe, only to end up doubting.

When we fail, the most difficult task is to forgive ourselves. It's fairly easy to receive forgiveness from God, but forgiving ourselves is tough. Coping with guilt means learning to forgive yourself. Besides, if God forgives you, who are you to not forgive yourself? Are you greater than God?

Pray this prayer of the psalmist if you are stuck in a place of guilt:

> Have mercy on me, O God, according to your unfailing love; according to your great compassion blot out my transgressions. Wash away all my iniquity and cleanse me from my sin. . . . Cleanse me with hyssop, and I will be clean; wash me, and I will be whiter than snow. . . . Create in me a pure heart, O God, and renew a steadfast spirit within me. Do not cast me from your presence or take your Holy Spirit from me. Restore to me the joy of your salvation and grant me a willing spirit, to sustain me. Then I will teach transgressors your ways, and sinners will turn back to you. . . . The sacrifices of God are a broken spirit; a broken and contrite heart, O God, you will not despise (Psalm 51:1-17).

God says, "Your sins are forgiven!" Now, forgive yourself.

Forgetting the Former Things   DAY 186

Everybody needs a new beginning from time to time. Here is God's challenge and promise to us: "Forget the former things; do not dwell on the past. See, I am doing a new thing! Now it springs up; do you not perceive it? I am making a way in the desert and streams in the wasteland" (Isaiah 43:18).

Let's focus today on God's challenge to forget the former things. We tend to remember the things we should forget and forget the things we should remember. It's like the man who said, "There are three things I always forget: names, faces, and the third . . . I can't remember."

Don't allow your life to become a museum. Don't waste time reliving the glory of the past, polishing trophies, and displaying blue-ribbon awards. While your accomplishments are great, and should be celebrated, your greatest achievements are yet ahead.

Someone asked Rembrandt, "Of all your paintings, which one is the greatest?"

He said, "I don't know. I haven't painted it yet."

One day Charles Schwab received a telegram from one of his salesmen telling him he had just sold the largest single order for steel in the history of the company. Mr. Schwab received the telegram the next day and wired back, "That's wonderful. What have you done today?"

Today is an opportunity to write a new chapter in the story of your life. God has a work for you to do today.

A New Thing! 　　　　　　　DAY 187

The reason we need to forget the former things and not dwell on the past is because God says, "I am doing a new thing." Then He asks a thought-provoking question: "Do you not perceive it?" (Isaiah 43:18). We never achieve more than we perceive.

Why do we fail to perceive the new things God is doing? Because we are too focused on the former things.

The story is told of two Buddhist monks walking together in a thunderstorm. They came to a swollen stream. A beautiful, young Japanese woman in a kimono stood there wanting to cross to the other side, but she was afraid of the currents. One of the monks said,

"Can I help you?"

"I need to cross this stream," replied the woman.

The monk picked her up, put her on his shoulders, carried her through the swirling waters, and put her down on the other side. He and his companion then went on to the monastery.

That night his companion said to him, "I have a bone to pick with you. As Buddhist monks, we have taken vows not to look on a woman, much less touch her body. Back there by the river, you did both."

"My brother," answered the other monk, "I put that woman down on the other side of the river. You're still carrying her in your mind."

Don't allow your mind to be cluttered with the past so that you fail to see the new things God is doing. Jesus told the religious leaders of His day, "You missed the day of God's coming to you" (see Luke 19:44). What a tragedy to miss the visitation of God. But they were so entrapped by their religious traditions they could not see the salvation of God that came to the world in Jesus.

You can't drive a car looking in the rearview window, and you can't live your life focusing on the past. Take time today to identify the new things God is doing in your life.

A Way in the Desert   DAY 188

I am sure we have all felt like the Israelites when they wandered in the desert 40 years. Sometimes we put ourselves in the desert by making bad decisions, and sometimes we are there because of other people's actions that affect us. When we are in the desert, God promises to do two things: "I am making a way in the desert and streams in the wasteland" (Isaiah 43:19).

The first thing you need to do to get out of the desert is to take God's way. He promises to guide, but we have to follow. The way of the Lord is a predominant theme in Scripture. Jesus talked about the narrow way of life and the broad way of destruction. Jesus said, "I am the way" (John 14:6). Christianity was originally called "the Way" (Acts 9:2).

Solomon cautions us: "There is a way that seems right to a man, but in the end it leads to death" (Proverbs 16:25). The way of the world is "the cravings of sinful man, the lust of his eyes and the boasting of what he has and does" (1 John 2:16). The way of the world is a wilderness life devoid of God's abundance.

God does not abandon us in the desert. Moses told the people that the Lord "went ahead of you on your journey, in the fire by night and in a cloud by day, to search out places for you to camp and to show you the way you should go" (Deuteronomy 1:33).

God also provides streams in the desert. Just as Moses brought water from the rock, God will give us the fresh water of the Holy Spirit to sustain us in the desert. Jesus said, "From his innermost being [the person who believes in Him] will flow rivers of living water [the Holy Spirit]" (John 7:38, *NASB*).

If you are in a desert experience, follow the way of faith and obedience. Listen to the voice of God. "Your ears will hear a voice behind you, saying, 'This is the way; walk in it' " (Isaiah 30:21). Take His way as He leads you through the desert to the land of promise.

What God Looks For   DAY 189

Did you know that there are some things God is looking for? Jesus said, "The Father seeks such to worship Him in spirit and in truth" (see John 4:23). God is looking for worshipers!

King Asa put it this way: "For the eyes of the Lord range throughout the earth to strengthen those whose hearts are fully committed to him" (2 Chronicles 16:9).

A.W. Tozer once referred to worship as the missing jewel of the church. The word *worship* simply means "worth-ship." It denotes the worthiness of a person who is the recipient of special honor. As the creation of God, we declare the glory of the Creator. Who is worthy of our praise?

- Is the earth worthy—has the soil given us life?
- Are the stars worthy—shall they guide our course?
- Is science worthy—will it save us from destruction and solve all our problems?
- Is the government worthy—is Big Brother our source of security?
- Is religion worthy—can we, through our creeds and good deeds, atone for our sins?
- Is man worthy—is he really the measure of all things?

We join the hosts of heaven and sing to Him who is seated on the eternal throne: "You are worthy, our Lord and God, to receive glory and honor and power, for you created all things, and by your will they were created and have their being" (Revelation 4:11).

Spiritual Worship   DAY 190

I once read that "joy is the flag flown from the castle of the heart where Christ rules as Lord." The word *worship* can also be translated "to kiss." The psalmist declared, "Kiss the Son, lest he be angry" (Psalm 2:12). To "kiss" here means to submit to the lordship of the Son of God.

The most frequent word for *worship* in Scripture (Hebrew, *saha*; Greek, *proskyneo*) means "to fall prostrate or to bow down." Bowing down speaks of looking toward God or beholding Him. David says he desires to "see the beauty of the Lord, and to behold Him in His temple" (see 27:4). "Come, let us bow down in worship, let us kneel before the Lord our Maker" (95:6). Worship means bowing our will to the will of God.

The first use of the word *worship* appears in Genesis 22:5 when Abraham went to Moriah to offer Isaac as a sacrifice. Abraham told his servants, "We will worship and then we will come back to you." God was testing his faith. Isaac's willingness foreshadowed Jesus' submission to the will of God on the cross.

Paul says, "Offer your bodies as living sacrifices . . . this is your spiritual act of worship" (Romans 12:1). He distinguishes spiritual worship from carnal worship, empty ritualism or worship in ignorance. Jesus says to worship God "in spirit and in truth" (John 4:24). The word *spiritual* in Romans 12:1 ("reasonable," KJV) is *logikos* (Greek) and means "worship offered by the mind and heart"—the worship which we, as rational creatures, should offer. This is our "reasonable service."

Worshiping God in love and obedience is the only logical, reasonable way to live in response to His great love for us.

Straining at the Oars   DAY 191

I have always been fascinated with the story of Jesus walking on the water. Not by the miracle of walking on the water—that was a piece of cake for Jesus—but the fact that He was going to walk right past the disciples who were in the boat.

The waters were choppy. The winds were strong. They were exhausted, "straining at the oars" (Mark 6:48). Jesus was not walking on the water to bail them out of their situation. In fact, "He was about to pass by them" (v. 48). When they saw Him, they thought He was a ghost and were terrified. He got in the boat with them, and the wind died down.

We think God will give us a struggle-free life. But here we see Jesus watching His disciples straining at the oars, yet He was going to walk right past them to His destination. (He had been alone in the mountains praying when they got in the boat to cross the Sea of Galilee.)

I believe Jesus took joy seeing them straining with such determination to get to the next place of their ministry assignment. He had told them to cross the Sea of Galilee to the other side because they had a job to do. God honors the strain we put into our efforts for His glory.

You see, straining is an important step in our personal development. Paul says we are to "strain for what lies ahead" (see Philippians 3:13). No pain, no gain. The word *strain* is an athletic term that describes an Olympic runner stretching out with all his energy to cross the finish line to win first place. With an all-consuming focus on the prize, the runner lunges forward, stretching out his body to cross the finish line with all the energy he can muster. That's what it means to strain.

Oswald Chambers, in *My Utmost for His Highest*, writes: "God does not give us overcoming life. He gives us life as we overcome." The strain is the strength. If there is no strain, there is no strength. Success belongs to that company of determined people who strain at the oars.

Seized by Christ   DAY 192

Theodore Roosevelt said, "If you are not actively pursuing the person you want to be, you are becoming the person you don't want to be."

Take a look at your future. What do you see ahead? Do you have a dream? What do you want to accomplish? Now is the time to get a clear sense of direction of what you want to do with your life and go for it with all your might.

Paul the apostle had a sense of destiny: "I press on to take hold of that for which Christ Jesus took hold of me" (Philippians 3:12). He believed that Jesus had taken hold of his life on the Damascus road for a particular purpose.

Every person is seized by Christ for a higher, spiritual purpose. Jesus Christ took hold of you when you came to know Him. He seized possession of your life that He might use you as an instrument of His praise. You have eternal significance and a divine destiny. Now go for it!

The will of God does not come to pass passively. We must, in Jesus' words, take the Kingdom by force (see Matthew 11:12). Many people are too passive in their pursuits. The blessings of God are not divine luck that arbitrarily makes some people successful and others mediocre. God's blessings are not random. They follow faith, obedience and perseverance.

Human nature tends to follow the path of least resistance. The good life belongs to those who travel the road not taken—the road of diligence, vision and commitment.

America is plagued by those who take the path of least resistance. Look at education and what we call the "dumbing down" of America. Instead of providing higher education, we lower the academic standards so that everyone can be an "A" student.

Athletics have eliminated the concept of losing so that everyone can be a winner, as if losing would damage a person's psyche. Losing happens to be fundamental in developing the qualities of determination and perseverance that are needed to achieve success. Everyone needs to experience the pain of losing so that he or she can appreciate the joy of victory.

The treacherous climb to the top of the mountain, the long journey through the hot desert sands, and the hardships experienced through endless trial and error are necessary ingredients in reaching one's highest potential.

God Knows What You Can Handle | DAY 193

Mother Teresa said, "I know God will not give me anything I can't handle. I just wish He didn't trust me so much."

God knows how much we can handle. "No temptation has seized you except what is common to man. And God is faithful; he will not let you be tempted beyond what you can bear. But when you are tempted, he will also provide a way out so that you can stand up under it" (1 Corinthians 10:13).

You are not alone. Whatever temptation or trial you are facing, others have faced, and have overcome it—and so can you. You can take courage in the fact that you are not alone. Even Jesus was tempted in all points as we are, so He is "touched with the feeling of our infirmities" (Hebrews 4:15, KJV).

God sets boundaries. God is sovereign. He will not allow you to be tempted beyond your capacity to overcome. He will give you grace to handle your problems. "My grace is sufficient for you" (2 Corinthians 12:9). In Revelation 12 we read how the devil, pictured as the "ancient serpent" (v. 9), threatens to destroy the people of God. Yet, God puts His people "out of the serpent's reach" (v. 14). Satan may rage against us, but we are out of his reach!

God provides a way. He provides both a way of escape and a way of endurance. Sometimes, God takes us out of our temptations and trials by way of deliverance. Other times, He takes us through the trials by way of perseverance so that we can "stand up under it." We prefer God to take us out of our problems, but God works in every circumstance of life to conform us to the image of His Son. God's way is not always the shortest route!

We are to trust God in the midst of trials and temptations, looking to Him for strength, direction and power. "Look to the Lord and his strength; seek his face always" (1 Chronicles 16:11).

Remember Lot's Wife   DAY 194

It sounded strange the day Jesus said it—"Remember Lot's wife" (Luke 17:32). It sounds even stranger to us today.

The disciples would have expected Jesus to say, "Remember Lot." Lot was Abraham's nephew. He was a righteous man. His heart was grieved over the sins of Sodom, where he and his family lived. When the angels came to lead them out of Sodom, Lot's wife looked back. As a result, she was turned into a pillar of salt. This means that she actually started back home to Sodom and was destroyed in the catastrophe. She had the opportunity to move on to a new life, but she went back to the old life.

Here's the lesson: Where you're going is more important than where you've been. You, too, may be looking back and failing to miss out on the moment. Look ahead to your future. Life is ahead of you, not behind you.

When Israel faced the challenges of the wilderness, they kept looking back to the comforts of Egypt (as if being slaves in Egypt was a comfortable life!). What they got for looking back was not a first-class ticket back to Egypt, but 40 years in the desert. Looking back keeps us out of the Promised Land and stuck in the desert.

U.S. diplomat and former Hollywood child star Shirley Temple Black told a story about her husband, Charles, and his mother. When he was a boy, he asked his mother what the happiest moment of her life was.

"This moment—right now," she responded.

"But what about all the other happy moments in your life?" he said. "What about when you were married?"

She answered, "My happiest moment then was then, and my happiest moment now is now. You can only really live in the moment you're in. So, to me, that's always the happiest moment."

Stop looking back and start looking ahead. The mercies of the Lord are new every morning! (Lamentations 3:23).

Finding Your Way Back to God   DAY 195

I had the privilege of hearing Dr. Condoleeza Rice, then national security adviser, speak at the National Prayer Breakfast in Washington, D.C. She shared her testimony of how she got away from her Christian upbringing but found her way back. She grew up in church. Her father was a pastor.

As a young adult, she got out of the habit of going to church. One Sunday morning she was shopping at the Lucky Grocery Store, when she said, "I should have been in church." She ran into a man in the aisle. He told her he was shopping for a church picnic that afternoon. He asked if she played the piano because they needed a pianist at their church. She said, "Yes."

She shared at the breakfast that she was shocked at just how far God's hand could reach—all the way into the Lucky Grocery Store. So she started playing piano for this Baptist church, but she had a hard time with their music, having been raised Presbyterian. She was trained in classical, but they were singing gospel music. The pastor would start singing in a key that didn't exist, and the musicians had to follow along.

She called her mother, who also played in church, and asked, "What should I do to keep up with them when I can't find the key they are singing in?" Her mother gave her great advice: "Just play in the key of C, and they'll come back to you." Dr. Rice added, "God always plays in C, and even though we may drift from Him, we will always find our way back."

Life begins with finding your way back to God. Of the Prodigal Son, we read: "When he came to his senses . . . he got up and went to his father" (Luke 15:17, 20). May this be the day you return to your heavenly Father if you have taken the way of the prodigal.

Don't Go Through It—Grow Through It! DAY 196

In his book *Profiles in Courage*, John F. Kennedy wrote, "Great crises produce great men and great deeds of courage." The fact is, it is how we respond to life's crises that either makes us or breaks us.

We don't have the luxury of choosing our circumstances, but we can choose how we will respond. "We also rejoice in our sufferings, because we know that suffering produces perseverance; perseverance, character; and character, hope" (Romans 5:3, 4). The word used here for sufferings (Greek, *thlipsis*) means "pressures." What a paradox! Praise is the answer to pressure.

Praise is an outward expression of a deep inner faith in the faithfulness of God. Don't just go through the pressures and pains of life—grow through them! Take full advantage of life's learning experiences, whether they are positive or negative.

We need perseverance to grow through suffering. The Greek word is *hupomone*, meaning "to endure patiently with expectant faith." It is the ability to hang in there when you feel like giving up. Satan's greatest weapon against us is discouragement.

We also need character development when we're in the crunch. The word *character* describes the process of purifying metal. Metal goes through the fire to be purified of all alloys and impurities so that it is strong. God refines our character so that we are strong enough to handle life. God is more concerned with what's going on within us than He is with what's going on around us. He cares more about our character than He does our circumstances.

Michelangelo described sculpting as "the making of men." He sought to free men from the prison of stone. He merely chipped away the excess stone until only the image was left. God does the same with us. *Finally, we need to hope.* A close friend of mine committed suicide because he ran out of resources. Some 17.6 million Americans suffer from depression—costing an estimated $23.8 billion annually in lost work and productivity and $12.4 billion in treatment costs.[13] God gives hope, which is "a confident expectation based on certain fundamental truths and actions" (Webster).

After the Babylonian invasion, Jeremiah sat on the hillside of Jerusalem overlooking the devastation of the city. But he wrote, "When I called this to mind, I had hope" (see Lamentations 3:21, 22). What did he call to mind? The promises of God. Paul says, "Hope does not disappoint us, because God has poured out his love into our hearts" (Romans 5:5).

Signs of the Times   DAY 197

Jesus gave prophetic signs signaling His return—chaotic world conditions, economic instability, persecution, global wars, and political instability (see Matthew 24:1-13).

The most significant sign is "This gospel of the kingdom will be preached in all the world as a witness to all nations, and then the end will come" (v. 14, *NKJV*). What will happen at the end of the world? Paul declares, "Then the end will come, when he [Christ] hands over the kingdom to God the Father after he has destroyed all dominion, authority and power. For he must reign until he has put all his enemies under his feet" (1 Corinthians 15:24, 25).

Even though Jesus gave prophetic signs, He said that no one knows the day nor the hour of His return, so we should be ready: "for in an hour that you do not expect, the Son of Man will come" (see Matthew 24:36-44). So why did He give the signs of His coming if we can never know the exact time of His return?

First, *to reassure us in chaotic times that God is in control.* He said that when we see the chaos coming on the world, "See to it that you are not alarmed. Such things must happen" (v. 6).

Second, *to prepare us to endure whatever the cost* because we know our final reward and eternal assurance. "He who stands firm to the end will be saved" (v. 13).

Third, *to confirm the eternal verity of His word.* "Heaven and earth will pass away, but my words will never pass away" (v. 35). Every headline of the newspaper and TV news report that verifies end-time prophecy reminds us that God's Word is true and gives us a firm foundation to stand on in uncertain times.

So, "when these things begin to take place," Jesus says, "stand up and lift up your heads, because your redemption is drawing near" (Luke 21:28).

The Prophetic Promise   DAY 198

If I were to ask you what promise of God is found over 300 times in the New Testament, what would you say? What subject does one out of every 25 verses in the New Testament address? The answer is the return of Christ.

While the Bible does not give every detail about His return and much prophecy is shrouded in mystery, sealed up until the time of the end, one fact is clear: Jesus will return to earth again—visibly, literally and victoriously.

Let me paint a portrait of His return.

A *glorious return.* "As the lightning comes from the east and shines as far as the west, so will be the coming of the Son of Man" (Matthew 24:27, *RSV*).

An *unexpected return.* "So you also must be ready, because the Son of Man will come at an hour when you do not expect him" (v. 44).

A *literal return.* "This same Jesus, who has been taken from you into heaven, will come back in the same way you have seen him go into heaven" (Acts 1:11).

A *sudden return.* "The day of the Lord will come like a thief in the night" (1 Thessalonians 5:2).

A *judgmental return.* "See, the Lord is coming with thousands upon thousands of his holy ones . . . to convict all the ungodly of all the ungodly acts they have done" (Jude 14, 15).

A *global return.* "Look, he is coming with the clouds, and every eye will see him" (Revelation 1:7).

A *triumphant return.* "He treads the winepress of the fury of the wrath of God Almighty. On his robe and on his thigh he has this name written: KING OF KINGS AND LORD OF LORDS" (19:15, 16).

An *imminent return.* "The Lord Himself will descend from heaven with a shout. . . . Then we . . . shall be caught up together with them in the clouds to meet the Lord in the air" (1 Thessalonians 4:16, 17, *NKJV*)

Keep your eye on the eastern sky. Live life in view of eternity. This could be the day our Lord returns!

Suffering Servant, Conquering King   DAY 199

The Old Testament clearly reveals two distinct appearances of the Messiah. First, as the suffering servant of the Lord: "He was wounded for our transgressions, He was bruised for our iniquities; the chastisement for our peace was upon Him, and by His stripes we are healed" (Isaiah 53:5, *NKJV*).

Second, He will come at the end of the age as the conquering king: "Then the Lord will go out and fight against those nations, as he fights in the day of battle. On that day his feet will stand on the Mount of Olives. . . . Then the Lord my God will come, and all his holy ones with him" (Zechariah 14:3-5).

How different the second coming of Christ will be from His first coming into the world as our Savior.

- When He came the first time, He was meek and lowly of heart, but He will return as Judge of all the earth.
- When He came the first time, He was born in a manger and was wrapped in swaddling clothes; but when He returns, He will be clothed with glory.
- When He came the first time, He was given a reed for a scepter; but when He returns, He will rule the nations with a rod of iron.
- When He came the first time, He wore a crown of thorns; but when He returns, He will be crowned with many crowns.
- When He came the first time, He was rejected, mocked and crucified; but when He returns, every knee will bow before Him and

every tongue confess that Jesus Christ is Lord to the glory of God the Father (Philippians 2:10, 11).

"The kingdom of the world [shall] become the kingdom of our Lord and of his Christ, and he will reign for ever and ever" (Revelation 11:15).

When Queen Elizabeth II was crowned by the Archbishop of Canterbury, he laid the crown on her head with the sure pronouncement, "I give thee, O Sovereign Lady, this crown to wear until He who reserves the right to wear it shall return."

How Should We Then Live! DAY 200

How should the promise of Christ's return affect the way we live? When Jesus gave the signs of His coming as recorded in Matthew 24, He also gave us some principles for living in view of His return.

1. *Watch out that no one deceives you!* (v. 4). He cautioned us against the rise of false prophets and Christs so that we would not be misled by those who manipulate the gospel for their own profit.

2. *See to it that you are not alarmed* (v. 6). Terrorism begets terror in the human heart. While the world is engulfed in fear, we face the future with faith (see Luke 21:26-28).

3. *Stand firm to the end* (Matthew 24:13). True faith in Jesus is present tense. Our decision to believe in Christ and to follow Him is daily. We must persevere in our faith. "We must through many tribulations enter the kingdom of God" (Acts 14:22, *NKJV*).

4. *Keep your eye on the eastern sky* (see Matthew 24:27). Live with expectancy. Think often of His return. Make an eternal investment with your time, talent and treasure. Don't get too earthbound.

5. *Learn the lesson of the fig tree* (see vv. 32-35). The fig tree parable means that His Word is true concerning His promise. Every prophetic sign we see fulfilled reminds us that all God has promised in His Word about the end of the age and the dawn of eternity will come to pass.

6. *Remember the days of Noah and the days of Lot* (see Luke 17:26, 28). We have to respond as did Noah and Lot. Just as people were dull to the message of Noah and to the warning of the angels in

Sodom, the world will not take the message of Christ's return seriously. It was life as usual during their times. But we do take it seriously and are ready to meet Him when He comes. Like Noah and Lot, we are to be faithful in proclaiming the gospel to this generation while there is still time to be saved.

What Is a Disciple? DAY 201

When you hear the word *disciple*, what comes to mind? Do you think of the Twelve? Or, perhaps, an outstanding Christian leader like Martin Luther, Billy Graham or Mother Teresa? Or, perhaps, a deeply devoted believer?

The fact is, every believer is a disciple of Jesus. The word *Christian* appears only three times in the New Testament. "The disciples were called Christians first at Antioch" (Acts 11:26). King Agrippa asked Paul, "Do you think that in such a short time you can persuade me to be a Christian?" (26:28). Peter said, "If you suffer as a Christian, do not be ashamed, but praise God that you bear that name" (1 Peter 4:16). The word *Christian* is a very meaningful and sacred name. However, the word *disciple* appears nearly 300 times.

What is a disciple? The word *disciple* simply means "a student." More specifically, a disciple is a follower: "Come, follow me" (Matthew 4:19). Disciples learn from Jesus' example: "Take my yoke upon you and learn from me" (11:29). Disciples imitate Christ: "A student is not above his teacher, but everyone who is fully trained will be like his teacher" (Luke 6:40). Disciples experience an ongoing radical change in their personalities, priorities and passions as a direct result of Jesus' lordship.

Jesus began His ministry calling disciples, and He finished it by telling us to "go and make disciples of all nations" (Matthew 28:19). When we move beyond casual Christianity into real discipleship, we experience joy unspeakable and full of glory. You will know the peace that transcends all understanding, and you will be empowered with His grace that is all-sufficient so that in every circumstance of life you can say, "For to me, to live is Christ and to die is gain" (Philippians 1:21).

The Time Has Come!

"A weakness of all human beings," Henry Ford said, "is trying to do too many things at once. That scatters effort and destroys direction. It makes for haste, and haste makes waste. So we do things all the wrong ways possible before we come to the right one. Then we think it is the best way because it works, and it was the only way left that we could see. Every now and then I wake up in the morning headed toward that finality, with a dozen things I want to do. I know I can't do them all at once."

When asked what he did about that, Ford replied, "I go out and trot around the house. While I'm running off the excess energy that wants to do too much, my mind clears, and I see what can be done and should be done first."

Seven times we read in the Gospel of John concerning Jesus, "The time has come." Jesus led a focused life. He was focused on what the Father had sent Him to do—namely, to redeem the world from sin and to establish the kingdom of God in human hearts.

Keeping our lives on track is a matter of managing our time according to His purpose. Set your goals and stick to them relentlessly. Dr. Howard Hendricks said, "The secret of concentration is elimination." When you know your plan and stick to it, you are empowered to succeed in your endeavors.

Most importantly, keep your faith focused on Jesus. Our faith is not focused on abstract theological concepts, but on a living Person. "Let us fix our eyes on Jesus, the author and perfecter of our faith" (Hebrews 12:2).

A Sense of Timing DAY 203

Public speakers, actors and comedians are trained to have a sense of timing in their presentations. A sense of timing is equally important for life. Jesus lived with such a sense of time. Seven times the Gospel of John uses the phrase "The time has come" about Jesus. Let's look at these passages to learn how to live with a sense of timing.

When you have a sense of timing, *nothing can distract you*. At a marriage in Cana the guests ran out of wine. Jesus' mother asked Him to intervene, but He said, "My time has not yet come" (John 2:3, 4). He was not being rude. He did turn the water into wine at her insistence. But He did not want to prematurely reveal Himself as Messiah by performing a miracle. He was on a mission and knew that *when* you do something is equally as important as *what* you do.

Mother Teresa was once asked why people lose their spiritual passion. She replied simply, "Distractions." An ancient proverb says, "If you want to defeat them, distract them."

When you have a sense of timing, *no one can manipulate you.* Jesus was caught up in a religious debate in the Temple. Some leaders opposed Him so severely that "they tried to seize him, but no one laid a hand on him, because his time had not yet come" (John 7:30; 8:20). People will try to manipulate you with guilt, making you feel over-obligated. When you know that your time has come, you will learn the power of saying "no" and "yes" to the right things. Operate on your own schedule, and don't let others manipulate your time.

Time Is on My Side DAY 204

Let's continue our review of the seven passages where John uses the phrase "The time has come" about Jesus. Taking charge of time is the key to living a life that matters. To waste time is to waste one's life, for life is time.

When you take charge of time, *nothing can frighten you.* As Jesus faced the cross, He said, "Now my heart is troubled, and what shall I say? 'Father, save me from this hour?' No, it was for this very reason I came to this hour" (John 12:27).

Purpose brings courage. I don't mean you won't have feelings of fear and anxiety. You will. But you will have a greater measure of courage when you know that your life is right on track with God's timing. Jesus knew that doing the will of God would require His utmost commitment, but He faced His fears with faith, knowing that He had power over death (see 10:17, 18). We, too, have power over death in Him. "To be absent from the body [is] to be present with the Lord" (2 Corinthians 5:8, *NKJV*). Jesus was the most courageous person who ever lived!

When you are in control of time, *nothing can isolate you.* "But a time is coming, and has come, when you will be scattered, each to his own home. You will leave me all alone. Yet I am not alone, for my Father is with me" (John 16:32). Loneliness is a painful feeling. But often it comes from a life that is passive rather than active. When something difficult happens, we tend to withdraw from others and from life itself. We get isolated, and loneliness takes over. That's when we need to get back in the game and find our place of service in the kingdom of God. Jesus faced the time of being alone, but not being lonely, because He practiced the presence of God.

Finally, when you take charge of time, *nothing can conquer you.* Jesus prayed, "Father, the time has come. Glorify your Son, that your Son may glorify you" (17:1). He faced the Cross in victory. He knew His time had come. He did not complain that He did not have a long life (He died at age 33). He shouted from the cross, "It is finished!" You're not running out of time, you're running into eternity with God!

Here is the lesson: When you have the right purpose and plan for life, you can face every opposition to your goals. When you know in your heart that you are where God wants you to be, doing what God wants you to do, you know that you will be victorious!

Winning Your Spiritual Battles   DAY 205

We all face spiritual battles. "For our struggle is not against flesh and blood, but against the rulers, against the authorities, against the powers of this dark world and against the spiritual forces of evil in the heavenly realms" (Ephesians 6:12). We face temptations to doubt and to disobey God. We battle oppressive thoughts that weigh us down.

The fight is on! So, how do we win?

Tap into the power of the prayer of agreement. Jesus said, "I tell you that if two of you on earth agree about anything you ask for, it will be done for you by my Father in heaven" (Matthew 18:19). You need a prayer partner, or should I say a battle partner? Paul ends his discourse on the armor of God by challenging us: "And pray in the Spirit on all occasions" (Ephesians 6:18). When we pray, we are strong in the Lord and the power of His might, we put on the whole armor of God, and we take our stand against the devil's schemes (vv. 10, 11).

Keep yourself in shape spiritually. "Be strong in the Lord and in his mighty power" (v. 10). When fighting a spiritual battle, it's easy to give in to temptation or to discouragement. Notice how the early church responded to the fight of faith: "Day after day, in the temple courts and from house to house, they never stopped teaching and proclaiming the good news that Jesus is the Christ" (Acts 5:42). Jesus said, "Watch and pray so that you will not fall into temptation. The spirit is willing, but the body is weak" (Matthew 26:41).

The only offensive weapon we have to fight deceptive thoughts is Scripture. It is the sword of the Spirit (Ephesians 6:17). The battle is often in the mind. By the power of the written Word, we "take captive every thought to make it obedient to Christ" (2 Corinthians 10:5). Jesus fought Satan by drawing on the Word. "It is written!" He declared, and Satan left him (see Matthew 4:1-11).

A Battle Strategy   DAY 206

L et's continue the battle strategy from yesterday's devotion.
Get on the offensive. Set goals to overcome your greatest spiritual struggles. Map out a strategy for your personal spiritual growth.

Mel Gibson plays the role of Lt. Col. Hal Moore in the movie *We Were Soldiers*. The movie depicts the first U.S. battle in Vietnam. The Americans were greatly outnumbered and under heavy attack. In one scene, a young soldier sees the mayhem and cries out, "We're all going to die!" Calmly, Moore surveys the scene with bullets flying and mortar shells going off, and responds with confidence, "We will win this fight." You and I have to know that we will win every spiritual battle we face, for "the Lord almighty is with us!" (Psalm 46:7).

Close any door of opportunity for the Evil One. "Do not give the devil a foothold" (Ephesians 4:27). We need to live in such a way that "Satan might not outwit us" (2 Corinthians 2:11).

Finally, *live in an atmosphere of praise.* Praise is a weapon. "May the praise of God be in their mouths and a double-edged sword in their hands" (Psalm 149:6). Praise brings joy, which, in turn, gives us strength to fight the good fight of faith. "The joy of the Lord is your strength" (Nehemiah 8:10).

Remember, above all things, "Greater is he that is in you, than he that is in the world!" (1 John 4:4, KJV).

A Time for Examination

Paul says, "Examine yourselves to see whether you are in the faith; test yourselves" (2 Corinthians 13:5). How does spiritual examination take place? God uses several means.

The Scripture is a probing instrument in the hand of the Holy Spirit, revealing our strengths and weaknesses, encouraging and convicting. "The word of God is living and active. Sharper than any double-edged sword, it penetrates even to dividing soul and spirit, joints and marrow; it judges the thoughts and attitudes of the heart" (Hebrews 4:12). Regular reading or listening of Scripture helps us live the examined life.

The Holy Spirit "searches our hearts" (Romans 8:27). Only God knows the heart. We need Him to reveal the hidden issues of our hearts and minds that defeat us. Pray often this prayer: "Search me, O God, and know my heart; test me and know my anxious thoughts. See if there is any offensive way in me and lead me in the way everlasting" (Psalm 139:23, 24).

Silence in God's presence is the key to self-examination. Pascal, the great scientist, said, "Man brings most of his troubles on himself by his inability to be still." God says, "Be still, and know that I am God" (46:10). "The Lord is in his holy temple; let all the earth be silent before him" (Habakkuk 2:20). Where is the temple of God? "Do you not know that your body is a temple of the Holy Spirit, who is in you, whom you have received from God?" (1 Corinthians 6:19). There is nothing so searching as being silent in God's presence. He speaks to us with a gentle whisper in the sanctuary of the soul.

Set aside time today for silence and listen to the voice of God. His searching of the soul leads to new strength.

Test Yourselves

We are looking at the challenge of Paul: "Examine yourselves . . . test yourselves" (2 Corinthians 13:5). No one likes an examination in any shape, form or fashion. We dread exams in school. We get test anxiety.

We dread going to the doctor for an exam. The soft music designed to relax us doesn't work. We worry what illness they may find if they look too closely with the probing instruments and X-ray machines.

But life requires examination. A friend of mine went for a routine medical examination. It revealed a severe heart problem. He went through multiple heart-bypass surgery and months of recovery. He asked his doctor what he should have noticed. The doctor said, "Most people would have never seen the heart attack coming." The exam saved his life. What is true physically is true spiritually.

God uses people to examine us. "Faithful are the wounds of a friend" (Proverbs 27:6, *NKJV*). A friend will tell you the truth to help you. Your enemy will tell you the truth to hurt or manipulate you. A friend knows the truth but keeps it a secret. An enemy will expose you to bring you down. We need people to whom we are accountable.

God uses experiences to test and refine us. "In all things God works for the good of those who love him" (Romans 8:28). The fact is, in all things God works. Times of prosperity test our sincerity in serving God. Have you ever had that feeling of fear when you are on the mountain peak wondering how long the good times will last?

Times of adversity test our motives for serving God and the limitations of our faith. Have you ever asked, "Where is God?" When life is difficult and you face tough times, God works in the soul to purify the heart, to refine faith, and to shape character.

Let us have the courage to live the examined life. "Examine yourself . . . test yourself" (see 2 Corinthians 13:5).

Future Shock

A study of hospital patients regarding life expectancy reportedly came to the conclusion that there exists a strong correlation between life expectancy and future-oriented thinking. That is to say that a patient who looks ahead to upcoming events in the year is more likely to live than one whose thinking is confined to the daily hospital routine.

This conclusion comes as no surprise. God created us to dream. Physically, we are confined to the moment; we can't step back in time to change the past; neither can we step into the future to know what will happen next. But mentally, we have the capacity to dream of the future, to plan and to hope for things not seen. In fact, the power of hope is the substance of faith (see Hebrews 11:1).

Take Abraham for example. God showed him the stars of the sky and told him that one day his descendants would be as numerous as the stars. Abraham knew that God calls those things that are not as though they were. His vision of the future gave him hope for the moment. "Against all hope, Abraham in hope believed and became the father of many nations" (Romans 4:18). He even looked beyond his earthly future to his heavenly future: "for he was looking forward to the city with foundations, whose architect and builder is God" (Hebrews 11:10).

The Christian hope is twofold. First, we believe that the quality of life here and now can always be better. We are agents of hope in a world of despair. I point this out because some have criticized the belief in the return of Christ, saying that we have a "blocked future"—a future that offers no hope for the present, only hope for eternity.

In reality, however, the world is a better place today because of the influence of the good news of Christ. Look at the hospitals, drug and alcohol recovery programs, and support groups. Look at the schools, universities, and social programs established by the church. Consider the moral and political action groups that keep the nation focused on Biblical values. Let us be agents of hope today, bringing positive change in the name of the Lord.

A Two-Sided Coin   DAY 210

Yesterday we looked at the meaning and power of being agents of hope in the world. Let's continue our thoughts on this subject.

We need to face the fact that after we have done all we can to make our world the best place it can be, the Bible tells us in no uncertain terms that evil will continue until the end of the world when Christ returns. "Then the end will come, when Christ hands over the kingdom to God the Father" (1 Corinthians 15:24).

But that does not mean that we can't and shouldn't work toward a better world today. If we take the return of Christ seriously, we know that we are accountable to God for how we take care of this present world. Heavenly rewards are based on earthly responsibilities.

We do not shy away from social, political and moral action in the arenas of life. While we know that our only utopia will come when Christ sets up His kingdom, we also assume our place as the light of the world and the salt of the earth.

But having said that, I must also say that our vision of hope goes beyond better schools, cultural influence, or an improved economic situation—we have an eternal hope, the kingdom of God. The return of Christ is the "blessed hope" of the world (Titus 2:13).

"Therefore, since we are receiving a kingdom that cannot be shaken, let us be thankful, and so worship God acceptably with reverence and awe, for our God is a consuming fire" (Hebrews 12:28, 29).

Heavenly-Minded   DAY 211

I'm sure you've heard the saying, "He's so heavenly-minded, he's no earthly good." The truth is, the One who was the most heavenly-minded did the most earthly good.

If the Bible gives us any resource for daily living, it gives us a healthy dose of heavenly-mindedness—an eternal perspective in a temporal world.

Paul the apostle shared his secret for dealing with stress: "Therefore we do not lose heart. Though outwardly we are wasting away, yet inwardly we are being renewed day by day. For our light and momentary troubles are achieving for us an eternal glory that far outweighs them all. So we fix our eyes not on what is seen, but on what is unseen. For what is seen is temporary, but what is unseen is eternal" (2 Corinthians 4:16-18).

Life without this eternal perspective is lived in a hopeless pessimism expressed in the words of H.G. Wells: "The experiment will be over, the crystals gone, dissolving down the waste pipe." Many people live their lives today in the same kind of pessimism often described in the classical Greco-Roman world: "Death reigned as king of terrors, spoiling men's enjoyment of the present with the intruding thought of the future, so that life could seem a gift not worth receiving, and death in infancy preferable to growing up to the conscious anticipation of having to die."

But in Christ, we are being renewed day by day as we keep an eternal perspective in a temporal world.

A New Outlook   DAY 212

What we need is a spiritual outlook on life. The philosopher Archimedes said, "Give me a place to stand, and I will move the world." The Bible gives us a place to stand on absolute truth so that we can move our world for the glory of God.

We face life with either fear or faith. Jesus said of the last days, "Men will faint from terror, apprehensive of what is coming on the world, for the heavenly bodies will be shaken" (Luke 21:26).

But there is a better way. He went on to say, "When these things begin to take place, stand up and lift up your heads, because your redemption is drawing near" (v. 28). That's the power of an eternal perspective—look up!

While in exile, John came to see life from heaven's vantage point. He was caught up to heaven in a vision. "There before me was a door standing open in heaven. And the voice . . . said, 'Come up here, and I will show you what must take place after this' " (Revelation 4:1).

The door in heaven is open for us. We can go there in prayer and catch a glimpse of the greatness of God. He, too, will show us things to come. God reveals to us in His Word that He is sovereign. He is in control. Life looks very different from the vantage point of heaven. When John was in heaven looking down on history, he saw things the way God sees them. He had the power of a new outlook on life.

Look at life vertically from the vantage point of heaven. You will realize that "in all things God works for the good of those who love him, to those who have been called according to his purpose" (Romans 8:28).

If your life is confusing, ask God to help you see what you are going through from His perspective. A heavenly perspective brings peace.

An Open Door   DAY 213

John the Revelator is not the first person in the Bible to see heaven open. The prophet Ezekiel saw heaven opened and described "visions of God" (1:1). When Jesus was baptized by John the Baptist in the Jordan River, heaven was opened (Matthew 3:16). Later in the

Revelation, John again sees heaven open as Jesus Christ returns in triumphant power at the end of the age (19:11).

What does all this business about heaven being open mean? The fact that heaven is opened, not closed, tells us that God has prepared a way for us to go to heaven. Remember that Jesus said, "I am the door of the sheep" (John 10:7, *NKJV*).

The *open door* means God is giving us a glimpse of what life down here on earth looks like from His perspective. That's why John was transported into heaven. He saw the throne of God and the very presence of God, the Father, on that throne (see Revelation 4).

The throne of God is the most frequently used symbol in Revelation, appearing 54 times. It represents the sovereignty of God. We join the heavenly host around the throne described in his vision and rejoice that our God reigns supreme. "Day and night they never stop saying: 'Holy, holy, holy is the Lord God Almighty, who was, and is, and is to come'" (v. 8). That means God is sovereign over the past, present and future!

The door to heaven is open for you today. Go to God in prayer and find grace to help you deal with every issue you are facing.

Sharing the Wealth DAY 214

Heaven is a place of reward. Jesus will reward His people for their faithfulness. "Hold on to what you have, so that no one will take your crown" (Revelation 3:11). What is this crown Jesus will give us in heaven?

The word for *crown* here is *stephanos* (Greek) and means "the victor's wreath." In the ancient Olympic Games, winners were awarded garlands to wear. The word for a king's crown is *diadem*, which the Bible uses to describe the crown of Christ. He has all power and authority.

The Lord will reward us for our faith and obedience. In fact, the New Testament describes this crown as an incorruptible crown (1 Corinthians 9:25), a crown of righteousness (2 Timothy 4:8), a crown of life (James 1:12), and a crown of glory (1 Peter 5:4).

True success is not measured merely by prosperity, power, position or pleasure. Success is measured when Christ places the victor's wreath around your neck and says to you and to me, "Well done, good and faithful servant. Enter into the joy of the Lord, the kingdom prepared for you since the foundation of the world!" (see Matthew 25:21, 23, 34).

The Los Angeles Times (Dec. 12, 1996) reported that David Suna and John Tu sold 80 percent of their company, Kingston Technology Corp., the world's largest manufacturer of computer memory products, for $1.5 billion. The two men decided to share their windfall with their employees. The average bonus payment their workers received was just over $75,000. Suna summarized their decision: "To share our success with everybody is the most joy we can have."

That's what Jesus is going to do in eternity. He's going to share the rewards of glory with us.

"The Spirit himself testifies with our spirit that we are God's children. Now if we are children, then we are heirs—heirs of God and coheirs with Christ, if indeed we share in his sufferings in order that we may also share in his glory" (Romans 8:16, 17).

A Wonderful Paradox   DAY 215

Consider these powerful words: "See, the Lion of the tribe of Judah, the Root of David, has triumphed. He is able to open the scroll and its seven seals. Then I saw a Lamb, looking as if it had been slain, standing in the center of the throne" (Revelation 5:5, 6).

What a paradox—the Lion who is a Lamb. "The Lion of the tribe of Judah" is a messianic title referring to the Davidic covenant portraying the Messiah's conquest over death. The image of the Lamb draws our attention back to the Passover lamb in Egypt. The Israelites were delivered from Egypt by the power of God and by the blood of the lamb.

In these two pictures, we see Isaiah's conquering king and suffering servant come together in Jesus (see 42:1-4; 53:4-6). The Lamb is mentioned 30 times in the Revelation. Whatever picture you have of Jesus, the greatest is the Lamb of God who takes away the sins of the world.

The largest crowd Charles Spurgeon ever addressed came the night he spoke in the Crystal Palace to 23,654 people. A mutiny had occurred in India, protesting Britain's rule over that land, and a service of national humiliation was planned. Spurgeon was selected to deliver the sermon.

The night before the service, he went to the Crystal Palace to test the acoustics since the building was not constructed with religious services in mind. As he stood on the platform, he repeated the verse, "Behold the Lamb of God who takes away the sin of the world!" (John 1:29). His words were heard by a man working somewhere in the building. The man came to Spurgeon several days later to say that the verse had touched his heart, and he had come to know the Lord Jesus Christ.[14]

"And they sang a new song: 'You are worthy to take the scroll and to open its seals, because you were slain, and with your blood you purchased men for God from every tribe and language and people and nation. You have made them to be a kingdom and priests to serve our God, and they will reign on the earth'" (Revelation 5:9, 10).

Peace Through Surrender   DAY 216

Peace comes through surrender. "Now may the Lord of peace himself give you peace at all times and in every way" (2 Thessalonians 3:16). Note the connection between the words *Lord* and *peace*. We can't have peace without the Lord of peace reigning in our hearts.

Isaiah called the Messiah the Prince of Peace. "Of the increase of his government and peace there will be no end" (Isaiah 9:7).

We don't make him Lord—He is Lord! That's the confession of the believer. "If you confess with your mouth, 'Jesus is Lord,' and believe in your heart . . . you will be saved" (Romans 10:9).

During the days of emperor worship, Roman citizens had to declare, "Caesar is Lord," as they pledged him their loyalty. But early Christians refused to make the confession. To them, the title "Lord" could only be ascribed to Jesus. While Rome confessed "Caesar is Lord," the church proclaimed, "Jesus is Lord." For that creed, they lived and died.

Have you surrendered your life to Jesus as Lord? Are there any unsurrendered attitudes, feelings, plans and desires in your heart?

The following letter was written by Cyprian, bishop of Carthage, in the second century to his friend Donatus, an official in the Roman government. He wrote the letter right after his conversion to show the way of surrender:

> It's a bad world, Donatus, an incredibly bad world. But I have discovered in the midst of it a quiet and good people who have learned the secret of life. They have a joy and wisdom which is a thousand times better than any pleasures of our sinful lives. They are despised and persecuted, but they care not. They are masters of their souls. They have overcome the world. These people, Donatus, are Christians, and I am one of them.

Reigning in Life DAY 217

I have always been intrigued with this passage of Scripture: "For if, by the trespass of the one man (Adam), death reigned through that one man, how much more will those who receive God's abundant provision of grace and of the gift of righteousness reign in life through the one man, Jesus Christ" (Romans 5:17).

The phrase "reign in life" leaps off the page to me. We all want to reign in life, but quite often life reigns over us. We are fully aware of the mess Adam got us into when he disobeyed God. Death reigns as a result of human sin. "The wages of sin is death" (6:23).

Are we equally aware of the miracle Jesus brought us? He has delivered us from the ruling force of sin and its effects. "Count yourselves dead to sin but alive to God in Christ Jesus" (v. 11). To be dead to sin means that it is rendered powerless. This is not to say that we don't ever sin. We know better than that. But Christ does give us a new heart with new desires. Our deepest desire is to live for God.

When we keep our trust in the Lord and endeavor to walk worthy of Him and to please Him in every way, we can reign in life over sin, fear, stress, failures, criticism, and every enemy of the soul we face.

I like the insights of Peg Rankin:

> We know that to take a job after unemployment is to conquer, even if the job lasts only temporarily. To become resigned to the death of a loved one is to conquer, even though we may have

to overcome moments of overwhelming depression. To receive physical healing is to conquer, even though we know that we will get sick again and even die. What does it mean to be "more than a conqueror"? Perhaps it means to go on with Christ in glory where conditions are permanent, not temporary. Perhaps that is why "the others" in Hebrews 11 did not accept deliverance. They were looking for a "better resurrection."[3]

Live with confidence that the Lord will give you abundant grace to reign in life!

Something to Sing About   DAY 218

When the noted agnostic Robert Ingersoll died, his funeral notice read: "There will be no singing at the funeral." There was nothing to sing about—no resource of faith in the crucible of life; no sound of praise in the face of death.

How different was my experience when I preached the funeral of a young woman in her mid-40s. In spite of her illness, she possessed a vibrant faith, which she shared openly and freely with everyone she met. The day of her funeral, her husband shared with me how inspired he had been by her faith. He said, "I would often stand next to her in church, knowing she was in tremendous pain; yet, as the congregation sang, she would lift her voice and give glory to God." Then he added, "She had peace in the midst of her pain."

Singing scarcely exists in religions outside of Judaism and Christianity. The Psalms, meaning "songs of praise," occupy a central place in the Old Testament. Hundreds of thousands of hymns have been composed during the church age. Today there is an explosion of new worship music being composed. A revival of worship is happening among God's people who have always been characterized by the song of the Lord.

C.S. Lewis said, "Praise is inner health made audible." Praise is the key to maintaining spiritual, mental and emotional health. Praise determines our attitudes, beliefs, values, philosophy of life, and lifestyle. What is praise? It is the adoration of God. It involves celebration, thanksgiving, worship and blessing God. Praise is expressed through singing, lifting hands, dancing, clapping, testifying, kneeling, and musical performance.

The word *praise* appears 200 times in Scripture. The word *hallelujah* appears only four times in the New Testament and all in Revelation 19. In fact, there are more references to praise in the Revelation than any other book in the Bible, except the Psalms. The Revelation is the hymnal of the New Testament.

"Hallelujah! For the Lord God Almighty reigns. Let us rejoice and be glad and give him glory!" (19:6, 7).

For Goodness' Sake DAY 219

I find it helpful to reflect on the goodness of God in a world where bad things happen. It's true—life is hard and sometimes unfair. Bad things happen to good people. But in the midst of it all, God is good.

David confessed, "I am still confident of this: I will see the goodness of the Lord in the land of the living" (Psalm 27:13). Nahum assures us, "The Lord is good, a refuge in times of trouble. He cares for those who trust in him" (1:7).

Jesus tells us, "If you, then, though you are evil, know how to give good gifts to your children, how much more will your Father in heaven give good gifts to those who ask Him!" (Matthew 7:11).

Here is profound truth: "And we know that in all things God works *for the good* of those who love him, who have been called according to his purpose" (Romans 8:28). What a reassuring promise. God is always working in every situation for our good.

This does not mean God causes everything. Far from it! God is not the source of trouble, hardship and suffering. But Paul assures that "in all things" God works as a master sculptor to conform us to Christ's image.

In the 15th century a great genius was born into the world—Michelangelo Buonarroti. He was not only a master sculptor, he was also an artist, architect, painter and scientist. His number one love was sculpting. He gave us such masterpieces as *David*, *The Pieta*, *Moses*, and *The Bacchus*. He often described the art of sculpting as the making of men. He considered the marble stone a prison which held captive living figures. "Freeing men from the prison of stone," is how he described his work.

God chips away the excess stone in us until only the image of Jesus remains.

When Bad Times Come

When bad times come our way, we have a variety of ways we can respond. *We can worry.* The Greek word for *worry* means "to be divided or inwardly distracted." The English word comes from an Anglo-Saxon word meaning "to choke or strangle." I like the beatitude that says, "Blessed is the man who is too busy to worry during the day, and too sleepy to worry at night."

When life is tough, *we can complain* like ancient Israel in the wilderness. They complained constantly against the Lord and the leadership of Moses. Even though God gave them one miracle after another, they continued to forget His goodness and doubt His promises. Their constant complaining led them into such unbelief that what should have been a temporary passing through the desert on their way to the Promised Land became a 40-year journey in the hot, dry wilderness of Judea.

When bad times come, *we can rebel.* Israel's complaint of the desert conditions eventually led the nation into rebellion against God. They built a golden calf and turned away from the Lord.

We can feel sorry for ourselves. All of us have been down the self-pity road, singing the old spiritual, "Nobody Knows the Trouble I've Seen." Like Elijah the prophet, we sit down under a broom tree and say, "Lord, I'm the only one You've got left" (see 1 Kings 19:4-10). If that's true, God is in serious trouble.

But there is a better way: "Cast your cares on the Lord and he will sustain you; he will never let the righteous fall" (Psalm 55:22). Stop worrying, complaining, rebelling, indulging in self-pity, and start "casting"!

C.S. Lewis said, "God whispers to us in our pleasure, speaks in our conscience, but shouts in our pain." No one is exempt from bad times. It's what you do when life hurts that really counts. E. Stanley Jones said, "Bitterness comes to all; sours some, sweetens others—I shall use it to sweeten my spirit."

I Raised My Eyes Toward Heaven

We worry because we lose sight of God's sovereignty. The classic example of a person who learned the hard way that God rules over all was the ancient Babylonian king, Nebuchadnezzar.

One day he walked out on the balcony of his palace. Gazing at the magnificence and grandeur of the city of Babylon with its majestic hanging gardens, he boasted, "Is not this the great Babylon I have built as the royal residence, by my mighty power and for the glory of my majesty?" (Daniel 4:30).

As the words came from his lips, he snapped psychologically with a psychotic disorder. He was reduced to acting like a brute beast of the field. His skin was toughened by the hot, arid climate of Iraq. His hair grew long, matted and coarse. His fingernails grew out like claws. Talk about falling off your pedestal!

But then Nebuchadnezzar made a comeback. Listen to his testimony, which was published and distributed throughout the kingdom:

> At the end of that time, I, Nebuchadnezzar, raised my eyes toward heaven, and my sanity was restored. Then I praised the Most High; I honored and glorified him who lives forever. His dominion is an eternal dominion; his kingdom endures from generation to generation. . . .
>
> At the same time that my sanity was restored, my honor and splendor were returned to me for the glory of my kingdom. My advisers and nobles sought me out, and I was restored to my throne and became even greater than before.
>
> Now I, Nebuchadnezzar, praise and exalt and glorify the King of heaven, because everything he does is right and all his ways are just. And those who walk in pride he is able to humble (vv. 34, 36, 37).

When we raise our eyes toward heaven, our peace is restored. When we look around we worry. When we look within, we get depressed. When we look up, we are filled with faith in God. "But they that wait upon the Lord shall renew their strength; they shall mount up with wings as eagles; they shall run, and not be weary; they shall walk, and not faint" (Isaiah 40:31, KJV).

Out of the Pit

We can respond to adversity with negativism or with praise. A minister friend of mine was the guest speaker at a leadership retreat. I sat spellbound as I listened to his testimony of healing from cancer. He had battled the disease for two years. The most touching part was when he said that during that time, he never got angry with God. Instead, every day he thanked the Lord for another day to live and sought to live it the best he could for the glory of God.

That's what happened to Handel when he wrote *The Messiah*. The year was 1741. George Frederick Handel was depressed, in debt and hopeless. He was 57 at the time. A minor poet named Charles Jenners delivered to Handel a collection of Biblical excerpts titled *A Sacred Oratorio*. Somewhat nonchalantly, Handel began reading its contents: "He was wounded for our transgressions and bruised for our iniquities . . . He was a man of sorrows, acquainted with grief" (see Isaiah 53:3, 5).

Handel came to identify with the sufferings of the Messiah. The Spirit of the Lord touched his heart as he began to read words that lifted his eyes to behold the greatness of God: "The kingdom of the world has become the kingdom of our Lord and of his Christ, and he will reign for ever and ever" (Revelation 11:15).

Under the power of divine inspiration, he began to compose a musical score to the lyrics. He remained in seclusion for 24 days, often going without food. At times, he said he was so overwhelmed with joy that he would jump to his feet and shout, "Hallelujah!" Later, when someone asked him how he came to compose *The Messiah* in a mere 24 days, he said, "I saw heaven open before me and God Almighty seated on His glorious throne." At one early performance in London, the king stood at "The Hallelujah Chorus" in honor to the true king, Jesus Christ. Since that time, audiences have stood whenever the chorus is sung.

Praise lifts us out of the pit of depression. "I waited patiently for the Lord; he turned to me and heard my cry. He lifted me out of the slimy pit, out of the mud and mire; he set my feet on a rock and gave me a firm place to stand. He put a new song in my mouth, a hymn of praise to our God" (Psalm 40:1-3).

Money Matters DAY 223

Did you hear about the economist who wrote a book about money titled *The Short Story of Money*? It contains only seven words: Here it is and there it goes!

I once read: "You write your autobiography in your checkbook." God has much to say in His Word about our possessions. One out of every 10 verses in the Gospels deals with money; 16 of Jesus' 38 parables concern money.

Money management is a matter of stewardship—being faithful with the resources God has entrusted to us. "It is required in stewards that a man be found faithful" (1 Corinthians 4:2, KJV).

Financial pressures cause marriage problems, personal stress, and business failures. Where do faith and finances meet? A delicate balance is found in Scripture on important money matters.

We are promised prosperity, yet warned against the dangers of wealth: "I pray that you may prosper" (3 John 2, *NKJV*). "Greed is idolatry" (see Colossians 3:5).

We are to honor God with our wealth, yet we are cautioned against its dangers: "Honor the Lord with your wealth" (Proverbs 3:9). "The love of money is a root of all kinds of evil" (1 Timothy 6:10).

We are told that we are worth more than our possessions, yet reminded that money management reveals our hearts: "A man's life does not consist in the abundance of his possessions" (Luke 12:15). "For where your treasure is, there your heart will be also" (Matthew 6:21).

We are to be content, yet we are rewarded for making wise investments: "Be content with what you have" (Hebrews 13:5). "Well done . . . you have been faithful with a few things; I will put you in charge of many things" (Matthew 25:21).

Consecrate yourself and your possessions to God and use everything He has entrusted to you for His glory.

God-Created but Self-Molded DAY 224

The *Phillips* translation of Romans 12:2 reads: "Don't let the world around you squeeze you into its own mold." We are responsible for our own development. We are God-created but self-molded.

Life itself is a process of being molded. We have to learn to put off the old self and put on the new self, "which is being renewed in knowledge in the image of its Creator" (Colossians 3:10).

Our goal is to be conformed to the likeness of Christ. Paul labored in prayer for believers "until Christ be formed in you" (Galatians 4:19). That's what spiritual growth is—the gradual work of grace in our hearts until Christ is fully formed in our thoughts, attitudes, beliefs, lifestyle, and ways of relating to others.

The word *conform* is *morpho* (Greek), meaning "to shape, to mold, and to change." In *Star Wars* there is a being called a "changeling" who is able to "morph," which means to change form. The morphing or molding of character is a lifelong process. So, how's your morphing coming along?

Mentoring helps in the molding process. We become like the company we keep. Company shapes character. "Iron sharpens iron" (Proverbs 27:17). Immature people don't have enough "iron" in their lives, while mature people have true mentors who can help mold or morph them.

So, keep iron in your relationships and allow godly people to help mold, or should I say morph, you into your God-ordained potential.

And So He Prospered
DAY 225

How can we achieve prosperity and manage it in a God-honoring way? In the Old Testament, *prosperity* means success, favor and victory. The Greek word for *prosperity* means "to help on one's way."

Divine prosperity speaks of the blessing and favor of God on what we put our hands to. "Carefully follow the terms of this covenant, so that you may prosper in everything you do" (Deuteronomy 29:9).

The life of King Hezekiah serves as a model for a prosperous life. Hezekiah was 25 when he became king of Judah. He was a descendant of David, and he reigned for 29 years. "He did what was right in the eyes of the Lord, just as his father David had done" (2 Chronicles 29:2).

He was a godly young man whose reign was marked by a time of spiritual revival in Judah. He forsook the idols of his father, King Ahaz, purified the Temple, consecrated the priests, then celebrated the greatest Passover with a celebration unequaled since the days of David and Solomon.

He prayed for the people: "May the Lord, who is good, pardon everyone who sets his heart on seeking God" (30:18, 19). When Sennacherib of Assyria threatened to destroy Jerusalem and marshaled his troops against the city, Hezekiah and the prophet Isaiah came together in prayer. God dispatched an angel from heaven who destroyed 185,000 Assyrian soldiers in one night. The Assyrian army fled.

So, the Chronicler summarized his life by saying, "And so he prospered" (31:21).

It Takes Action DAY 226

I'm sure you've heard the saying, "Attitude is everything." Believe me, it's not. Attitude is important, but it must be accompanied by action.

"In everything he did he had great success, because the Lord was with him," we read of King David (1 Samuel 18:14). The emphasis is on the word *did*.

Success is based on what we do, not what we plan to do, or want to do, or think about doing, or get prepared to do. The saying goes: "The road to hell is paved with good intentions." At the end of the day, there is only what we do in life.

We fail to act because we are afraid of failing. The only people who never fail are those who never attempt anything. *Procrastination* is the product of the fear of failure.

James tells us: "Be doers of the word, and not hearers only, deceiving yourselves" (1:22, *NKJV*). "Faith by itself, if not accompanied by action, is dead" (2:17).

We need to move from planning and praying to doing if we expect to see results. There is a time to wait, and there is a time for action.

When Joshua's army was defeated at Ai, he prayed and asked God "Why?" But God said to him, "Stand up! What are you doing down on your face?" (7:10). Israel had sinned at Jericho by taking things from the city. God told Joshua to take action and remove those things. "Go, consecrate the people . . . you cannot stand against your enemies until you remove it" (v. 13).

What projects have you been planning to do but still haven't gotten around to doing? House repairs? Writing a book? Composing a song? Volunteering in ministry? Getting an education? Going to a career enhancement seminar? Making a financial investment? Writing a will?

Today is the best day to get started. Now is the time for action.

Simple Obedience   DAY 227

Jesus said, "If you love me, you will obey what I command" (John 14:15). *To obey* means "to comply with the commands or requests of another who is in authority; to execute the commands; to be guided, controlled or actuated by one's instincts."

The word *obey* comes from Latin, meaning "to give ear." Hearing is the same as doing in a Biblical sense of the word. "Hear, O Israel: the Lord our God, the Lord is one. Love the Lord your God with all your heart" (Deuteronomy 6:4, 5). When we truly hear the Word of God, we obey. We not only believe the gospel, we obey the gospel to repent and put our faith in Christ Jesus.

Obedience involves the total self. It is more than outward compliance. A little girl was put in time-out by her mother. Plopping herself down in the chair, she boasted, "Mother, I may be sitting down on the outside, but I'm standing up on the inside."

Real obedience is an expression of love. God blesses our obedience to Him. "All these blessings will come upon you and accompany you if you obey the Lord your God" (28:2).

E. Stanley Jones tells of going to the Cathedral at Copenhagen to see Thorwaldsen's statue of Christ. Along the walls are life-sized statues of the 12 apostles, with the magnificent statue of Christ at the front. The statue is unique, with Christ holding out His hands as if to say, "Come unto Me." His face is looking down so you can't see it.

Jones commented to a friend with him, "I can't see the face of Jesus." He replied, "Stanley, you'll have to get on your knees to look into the face of Jesus."

Called of God

Cartoonist Ralph Barton, although successful and in demand, took his own life, leaving a note nearby that included these words: "I am fed up with inventing devices to fill up 24 hours of the day." Ralph Barton failed to connect with the calling of God.

The thought of being called of God can be exhilarating or intimidating, depending on how you look at it. Such a calling carries a deep sense of responsibility and humility. Yet, God has called every person first to know Him and then to serve Him in some capacity.

One of the most powerful aspects of Jesus' ministry was the way in which He called people from all walks of life and cut across all ethnic and gender lines. He called entrepreneurs, politicians, tax accountants, the wealthy, the poor, Jews, Gentiles, women, children and religious leaders.

The call of Christ is both comforting and challenging. But He promises to empower us to fulfill His calling. "Come, follow me, and I will make you fishers of men" (Matthew 4:18). If we follow, He will make us.

What exactly has Christ called us to be and to do? Peter gets a hold of this truth when he tells us that we are called to follow in the steps of Jesus. "To this you were called . . . that you should follow in his steps" (1 Peter 2:21).

We are called by Gods' name (Isaiah 43:1), "called to belong to Jesus Christ . . . and called to be saints" (Romans 1:6, 7), "called according to his purpose" (8:28), "called to be free" (Galatians 5:13), called "to live a holy life" (1 Thessalonians 4:7), and "called . . . out of darkness into His marvelous light" (1 Peter 2:9, *NKJV*).

You are not here by accident. You are called of God. Shake off feelings of self-doubt and inadequacy. "Make your calling and election sure!" (2 Peter 1:10).

With God on Your Side

There is a verse tucked away in Proverbs that motivates me: "When a man's ways please the Lord, He makes even his enemies to be at peace with him" (16:7, *NKJV*). I am challenged to please the Lord. I am comforted by the fact that God will look out for me.

To please the Lord means to live with integrity. Paul describes integrity this way: "Therefore, since through God's mercy we have this ministry, we do not lose heart. Rather, we have renounced secret and shameful ways; we do not use deception, nor do we distort the word of God. On the contrary, by setting forth the truth plainly we commend ourselves to every man's conscience in the sight of God" (2 Corinthians 4:1, 2). He adds, "We are taking pains to do what is right, not only in the eyes of the Lord but also in the eyes of men" (8:21).

Charles Allen gives four questions to ask when making moral decisions:

1. Would you need to keep it a secret?
2. Where will it lead you?
3. Which is your best self?
4. What would the person you admire the most do if he were in your situation?

Reuben Gonzales was in the final match of a pro racquetball tournament. In the fourth and final game, at match point, Gonzales made a super kill shot into the front wall to win the game. The referee called it good. Two linesmen affirmed that the shot was in. But Gonzales, after a moment's hesitation, turned around, shook his opponent's hand, and declared that his shot had hit the floor first. As a result, he lost the match and walked off the court. Everybody was stunned. They couldn't believe that a player with everything officially in his favor, with victory at hand, disqualified himself at match point and lost!

When asked why he did it, Reuben said, "It was the only thing that I could do to maintain my integrity. I could always win another match, but I could never regain my lost integrity."

Blessed to Be a Blessing   DAY 230

We talk a lot about the good life and how to get it. Peter offers this counsel: "Whoever would love life and see good days must keep his tongue from evil and his lips from deceitful speech. He must turn from evil and do good; he must seek peace and pursue it" (1 Peter 3:10, 11). Obviously, the good life is more about pursuing values than possessing valuables.

Everyone would like to be in the place where they "love life and see good days." God has called us to be blessed and to be a blessing. The first thing God did when He created Adam and Eve was to bless them. God desires us to experience the fullness of His blessings. Jesus blessed everyone He touched. One of the most touching scenes in Jesus' life is when "he took the children in his arms, put his hands on them and blessed them" (Mark 10:16).

We often feel that we don't deserve His blessing. We battle low self-esteem. The answer is to know that God loves you "with an everlasting love" (Jeremiah 31:3). You are God's "crown of glory . . . a royal diadem" (Isaiah 62:3, NKJV). You have been "blessed . . . in the heavenly realms with every spiritual blessing in Christ" (Ephesians 1:3).

We may feel guilty about the blessings we enjoy. I saw a sign in an office that read: "Your success has nothing to do with someone else's failure." You will fail to enjoy the blessings of God if you have unrealistic guilt. God wants you to live with gratitude, not guilt. "There is therefore now no condemnation to those who are in Christ Jesus" (Romans 8:1, NKJV).

We have to sow blessings in order to reap them. We get out of life what we put into it. "A man reaps what he sows" (Galatians 6:7). We are blessed to be a blessing. The blessing of the Lord is intended to be put into circulation. Whatever God gives you, give away to others.

Thomas Aquinas prayed: "Give me, O Lord, a steadfast heart, which no unworthy affection may drag downwards; give me an unconquered heart, which no tribulation can wear out; give me an upright heart, which no unworthy purpose may tempt aside."

Joy Unspeakable   DAY 231

C.S. Lewis said, "Joy is the serious business of heaven." Joy is the keynote of the Christian life. If we truly believe what we say we believe as followers of Jesus Christ, we will experience "joy unspeakable" (1 Peter 1:8, KJV).

If we believe that our sins are forgiven, never to be remembered against us, we will have joy. If we believe that we are sons and daughters of God, justified by faith, and heirs of God, we will have joy. If we believe that heaven is our home, we will have joy. While we know that our relationship to God is not based on our feelings, there is an emotional result of faith, and that emotion is joy.

What is joy? *Joy* is "an intense feeling of happiness; delight; gladness; a state of contentment or satisfaction." Joy is an unconquerable sense of gladness even in the face of adversity. Spiritual joy is a gift from God. "I will clothe her priests with salvation, and her saints will ever sing for joy" (Psalm 132:16).

Everyone battles discouragement, sadness and depression. Joy is not perpetual euphoria. It is, however, that inner sense of gladness that comes from knowing we are held in the palm of God's hand, and He will never leave us nor forsake us. Only real joy can sustain us in tough times: "In all our troubles my joy knows no bounds" (2 Corinthians 7:4).

Here is the key to real joy: Peter says of every believer about their personal faith in Jesus: "Though you have not seen him, you love him; and even though you do not see him now, you believe in him and are filled with an inexpressible and glorious joy" (1 Peter 1:8). That means "joy unspeakable and full of glory" (KJV), "a joy that words cannot express" (*Ph.*), and an "inexpressible and glorious (triumphant, heavenly) joy" (*Amp.*).

The joy of the Lord is your strength!

Handling Your Hurts   DAY 232

What do you do when life hurts? When you have played by the rules, done what's expected and lived a responsible life, then the bottom falls out?

We get hurt in many ways—illness, injustice, criticism, adversity, loss, stress, suffering. We feel confused and disappointed. Job felt this way, yet he kept his faith in God and came through his suffering victoriously. "Though He slay me, yet will I trust Him" (13:15, *NKJV*).

How did Job handle his hurts? What can we learn from him?

Reconnect with God. The first thing he did was worship. He "fell to the ground and worshiped" (1:20, 21, *NKJV*). Praise brings peace and inner strength.

Find a support base. His friends came to visit him. Unfortunately, they sat and stared at him for the first seven days. Some friends! They ended up blaming him in one way or another. People tend to judge because they are afraid of getting too close to suffering, lest it come their way. Our judgment of others is a denial of the possibility that we could go through the same thing. But we need a support base of friends.

Trust God when you don't understand why. What peace we would have if we truly believed that God works out all things in conformity to the purpose of His will. Charles Spurgeon said, "When you can't trace God's hand, trust His heart."

Learn what you can from the experience. God revealed Himself to Job during his suffering (see chs. 38-41). Job came to know God better through the experience. The Lord answered Job "out of the whirlwind" (38:1, *NKJV*). When you are in the whirlwind, God will speak. God uses whirlwinds to get our attention. Job repented and learned to see God in a new light (42:5, 6).

Forgive others. "After Job had prayed for his friends, the Lord made him prosperous again" (v. 10). We need to turn things loose and not hold on to hurt feelings. His situation turned around only after he prayed for his friends.

Expect a turnaround. The story ends with Job and his wife recovering, having more children and experiencing a double blessing. "The Lord blessed the latter part of Job's life more than the first" (v. 12).

Larger Than Life   DAY 233

If I could chose one word to describe the life of faith, it would be the word *transcendence*. Faith gives us the power to transcend life's challenges, disappointments and adversities. To transcend means to rise above and to be above and beyond in excellence or degree. We can be larger than life.

There are times when God delivers us out of a bad situation. Miracles are real. There are also times when God gives us the strength to endure and to overcome. He gives us the power to transcend, to rise above, and, thereby, to overcome the world. "This is the victory that has overcome the world, even our faith" (1 John 5:4).

If there is any person who learned how to transcend, or, better said, to live larger than life, it was the apostle Paul: "We are hardpressed on every side, but not crushed; perplexed, but not in despair; persecuted, but not abandoned; struck down, but not destroyed" (2 Corinthians 4:8, 9). I like the *Phillips* translation: "We may be knocked down but we are never knocked out!"

Paul tells us clearly about the tough times he faced. He even had a mysterious "thorn in the flesh" that he pleaded with God to take away from him. God gave him grace to transcend the thorn instead of taking it away. So Paul wrote: "I will boast all the more gladly about my weaknesses, so that Christ's power may rest on me. . . . For when I am weak, then I am strong" (12:9, 10).

He had a transcendent faith that could say, "In all our troubles my joy knows no bounds" (7:4). What was the secret? Here it is: "We have this treasure in jars of clay to show that this all-surpassing power is from God and not from us" (4:7). God gives inner power greater than external pressure when we put our faith in Him.

Life's Not Fair! DAY 234

Let's get historical. A man said to his friend at work, "Last night my wife and I had a sharp disagreement, and she went completely historical." "You mean hysterical," the man replied. "No, I mean historical. She told me everything I have ever done wrong in the history of our marriage."

Let's face it: Life's not always fair. We don't always get what we rightfully deserve. But on the other hand, we also have gotten by with many things we should have been punished for. Life has a way of balancing out. We resent it when we get a raw deal.

If there ever existed a person who had to learn to conquer resentment, it was Joseph. His brothers were jealous of him and sold him into slavery. He spent 12 years in an Egyptian prison. Yet, God had him promoted to second in power to Pharaoh himself!

Later, he was reconciled to his brothers when they came to Egypt for help during a famine. They thought he had been dead for years. Then the day came when he revealed himself to them. They were terrified.

But Joseph reassured them of his love and vowed to take care of them. Triumphant faith said, "You meant evil against me, but God meant it for good" (Genesis 50:20, *NKJV*). What a perspective!

His victory over resentment is seen in the names of his sons: *Manasseh*, "God has made me forget," shows healing from the past; *Ephraim*, "God has blessed me twice over," shows his hope for the future.

Of King Henry VI of England, it was said, "He never forgot anything but injuries." Emerson said of Lincoln, "His heart was as great as the world, but there was no room in it for the memory of a wrong."

Stepping on Suffering DAY 235

The story of Job is known to nearly everyone. The name *Job* itself is synonymous with suffering—unjust suffering. Suffering is a double-edged sword. First, there is the sheer pain of suffering; and second, there are the unanswered questions.

Listen to his lament:

- "After this, Job opened his mouth and cursed the day of his birth" (3:1).
- "[Oh] that God would be willing to crush me, to let loose his hand and cut me off!" (6:9).
- "I loathe my very life; therefore I will give free rein to my complaint and speak out in the bitterness of my soul" (10:1).
- "My spirit is broken, my days are cut short, the grave awaits me" (17:1).
- "I am reduced to dust and ashes" (30:19).
- "The churning inside me never stops; days of suffering confront me" (v. 27).

In spite of these feelings, he worshiped God. "I know that my Redeemer lives. . . . When he has tested me, I will come forth as gold. . . . I have treasured the words of his mouth more than my daily bread" (19:25; 23:10, 12).

His faith boiled down to one great affirmation: "Though He slay me, yet will I trust Him" (13:15, *NKJV*). God restored to Job what he had lost. Job could have ended in tragedy, being bitter toward God, forsaking his faith, maybe even dying by suicide. Instead, he rose on the wings of faith and became more than a conqueror.

I once visited a young man dying of Lou Gehrig's disease. When I walked into his room to pray for him, he greeted me with a big smile. Talking was extremely difficult for him because of the breathing apparatus. He gasped for every breath, yet he shared with me the joy that Christ had brought into his life. I prayed for him and bid him goodbye. As I turned to leave he said to me, "Pastor, I may give out, but I will never give up."

Good Grief   DAY 236

Grief is a feeling of sorrow due to the loss of a person, position or power. It is also associated with the disruption of old living patterns such as traditions. The death of someone we love is the greatest loss. Divorce brings on deep grief.

King David was bound in the throes of grief after his fall with Bathsheba. The son she gave birth to was ill at birth. For seven days David fasted, prayed, and stayed in his bedroom in the palace. He would receive no consolation from anyone. Then the child died. His attendants were afraid to tell him because he was so distressed. When he learned of the child's death, his actions baffled everyone. He freshened up, changed clothes, and went to the Temple to worship God. Then he returned to his palace and asked for a meal.

"Why are you acting this way?" his attendants asked him. "While the child was alive, you fasted and wept, but now that the child is dead, you get up and eat!" (2 Samuel 12:21).

His response is a powerful confession of faith and a triumphant attitude in times of grief: "While the child was still alive . . . I thought, 'Who knows? The Lord may be gracious to me and let the child live.' But now that he is dead, why should I fast? Can I bring him back again? I will go to him, but he will not return to me" (vv. 22, 23).

David rested in God's answer to his prayer, even though he didn't like the answer. His faith was strong enough to hear "no" from God as well as "yes." David had a grip on the reality of eternal life: "I will go to him." You and I will one day see our loved ones we have lost in this life when we arrive in heaven.

Make the Most of Your Losses ✠ DAY 237

The gospel of Christ, with the promise of eternal life, is the only definitive answer to grief. Grief is a feeling of sadness following the loss of something valuable to us or someone dear to us.

In the French Academy of Science, there is a rather plain, old shoemaker's awl on display. To look at it, one would never suspect that the simple tool could be responsible for anything of consequence. In fact, it caused tremendous pain.

This was the very awl which fell from the shoemaker's table and put out the eye of his 9-year-old son. The injury was so severe that the boy eventually lost vision in both eyes. He was enrolled in a special school for children who were blind. The boy learned to read by handling large, carved wood blocks.

Years later, when the shoemaker's son became an adult, he thought of a new way to read. It involved learning a system of dots which were translated into the letters of the alphabet that could be read from a piece of paper on any flat surface. Louis Braille actually used the awl which had blinded him as a boy to form the dots into a whole new reading system for the blind—known simply today as Braille.

Pour out your grief to the Lord in prayer. Put your faith in Him and claim His promise of restoration: "I will repay you for the years the locusts have eaten . . . you will have plenty to eat, until you are full, and you will praise the name of the Lord your God" (Joel 2:25, 26).

God will restore to you everything and everyone you have lost, either in this life or in the life to come. Jesus said, "I am the resurrection and the life. He who believes in me will live, even though he dies; and whoever lives and believes in me will never die" (John 11:25, 26).

If Only...

Contentment is a virtue. We live in a culture of consumerism. The biggest addiction in America is *more*.

Sure we need future goals. Dream big dreams and go for them with all your heart, but enjoy the journey toward your destination. The only thing ahead of you is your funeral, so slow down. I read recently: "The happiest people don't necessarily have the best of everything. They just make the best of everything."

Once while Francis of Assisi was hoeing his garden, he was asked, "What would you do if you were suddenly to learn that you were to die at sunset today?" He replied, "I would finish hoeing my garden."

The danger we face is discontentment. Discontentment leads to covetousness, which comes in two forms: jealousy of others and resentment toward others. *Covetousness* comes from a Greek word meaning "grasping for more." Tim Kimmel says that covetousness is "material inebriation. It's an addiction to things that don't last and a craving for things that don't really matter."

Discontentment complains, "If only..."

- If only I had...

  a job, a better job, a more understanding boss, enough money to retire on, a bigger house, a thinner waist, a better education, a husband, a different husband, a child, a lifestyle like...

- If only I hadn't...

  dropped out of school, been forced to get married, had an abortion, started drinking, been fired, run up so many debts, neglected my wife, quit that job, sold that stock.

- If only they had...

  given me more playing time, recognized my potential, offered me the job, encouraged me in my sports, been honest with me, stuck with me.

- If only they hadn't...

  abandoned me as a baby, discouraged me, prejudged me, pushed me so hard to achieve, lied to me, been so interested in making money, been ashamed of my handicap.

If only... if only... if only.[15]

In the Lap of Luxury DAY 239

Oscar Wilde came to the United States for a visit in 1882. When asked by customs if he had anything to declare, he replied, "Only my genius." Fifteen years later, alone and broken in prison, he reflected on his life of waste and excess. He wrote: "I have been a spendthrift of my genius . . . I forgot that every little action of the common day makes or unmakes character."

Oscar Wilde isn't the only man to forget that valuable lesson. The Israeli judge Samson forgot it as well. Samson is one of the most popular Biblical personalities. Everyone knows of Samson's downfall at the hands of Delilah.

On a humorous note, I read about a church's Sunday bulletin that listed the pastor's sermon title, "The Head of Samson in the Lap of Delilah." Underneath it was printed the closing hymn, "Leave It There."

Samson served as a judge in Israel. The judges governed Israel for about 330 years, from the time of Joshua's death to the rise of Saul, the first Israeli king. God raised up Samson (meaning "sun" or "brightness") to deliver Israel from the Philistines.

Samson had many notable qualities, but he also had strange contradictions. He was separate as a Nazarite, but he engaged in ungodly associations. He showed spiritual passion, but he was at times controlled by his appetites. He was immature in his plans, but he was courageous in battle. He possessed great physical strength, but he was weak in the face of temptation.

What went wrong? Samson sacrificed his future for the present. He lived for the moment. He sowed the wind and reaped the whirlwind. The result was, "He did not know that the Lord had left him" (Judges 16:20).

Life needs to be governed by purpose, not pleasure. "He who loves pleasure will become poor" (Proverbs 21:17). God wants us to enjoy life, but pleasure is balanced by a spiritual purpose for life: "For to me, to live is Christ and to die is gain" (Philippians 1:21).

Power Plus Purpose

God empowers us for His purposes, not our own. Jesus said, "You will receive power . . . you will be my witnesses" (Acts 1:8). Spiritual power follows spiritual purpose. When we ask God to give us power, He asks us why we want it.

Samson was a man who used spiritual power for his own purposes and ended up losing it. When reading his exploits, we ask: Is Samson furthering the purpose of God or his own agenda? Does he see himself as an instrument of God, or is he waging his own private war? Take, for example, Judges 15:3, when he says, "This time I have a right to get even with the Philistines; I will really harm them."

Where did Samson go wrong?

First, *he lacked dependency on God.* No record is found of him seeking God about his encounters with the Philistines. No recorded prayers. Compare him with David, who walked down into the valley of Elah to face Goliath, saying: "I come against you in the name of the Lord Almighty" (1 Samuel 17:45). David captures the meaning of depending on God in Psalm 20:7: "Some trust in chariots and some in horses [we would say "fighter planes and cruise missiles"], but we trust in the name of the Lord our God."

Second, *Samson failed to give praise to God.* He took credit for his successes. But when David returned from battle, he praised God for victory: "Through you we push back our enemies; through your name we trample our foes. I do not trust in my bow, my sword does not bring me victory; but you give us victory over our enemies, you put our adversaries to shame. In God we make our boast all day long, and we will praise your name forever" (44:5-8).

Power comes when we submit to God's purpose, live in dependency on His wisdom and strength, and give God praise in and for everything.

Making a Comeback

Judges 16:1 reads: "One day Samson went to Gaza, where he saw a prostitute. He went in to spend the night with her." Doesn't that verse strike you as odd for an anointed man of God? The story of Samson presents serious issues for us. *How could God use such a man? Why did God use such a man?* Why is he listed among the heroes of faith in Hebrews 11? Several lessons are important in the study of Samson.

God's sovereign prerogative to use Samson in no way excused or condoned Samson's behavior. God also used Pharaoh, Cyrus, and even the pagan nations of Assyria and Babylon as instruments of discipline against Israel. But this did not let them off the hook from God's discipline regarding their own actions. God works to accomplish His purposes, not ours.

The Hebrews 11 narrative of the great Old Testament heroes of faith, and Samson in particular, focuses exclusively on the miracles of God, not the sum total of their character traits and deficiencies.

God's patience is seen in Samson. He was allowed to judge or lead Israel for 20 years. God's patience and long-suffering with us is a testimony to His great love. Where would any of us be today if God were not patient with us? "He is patient with you, not wanting anyone to perish, but everyone to come to repentance" (2 Peter 3:9).

Samson was eventually defeated by the Philistines. They took out his eyes and made him thresh grain as an ox. In the end, Samson turned back to God, rededicated his life, and won a great victory over the Philistines in his death.

If you have strayed from your faith in God, make a comeback today. Rededicate yourself to His purpose for your life.

Good News DAY 242

Do you ever feel like you're bombarded with bad news? Bad news internationally—wars, poverty, political unrest, human-rights violations. Bad news nationally—higher taxes, national debt, corporate downsizing, rising crime, political scandals. Bad news personally—relationship conflicts, depression, personal tragedies, disappointments.

To be honest, there are days when I intentionally avoid the news. I just don't want to hear another story of tragedy, failure or disappointment. Life itself is a series of bad news and good news.

When Jesus came into the world, He was and is God's message of good news to us. Into a world of great unrest, there appeared the star of Bethlehem. Angels appeared to shepherds in the fields of Bethlehem with a message for all time: "Do not be afraid. I bring you good news of great joy that will be for all the people. Today . . . a Savior has been born to you; he is Christ [Messiah] the Lord" (Luke 2:10, 11).

Above all things, Jesus is the Savior of the world. What does this mean? The word *salvation* (Greek, *sozo*) means "to deliver, to set free, to make whole, and to preserve." Saved from what? The power, the penalty, and the punishment of sin.

There are two vital truths we need to know: (1) Humanity is lost and incapable of saving itself, and (2) God has provided salvation as a gift.

Jesus said, "The kingdom of God is near. Repent and believe the good news!" (Mark 1:15). He did not bring a gospel of religion, good works or self-help therapy.

Salvation is not an idea or theological concept; it is a Person. The world has many teachers, prophets and sages—but only one Savior. "Salvation is found in no one else, for there is no other name under heaven given to men by which we must be saved" (Acts 4:12).

Trusting, Not Trying   DAY 243

We all share a common need—the need to be reconciled to God. Sin is a universal problem. "All have sinned and fall short of the glory of God" (Romans 3:23). God met our need for salvation by sending His Son, Jesus Christ.

- If we needed an education, God would have sent us a teacher.
- If we needed prosperity, God would have sent us an economist.
- If we needed therapy, God would have sent us a psychiatrist.
- If we needed healing, God would have sent us a physician.
- If we needed technology, God would have sent us a scientist.
- If we needed knowledge, God would have sent us a philosopher.

But what we needed most was redemption, so God sent us a Savior!

To be saved means to be delivered from the penalty and power of sin. God frees us from the guilt, shame, and condemnation of sin when we confess our sins and receive Christ as our Savior. It takes humility to be saved. We have to come to the end of ourselves and admit we are powerless to save ourselves.

As Paul wrote: "For it is by grace you have been saved, through faith—and this is not from yourselves, it is the gift of God—not by works, so that no one can boast" (Ephesians 2:8).

"Not by works" means we cannot be saved by trying to live a better life. We need God to do a miraculous work in our hearts. That miracle is called *salvation*. Jesus called it "being born again"! When John Wesley became a Christian, he wrote in his journal: "I felt I did trust Christ—Christ alone as my Savior."

Here's the greatest news of all: Salvation is personal. Sure, Jesus came to save the whole world, but He came for you. When Jesus was born in Bethlehem, the angels announced: "A Savior has been born to *you*" (Luke 2:11).

God is deeply concerned about the quality of our lives and our eternal salvation. When Christ came into the world, He had you in mind.

Who Is the Lord? DAY 244

W hen Moses confronted Pharaoh with the message of God, "Let my people go," he responded, "Who is the Lord, that I should obey him?" (Exodus 5:2).

The question continues to be asked—Who is the Lord? While the overwhelming majority of people say that they believe in God, their picture of God is somewhat hazy. God is out of focus for them.

My son, David Paul, got his first pair of glasses when he was 3 years old. An eye exam revealed that he was extremely farsighted. I'll never forget the day we went to pick up his new glasses. Standing in the store, I put the glasses on him, and he opened his eyes as big as saucers. He jerked the glasses off and said, "Dad, everything is so big!"

"Put them back on, Son," I replied. "For the first time in your life, you're seeing the world the way it's supposed to look."

So many people have never seen God the way He really is. They are spiritually farsighted. But when they put on the glasses of the Bible, they see the greatness of God more clearly than they have ever seen Him.

In the Old Testament, God is called by several names. God is *Elohim*, the Creator, the Faithful One who binds Himself on oath. He is *El Olam*, the everlasting God. He is *El Shaddai*, literally, the God of the Mountain. The name also means the Almighty and the All-Sufficient One who provides for His people. *El Shaddai* has a feminine quality, referring to a mother nursing her children. God is called *Adonai*, meaning "Lord, Ruler and Sovereign King."

Most importantly, God's name is *Yahweh*, or *Jehovah*. The name Jehovah appears some 6,800 times in the Old Testament. Jehovah is the covenant name of God. It really means "the Promise Keeper." God gave Israel this name to remind them that He is faithful to His promises.

Today, reflect on the faithfulness of the Promise Keeper in your life. "There has not failed one word of all His good promise" (1 Kings 8:56, *NKJV*).

The Knowledge of the Holy — DAY 245

Perhaps the reason so many people have an identity crisis is that they don't understand who God is. Since we are made in His image, our self-concept is directly connected to our understanding of God. Proverbs 9:10 states, "The fear of the Lord is the beginning of wisdom, and knowledge of the Holy One is understanding."

Any portrait of God, apart from the understanding of God that we have in the Bible and in Jesus, is inadequate and distorted. The wrong image of God weakens morality. A.W. Tozer, in *The Knowledge of the Holy*, writes: "It is impossible to keep our moral practices sound and our inward attitudes right while our ideas about God are erroneous and inadequate."[16]

Ninety percent of American adults, when questioned, said they believe in God. But what kind of God? In his book, *Your God Is Too Small*, J.B. Phillips puts his finger on our problem: "The trouble with many people today is that they have not found a God big enough for modern needs."[17]

Jesus "is the image of the invisible God" (Colossians 1:15). He taught us that God is love. We are the masterpiece of His creation. His love was shown most clearly when He gave His Son for us on the cross. "God so loved the world that He gave His one and only Son" (John 3:16).

You don't have to do anything for God to love you. You don't have to have great faith, or live a perfect life, or perform courageous acts for God to love you. You are loved by God just the way you are.

God does what He does for us because He loves us. His love is unconditional. God not only loves us—He is love! His love is constant. It never changes. There is nothing good you can do to cause God to love you more. There is nothing so bad that you can think or do to cause God to love you less.

Love and Obey   DAY 246

True love is exclusive. When we say "I do" at the marriage altar, we also say "I don't" to all the other potential candidates! Now, if we know God loves us, it follows naturally that we will love Him in return. "We love because he first loved us" (1 John 4:19).

Loving God means obedience to Him. "We know that we have come to know him if we obey his commands" (2:3). Here's the fly in the ointment—we don't like obedience. We don't want anyone, including God, telling us how to run our lives. But God has the audacity to invade our privacy and freedom with commandments. How dare He!

Our tendency to rebel against God is cured when we realize that His law is the pathway to life. Your quality of life will not be diminished in any way by obeying God's commandments. Your life will be enriched greatly. God's law reflects His love and His desire for us to enjoy the best that life has to offer.

Submission to God is the secret of the good life for which we search. Did you know that the most frequently used word in the Bible for *worship* means "to bow down," or "to fall prostrate before God"? *Worship* means surrendering ourselves to the will of God in joyful obedience.

In fact, the first use of the word *worship* in the Bible occurs when God told Abraham to offer his son Isaac as a sacrifice. In spite of all his unanswered questions, he set out in faith to the appointed place in obedience to God.

God was testing his faith. Abraham's words to his servants still stir the human soul: "Stay here with the donkey while I and the boy go over there. We will worship and then we will come back to you" (Genesis 22:5). What faith! What obedience! What surrender!

Surrender!

A true, meaningful relationship with God is a matter of surrender, not striving. Learning to surrender our will to His will is the key to life. We often strive against God's will.

Like Jacob, we wrestle with God instead of surrendering to Him. Finally, after wrestling with the angel all night to obtain a blessing, Jacob surrendered to God, confessed his need, and found a new level of closeness to God. After surrendering, God changed his name from *Jacob*, meaning "deceiver," to *Israel*, meaning "a prince with God." Jacob said, "I saw God face to face" (see Genesis 32:22-31).

Mendelssohn, the gifted German composer and conductor, once visited the cathedral at Friedberg, which featured a majestic pipe organ. Unknown by the resident organist at the cathedral, Mendelssohn requested to play the organ. The resident organist refused.

Mendelssohn tried to persuade him. "You can stand next to me as I play. I only want to hear its majestic sound." Finally, the organist yielded. As Mendelssohn touched the keyboard, the thunder of the organ filled the cathedral.

The organist placed his hand on Mendelssohn's shoulder and asked, "Who are you?"

"My name is Mendelssohn," he replied.

The organist was shocked, apologized, and said, "Just think of it. The master composer was here, and I almost refused to let him touch this instrument."

Only when we surrender to God's will do we reach our full human potential. "I desire to do your will, O God; your law is within my heart" (Psalm 40:8).

Why We Worship

W hy should we love God exclusively? Is God on some kind of a cosmic ego trip, needing our constant attention so that He can feel good about Himself? Is God the Eternal Egoist?

This may shock you, but God doesn't need our love or worship. God enjoys our love and worship, but He doesn't need it. God is self-existent. He doesn't need anything. Worship is God's gift to us. We're the ones who need to worship. Worship guides us on the pathway to really knowing God.

We worship God for two reasons: Because of who He is and because of what He has done for us. Listen to the first commandment: "I am the Lord your God, who brought you out of Egypt, out of the land of slavery. You shall have no other gods before me" (Exodus 20:1-3). It is because God brought us out of the slavery of sin that we are free to worship Him. True worship is our response of love to the love of God. We have been redeemed from the slavery of sin and set free.

God redeemed Israel from slavery in Egypt by His power, seen in parting the Red Sea and by the atonement of the Passover Lamb. God has also redeemed us from sin by His power of Christ's resurrection and by the blood of Jesus given for our sins on the cross.

Jesus fulfilled all the Old Testament expressions of redemption—the Passover, the Day of Atonement, and the Levitical offerings. "Christ, our Passover Lamb, has been sacrificed" (1 Corinthians 5:7).

Redemption means, "You are not your own; you were bought at a price" (6:19, 20). We are no longer our own. Therefore, let us glorify God with our lives. Remember, your life is God's gift to you; what you do with your life is your gift to God.

Taste Is Everything DAY 249

Image is everything! Or, so the advertising world would have us believe. Advertisements entice us to buy what we see. That way, we'll look the best, have the best, and be the best.

Americans are very image-conscious. We dress for success to project an image of confidence and achievement. A young businessman in Atlanta got himself into financial jeopardy. He financed the right business image by buying an expensive car, expensive suits, and dining at the best restaurants all to impress his potential clients, only to amass a crippling debt. He tried to buy an image of success rather than achieving success the proper way. He told me, "I have to have all of this stuff in order to do business." But his need for the right image nearly put him out of business.

We focus heavily on building self-image but not as much on character development. Many people project an image of happiness, success, and even wealth, but their lives tell another story.

"But you and your wife looked so happily married," I overheard someone say to a man recently divorced. "It was all an image we put on for others," he replied.

Quite often, there's a world of difference between image and reality. This brings up the issue of faith. Do we really know God? Do we trust Him regardless of circumstances? Do we really love and serve Him? Or, is our faith more image than reality?

The Sprite commercial has it right—"Image is nothing. Taste is everything!" Well, the image of faith is nothing, reality is everything.

What we need is real faith—a sincere trust in the living God. "Without faith it is impossible to please God, because anyone who comes to him must believe that he exists and that he rewards those who earnestly seek him" (Hebrews 11:6).

A Jealous God   DAY 250

God comes right out and tells us He is a jealous God (Exodus 20:5). We think of jealousy as one of the seven deadly sins. Shakespeare called jealousy the "green-eyed monster."

Jealousy is an intense emotion which can take the positive form of zeal or the negative form of envy. The Hebrew word *quana*, translated *jealousy*, means "to become red," describing the colors of the human face when experiencing this emotion. The Greek word *zeloo* means "to boil."

God is jealous in the sense that He alone has the exclusive right to be worshiped and obeyed (Exodus 34:14). He is jealous for the well-being of His people (see Zechariah 1:14). He's called "a consuming fire" because He fills us with His all-consuming love (Deuteronomy 4:24).

There's a verse in the Book of James that helps us understand the jealousy of God. James tells us "the spirit he caused to live in us envies intensely" (4:5). You could translate the phrase, "God jealously longs for the spirit that He made to live in us." Or, "the Spirit He caused to live in us longs jealously." When the human spirit is touched by the Holy Spirit, we are drawn by God's love into a life of devotion.

This is what Elijah meant when he prayed, "I have been very zealous for the Lord God Almighty" (1 Kings 19:10). The disciples noted that Jesus was "consumed with the zeal of the Lord" (see John 2:17). And Paul said, "I am jealous for you with a godly jealousy" (2 Corinthians 11:2). Since God is jealous for us, let us be jealous for Him.

Jealous for God DAY 251

Whenever Michelangelo was meditating on some great design for a painting or a sculpture, he would close himself off from the outside world. "Why do you lead such a solitary life?" a friend inquired of him. "Art," he replied, "is a jealous god; it requires the whole and entire man." During his years of intense labor on the Sistine Chapel, he often refused to have communication with any person, even at his home, lest he be distracted from his commitment to the project.

Are we filled with jealousy for the Lord? Does our passion for God motivate us to live for Him? Or, has the holy fire of spiritual passion that once burned so brightly in our hearts dimmed to a flickering flame?

If so, renew your spiritual passion for God. "Never be lacking in zeal, but keep your spiritual fervor, serving the Lord" (Romans 12:11). "Fan into flame the gift of God, which is in you" (2 Timothy 1:6).

Everybody gets burned-out spiritually. We can have fresh fire rekindled on the altar of our hearts when we get alone with God. His presence and His Word are like fire "shut up in our bones," as Jeremiah said (see 20:9). Get rid of those things that are snuffing out your spiritual fire. Ask the Holy Spirit to baptize you with His sacred fire as He did for the early believers on the Day of Pentecost.

The Christian group 2nd Chapter of Acts sings a song titled "Purify Me." As you read the lyrics, ask God to rekindle your first love for Him.[18]

Living God, consuming fire,
Burn the sin from my life.
Make Your will my desire,
Take my life in Your hands.
Purify me with Your love,
Till I shine far brighter than purest gold,
In Your eyes, Living God.

President or Resident? DAY 252

P aul describes a true relationship with Jesus this way: "I pray that
    ... Christ may dwell in your hearts through faith" (Ephesians 3:16,
17). The word *dwell* means "to be at home at," or "to take up permanent
residence." Some people relate to Jesus as more of an occasional visitor
than a permanent resident in their hearts. Not only does Jesus want to
reside in our hearts, He wants to preside as Lord over every aspect of
our lives.

Have you ever received a telephone call on a Saturday afternoon
from a friend or family member who says, "I just got in town, and
I'll be over in a few minutes"? The house is a mess. You're not ready
for company. So, what do you do? You run through the house hiding
everything you can, wherever you can, as fast as you can. You throw
things in the closets and the bedrooms, shut the doors, tidy up the kitch-
en and family room, and then greet your guest at the front door with a
big smile.

They walk in, look around and say, "Your home is so lovely! I wish
our house looked this nice all the time." (If they only knew the truth!) But
you don't want them walking into the bedrooms or looking in the closets.
Although we tell them, "Make yourself at home," we don't really mean it.
That's just a Southern colloquialism.

We don't want them to be that much "at home." We don't want them
to dwell with us. We prefer that they visit for a while and then leave.
You see, a guest stays in his or her designated area, but a permanent
resident—a member of the family—goes wherever he or she wants to
go. So it is with Jesus.

Do you keep Him in His designated area, or does He dwell with you?
Is He at home in your heart? Do you allow Him to go into the closets of
bitterness, resentment, and sin and clean up the mess? Is He Lord over
your time, talents and treasure? Is He welcome to go into the attic of your
mind and the basement of your beliefs to transform your thinking so that
you live by the mind of Christ?

Let Christ *dwell* in your heart by faith!

Standing at the Crossroads

In Lewis Carroll's classic, *Alice in Wonderland*, Alice comes to a fork in the road. Confused, she asks the Cheshire Cat which road to take.

"Where do you want to go?" asks the Cat.

Alice replies, "I don't know."

"Then," says the Cat, "it doesn't matter which way you go."

The word of the Lord spoken by Jeremiah is apropos for our times: "Stand at the crossroads and look; ask for the ancient paths, ask where the good way is, and walk in it, and you will find rest for your souls" (6:16).

Will we choose the ancient path—the tried-and-tested way of faith and obedience to God? Or, will we follow the misguided philosophies of the day? Man tries in futility to build the city of man without the city of God, as Augustine, the early church leader, observed. Can it be done?

The 19th-century novelist Dostoyevsky asks in the classic, *Brothers Karamazov*, "Can man live without God?" Then reminds us, "If God does not exist, everything else is permissible."

When the British statesman Lord Gladstone was asked if there was anything that frightened him about the future, he replied, "Yes, one thing; the fear that God seems to be dying out in the minds of men." God lamented, "My people have forgotten me, days without number" (Jeremiah 2:32).

When God is foremost in our minds and thoughts, our lives will be lived at the highest level. We do nothing by ourselves. The living God is the breath we breathe, the life we enjoy, the bread we eat, the water we drink, the wealth we enjoy, the light by which we see. "In him we live and move and have our being" (Acts 17:28).

May we be like David, who prayed, "[Lord,] I think of you through the watches of the night" (Psalm 63:6).

Trusting God

The one word that best describes our relationship to God is *trust*. The Hebrew concept of trust that runs throughout the Old

Testament means "to roll the weight upon, to rely upon, to lean upon, and to take refuge in the Lord." The psalmist wrote, "Some trust in chariots and some in horses, but we trust *in the name* of the Lord our God" (Psalm 20:7). To trust in His name is to trust in who He is.

We only trust to the degree that we know someone. The same is true in our relationship to God. People don't trust God because they don't really know Him. We can trust His *wisdom* because He knows what is best for us. "'For my thoughts are not your thoughts, neither are your ways my ways,' declares the Lord. 'As the heavens are higher than the earth, so are my ways higher than your ways and my thoughts than your thoughts'" (Isaiah 55:8, 9).

We can trust His *goodness* because He only desires what is best for us. "The Lord is good, a refuge in times of trouble" (Nahum 1:7).

And we can trust His *power* because He is able to do what is best for us. "Now to him who is able to do immeasurably more than all we ask or imagine, according to his power that is at work within us" (Ephesians 3:20).

Corrie ten Boom said trusting God means "Don't doubt in the dark what God has shown you in the light." Trust God when you're in the valley of defeat as much as you do when you stand on the mountain peak of victory. Anybody can trust God when everything is going the way they planned. But only a person of true faith can trust God in tough times. "The one who trusts in him will never be put to shame" (Romans 9:33).

Power in His Name   DAY 255

Jesus taught us to pray in His name. "You may ask me for anything *in my name*, and I will do it" (John 14:14). What does that really mean? Can we manipulate God just by saying the words "in Jesus' name?" Not at all.

To pray in Jesus' name means that the content of prayer is in harmony with His will and character. To pray in His name means to pray according to His will and purpose. It is to pray, "Your kingdom come, Your will be done." This is a missing element from modern praying because we operate from our own agenda instead of God's agenda.

Humanism has conditioned us to place the self at the center of life and to be over-preoccupied with the self. We even interpret Scripture from the standpoint of "What's in it for me?" We have misread passages on faith, thinking that if we just say the magic words "in Jesus' name," then all our prayers will be answered just the way we want. But answered prayers are in accordance with His will. Since God knows the end from the beginning, we trust Him to do what is best for us.

In ancient times, the name of a person represented the person himself. The names of God given in Scripture reflect who God is. The name *Jesus* means Savior. When God worked in people's lives a special work of grace, He often changed their name. Jacob's name was changed to *Israel* after he wrestled with the angel. *Israel* means "a prince with God." Simon's name was changed to *Peter*, meaning "a rock," when he met Jesus.

When we pray in Jesus' name, we are putting our faith in His power, we are confessing Him as Lord of our lives and of the situations we are facing, and we are submitting to His will. He hears, and He answers!

The Blessing   DAY 256

When you hear the word *blessing*, what comes to mind? We use the word in a variety of ways. We speak of saying the blessing over a meal, or praying that God will bless others. When someone sneezes, we say "Bless you."

Let me share with you a story about my daughter, Charlsi. Our family was eating lunch one day when she was 7 years old. She sneezed abruptly. I mean, she really sneezed. No one said anything. She looked around, waiting for someone to say "Bless you." But no one did. So she said, "Bless me," and went on eating her lunch.

The word *blessing* occupies an important place in the Bible. The Hebrew verb *barak* occurs 330 times in the Bible and means "to kneel, to honor, to bless." The Greek verb *eulogeo* means "to speak well of" and "to bestow favor upon." It is used in reference to praising God, as well as the blessings God gives us.

We are to give the blessing of God to others. To bless another person means to speak well of them, to honor them, to praise them, to affirm them, and to seek their highest good. Everyone needs praise. The greatest gift we can give another person is praise, which builds their confidence, self-esteem and self-worth.

Here's a blessing you can speak over others: "The Lord bless you and keep you; the Lord make his face shine upon you and be gracious to you; the Lord turn his face toward you and give you peace" (Numbers 6:24-26). The priests spoke this blessing over the Israelites. Notice what God told Moses about the power of this blessing: "So they will put my name on the Israelites, and I will bless them" (v. 27).

The Offense of the Cross   DAY 257

B renda Nichol, a teacher's aide in southwestern Pennsylvania, was suspended for a year without pay for wearing a cross necklace to work. She "believes [that] to remove or hide that cross beneath her clothing is an act of denying Christ as her Lord and Savior, which she cannot do without violating her religious convictions," said her American Center for Law and Justice lawyer. But an 1895 Pennsylvania law specifically prohibits teachers from wearing religious symbols at work.

Christians aren't permitted to wear crosses in Saudi Arabia either, so when retired Army captain Todd M. Bair (sadly killed in recent terrorist bombings) was working in the country as a contractor, he turned to an ancient solution.

He asked a local jeweler to make three gold "ICTHUS" (which is an acrostic in Greek for "Jesus Christ Son of God Savior") fish necklaces. Bair's mother told the news chief of Winter Haven, Florida, that when he went back to the store, the owner asked about the fish. "It's just something special between me and my boys," he replied. Special indeed: Christians used the fish symbol to avoid persecution while identifying themselves and places of worship. The jeweler reportedly made more fish and quickly sold out.[19]

The cross of Christ is a paradoxical symbol—one of hope, yet one of offense. Paul speaks of "the offense of the cross" (Galatians 5:11). Yet, he can say, "May I never boast except in the cross of our Lord Jesus Christ, through which the world has been crucified to me, and I to the world" (6:14).

Why Christ Died

Let's continue today considering what Paul calls "the offense of the cross." What is so offensive about the cross? Just the image of the cross takes us back to the actual crucifixion of Jesus, which raises important spiritual questions:

- Why did Christ die?
- Who put Him to death?
- Why was the cross necessary in our salvation?
- If He did die for our sins, how can we be saved if we neglect so great a salvation?

The Greek word Paul uses for the offense of the cross is *skandalon* and means "to put a snare, like the bait in a trap or a stumbling block in the way; something which trips a person up." The message of the Cross is, "But we preach Christ crucified: a stumbling block to Jews and foolishness to Gentiles, but to those whom God has called, both Jews and Greeks, Christ the power of God and the wisdom of God. For the foolishness of God is wiser than man's wisdom, and the weakness of God is stronger than man's strength" (1 Corinthians 1:23-25).

The Cross answers our deepest spiritual need. It is through the Cross that our sins are forgiven, we are reconciled to God, and we receive eternal life. "For the message of the cross is foolishness to those who are perishing, but to us who are being saved it is the power of God" (v. 18).

Isaiah prophesied of the power of the Cross in his vision of the sufferings of the Messiah: "Surely he took up our infirmities and carried our sorrows, yet we considered him stricken by God, smitten by him, and afflicted. But he was pierced for our transgressions, he was crushed for our iniquities; the punishment that brought us peace was upon him, and by his wounds we are healed" (Isaiah 53:4, 5).

George Grenfell, missionary to Africa, ministered among tribes that were given to idolatry and violence. After some time he returned home for a short stay, wondering if he had made any impact for Christ on those tribes.

Sometime later he returned to that same area to resume his ministry. He recalls turning into a tributary of the Congo River and being met by a large group of warlike tribesmen. They began to sing powerfully in their native tongue, "All hail the power of Jesus' name, let angels prostrate fall, bring forth the royal diadem and crown Him Lord of all." Only years before, Grenfell had witnessed horrible acts of cruelty and hatred. Such is the power of the Cross.

Only God Can Save — DAY 259

The cross of Christ offends our wisdom and our self-sufficiency. We can't make sense of the sufferings of Christ, so we dismiss them. We think good works are sufficient for salvation, or we think we're not nearly as bad as other people, so we don't trust Christ to save us.

Paul speaks to our intellectual struggle with the Cross: "Where is the wise man? Where is the scholar? Where is the philosopher of this age? Has not God made foolish the wisdom of the world? For since in the wisdom of God the world through its wisdom did not know him, God was pleased through the foolishness of what was preached to save those who believe. . . . Christ the power of God and the wisdom of God. For the foolishness of God is wiser than man's wisdom, and the weakness of God is stronger than man's strength" (1 Corinthians 1:20-25).

He continues: "But God chose the foolish things of the world to shame the wise; God chose the weak things of the world to shame the strong. He chose the lowly things of this world and the despised things—and the things that are not—to nullify the things that are, so that no one may boast before Him. . . . Therefore, as it is written: 'Let him who boasts boast in the Lord'" (vv. 27-31).

We cannot save ourselves. We cannot devise a cure for sin. We believe we can cure anything. We are like Adam and Eve, covering our sins. The Cross offends us because it shows us our utter sinfulness. But only God can forgive sins. And God's way is through the Cross. Here's the good news: "If we confess our sins, He is faithful and just to forgive us our sins and to cleanse us from all unrighteousness" (1 John 1:9, *NKJV*).

Look at the Wounds — DAY 260

The one question people have asked me repeatedly about the movie *The Passion of the Christ* was the scene where Mary wiped up the blood with a linen cloth given to her by Claudia Procles, Pilate's wife. This scene comes from a book of visions by a nun named Anne Catherine Emmerich, who lived in the late 18th and early 19th century. Her visions are recorded in her book *Dolorous Passion of Our Lord*.

Blood is a synonym for life in Scripture. Of the Old Testament sacrifices, we read: "The life of a creature is in the blood, and I have given it to you to make atonement for yourselves on the altar; it is the blood that makes atonement for one's life" (Leviticus 17:11). The blood is mentioned over 700 times in Scripture. Jesus gave His life in exchange for our life.

Augustine's mentor told him, "Look at the wounds." There are five wounds of Jesus that we need to consider. Let's look at two:

The crown of thorns on His head. The head is a symbol of authority. Jesus has all power and authority. He could have summoned a legion of angels to free Him from His sufferings. Yet, love and obedience to the Father's will kept Him on the cross. He said of Himself, "I lay down my life. . . . No one takes it from me" (John 10:17, 18).

His back. The back represents carrying a burden or responsibility. He carried the cross down the road leading outside of Jerusalem to Golgotha. He bore the sins of the world in His own body (1 Peter 2:24). He was scourged by the Romans, taking it as a punishment for our peace. Surely, by His wounds, we have been healed!

He Took Our Place   DAY 261

Jesus took our place on the cross. He died for us that we might live eternally. "I have been crucified with Christ and I no longer live, but Christ lives in me. The life I live in the body, I live by faith in the Son of God, who loved me and gave himself for me. I do not set aside the grace of God, for if righteousness could be gained through the law, Christ died for nothing!" (Galatians 2:20, 21).

Let's consider today the remaining three wounds of Jesus from our devotion yesterday.

His hands. The hand is a symbol of redemption. The hand of God brought Israel out of Egypt (see Exodus 15:6). His hands had fed the multitude, touched the leper, held little children. Then He stretched out His hands on the cross as though He were reaching across the globe to gather in the lost. His hand reaches out to you today.

His feet. The feet represent His mission of peace and good news. "How beautiful upon the mountains are the feet of him who brings good news, who proclaims peace" (Isaiah 52:7, *NKJV*). He came from heaven and walked the earth to reveal the love of God. One day He will come again and place His feet on the Mount of Olives (Zechariah 14:4). When the Revelator saw Him, "His feet were like bronze glowing in a furnace" (Revelation 1:15). He will come again to judge the world and establish the kingdom of God.

His side. When the soldier thrust the spear in Jesus' side, a stream of blood and water flowed out. His blood atones for our sins. The water represents cleansing that gives us life.

How to Get to Heaven
DAY 262

Bishop Fulton Sheen was scheduled to speak in Philadelphia at the Town Hall. He decided to walk from his hotel, even though he was unfamiliar with the city. Sure enough, he got lost and stopped to ask some boys playing in the street how to get there.

One of the boys asked him, "What are you going to do there?"

Sheen replied, "I'm going to give a talk."

"What about?" the boy asked.

Sheen said, "I'm going to give a talk about how to get to heaven. Would you like to come along and listen?"

"Are you kidding?" the boy replied. "You don't even know how to get to Town Hall!"

I was watching a program on capital punishment. A man who was awaiting execution was being interviewed. The study was about the impact of Christianity in prisons and on death-row inmates. The interviewer asked the inmate, "Do you believe in hell?" He said, "Yes." "Do you believe in heaven?" He said, "Yes." The interviewer then asked, "What does it take to get to heaven?" The man replied, "You have to be as Christlike as you can." Then he added, "I don't think I have done well enough."

When Jesus talked to His disciples about heaven, He said, "In My Father's house are many dwelling places . . . I go to prepare a place for you" (John 14:2, *NASB*). They asked Him how to get there, and He replied, "I am the way and the truth and the life" (v. 6). Individuals get to heaven by simply trusting Jesus to save them from the law of sin and death and to give them a new heart. Heaven is a gift to be received, not an accomplishment to be earned.

When you know heaven is your home, you are then able to bring heaven to others here and now. André Crouch sang a song with this lyric:

> If heaven never was promised to me . . .
> It's been worth just having the Lord in my life.
> Living in a world of darkness,
> He came and brought me the light.

Try Again! DAY 263

Success is largely a matter of trial and error. Perseverance is a must to succeed. Our patience is tested, as well as our character, when we set out to accomplish anything of significance.

People often give up too soon in their goals. Discouragement sets in, and they quit. But if you stick to your plan and try new strategies, you can make your dreams come to pass.

Paul said, "Therefore, my dear brothers, stand firm. Let nothing move you. Always give yourselves fully to the work of the Lord, because you know that your labor in the Lord is not in vain" (1 Corinthians 15:58).

Cicero practiced speaking before his friends for 30 years to perfect his oratorical ability. Bryant rewrote one of his poetic masterpieces 99 times before publication.

In the British Museum one can see 75 drafts of Thomas Gray's classic, *Elegy Written in a Country Courtyard*. Hemmingway reviewed and rewrote the manuscript to *The Old Man and the Sea* 80 times.

Beethoven painstakingly rewrote his music before he got it the way he wanted. Hardly a bar was not rewritten a dozen times. Michelangelo developed some 2,000 studies of his painting *Last Judgment*, one of the 12 master paintings of the ages.

Leonardo da Vinci worked on *The Last Supper* for 10 years, trying to perfect it. Charles Goodyear worked, studied, and endured poverty for 10 years trying to develop hard (vulcanized) rubber.

Go out and meet your challenges with renewed determination to try again!

Success and Failure

The longer I live, the more I realize there is a fine line between success and failure. Great success often results from previous failure. We learn through failure. We think creatively when we fail and discover better ways of doing things.

When the disciples of Jesus failed Him by abandoning Him at His trial, He didn't reject them. After His resurrection, He restored them to their calling. Those were the same men who turned their world upside down. They rebounded from failure. Failure made them stronger in their faith. Later, when Peter and John were flogged for their preaching, they left "rejoicing that they were counted worthy to suffer shame for his name" (Acts 5:41). Those were the same guys who left Him at His trial, arrest and crucifixion.

Speaking of failure, did you know that . . .

- Henry Ford failed to put a reverse gear in his first car?
- Thomas Edison failed in 2,000 experiments before he finally invented the lightbulb?
- Abraham Lincoln lost nine elections for political office and failed in business twice before finally being elected president?
- Albert Einstein was dismissed from school because he lacked interest in his studies, failed an entrance exam to a school in Zurich, and was later fired from his job as a tutor?
- Beethoven's music teacher, the brilliant John Albrechtsberger, said Beethoven would never compose any worthwhile music because he failed to follow the rules of musical composition?
- When Bob Dylan performed at a high school talent show, his classmates booed him off the stage?
- W. Clement Stone, successful insurance company executive and founder of *Success* magazine, was a high school dropout?
- Michael Jordan failed to make the junior varsity basketball team when he tried out? Later, the school principal told him to consider enlisting in the Air Force Academy after high school, which would be his best option for a career.

Who's Influencing You?

We live under constant pressure to conform. It starts the moment we go to kindergarten and experience peer pressure. It continues throughout life. Paul says, "Don't let the world around you squeeze you into its own mold" (Romans 12:2, *Ph.*).

Betty Wean retells an old tale she heard from Ely Wisely. A just man comes to Sodom hoping to save the city. He pickets. What else can he do? He goes from street to street, from marketplace to marketplace, shouting, "Men and women, repent. What you are doing is wrong. It will kill you; it will destroy you."

They laugh, but he goes on shouting, until one day a child stops him.

"Poor stranger, don't you see it's useless?"

"Yes," the man replies.

"Then why do you go on?" the child asks.

"At first I was convinced that I would change them. Now I go on shouting because I don't want them to change me."[20]

Are you being shaped by external pressure or molded into the person God wants you to be by the inner work of Christ in your heart?

We need to take two action steps to avoid being shaped by pressure. First, *take your cues from Jesus.* He is our example for how to think, relate to others, face temptation, manage money, conduct business, and make decisions.

Second, *think for yourself.* Don't follow the crowd. Use the power God gave you to think, judge, discriminate, and decide for yourself. Too many people get caught up in "group think" and just follow the party line of their peer group or ethnic group. But you are an individual. As Shakespeare said, "To thine own self be true."

Faith That Dispels Fear

The last appearance of Jesus in the Bible occurs in the Revelation. John the apostle had been exiled to the island of Patmos by Rome. While there, Jesus appeared to him and gave him the unfolding drama of the church age and the end of the world.

John was so overwhelmed by Jesus' visitation: "When I saw him, I fell at his feet as though dead" (Revelation 1:17). For He was "dressed in a robe reaching down to his feet and with a golden sash around his chest. His head and hair were white like wool, as white as snow, and his eyes were like blazing fire. His feet were like bronze glowing in a furnace, and his voice was like the sound of rushing waters. In his right hand he held seven stars, and out of his mouth came a sharp double-edged sword. His face was like the sun shining in all its brilliance" (vv. 13-16).

But then we see a deeper meaning of the Savior's power: "Then he placed his right hand on me and said: 'Do not be afraid. I am the First and the Last. I am the Living One; I was dead, and behold I am alive for ever and ever! And I hold the keys of death and Hades'" (vv. 17, 18). The most awesome display of God's power is His love and mercy. Just as Jesus placed His right hand on John, He touches us at the point of our fears and declares, "Fear not!"

The message "Fear not!" appears 80 times in Scripture as God's reassurance of His presence, power and providential care. Even when John saw the seals broken, the Antichrist rise, the mark of the Beast, the persecution of the righteous, and the Battle of Armageddon, the message was "Fear not!"

Today the Lord lays his hand on you and says, *"Fear not!"*

The First and the Last   DAY 267

W hy did Jesus tell John the Revelator not to fear the prophetic visions he would see of the judgments coming on the world, the Antichrist empire, and the Battle of Armageddon? In Revelation 1:17, 18, Jesus gave three reasons why we are not to fall prey to fear. We will look at the first one here.

Fear not, I am the First and the Last (v. 17). Jesus is the beginning of creation and the ultimate goal of history. The purpose of God is stated clearly by the apostle Paul: "And he made known to us the mystery of his will according to his good pleasure, which he purposed in Christ, to be put into effect when the times will have reached their fulfillment—to bring all things in heaven and on earth together under one head, even Christ" (Ephesians 1:9, 10).

I find it very comforting that God had the first word in history, and He will have the last. History is not spinning out of control or repeating itself in meaningless cycles. History is linear. It begins in Genesis with the Creation and is completed in Revelation with a new creation. Just as we began the human story in Paradise (Garden of Eden), God will restore the world to paradise when Christ returns. "To him who overcomes, I will give the right to eat from the tree of life, which is in the paradise of God" (Revelation 2:7).

Are you an overcomer? Are you overcoming fear by trusting God to provide everything you need? Have you surrendered your fears to His power? Remember, paradise is your ultimate home.

"Who is it that overcomes the world? Only he who believes that Jesus is the Son of God" (1 John 5:5).

From Genesis to Revelation   DAY 268

What God started in Genesis, He will complete in Revelation. In Genesis, Satan became the god of this world. In Revelation, Satan is destroyed. In Genesis, man was separated from God by sin. In Revelation, man is reconciled to God in the New Jerusalem.

In Genesis, sin brought the curse. In Revelation, there will be no more curse. In Genesis, death and hell came into existence. In Revelation, death and hell are destroyed. In Genesis, the gates of Paradise are closed. In Revelation, paradise is opened, and we have the right to eat from the Tree of Life. In Genesis, suffering, sorrow and death became part of the human experience. In Revelation, there will be no more death or pain or sorrow. In Genesis, man lost his inheritance. In Revelation man will inherit all things.

Fear not, I am the Living One (Revelation 1:18). This is Jesus' second message to His people. All early extra-Biblical sources agree that the tomb of Jesus was empty three days after He was buried in it. Even the Roman government testified to the fact of the empty tomb after the Roman seal on the tomb had been broken and that the guards were terrified by an angelic visitation. The resurrection of Jesus is the foundation of our faith today and our hope for tomorrow.

As C.S. Lewis observed: "The first fact in the history of Christendom is a number of people who say they have seen the resurrected Christ. If they had died without making anyone else believe this 'gospel,' no Gospels would have ever been written."

Abraham, the father of Judaism, lived 19 centuries before Christ—he has not risen. Buddha lived five centuries before Christ and died at age 80—he has not risen. Muhammad lived six centuries after Christ and died in A.D. 632. He is buried in Mecca—he has not risen. But when we visit the tomb of Jesus in Jerusalem, the angelic announcement of hope can still be heard: "Why do you look for the living among the dead? He is not here; he has risen!" (Luke 24:5, 6).

The Keys of Death   DAY 269

Our greatest fear is death. Jesus destroyed death for us when He rose again. He reassures us, "Because I live, you will live also" (John 14:19, *NKJV*). Jesus reminded John the apostle of the promise of eternal life when He appeared to John on the island of Patmos and gave him the Book of Revelation.

We have looked at the first two reasons Christ gives us why we should not live in fear: "I am the First and the Last" (1:17)—He controls the outcome of history; "I am the Living One" (v. 18)—He is risen and has promised us eternal life.

Finally, *Fear not, I hold the keys of death and Hades* (v. 18). The keys represent Christ's power and authority. That means Jesus controls everything that happens in this world and even in our personal lives. At His ascension He declared, "All authority in heaven and on earth has been given to me. Therefore go and make disciples of all nations" (Matthew 28:18, 19).

As His disciples, we minister in the power and authority of the risen Lord. That's why, even in the face of emperor worship, first-century Christians refused to confess, "Caesar is Lord" because he wasn't lord of anything or anybody. Instead, they boldly declared, "Jesus Christ is Lord!"

It is a misnomer for Christians to speak of making Jesus Lord. We don't make Jesus Lord—He is Lord! An early Christian hymn says it best: "Therefore God exalted him to the highest place and gave him the name that is above every name, that at the name of Jesus every knee should bow, in heaven and on earth and under the earth, and every tongue confess that Jesus Christ is Lord, to the glory of God the Father" (Philippians 2:9-11).

Take three action steps today to defeat fear: (1) Confess that Jesus is Lord of your life. (2) Give your fears to Him in prayer and believe that He will provide for you. (3) Affirm your commitment to obey Him as Lord.

The Kingdom of God DAY 270

Jesus began His ministry in a time when the Jewish people longed for the Messiah to deliver them from Roman oppression and to establish the Davidic kingdom of old.

While Jesus deliberately avoided the title *Messiah*, He spoke freely of Himself as the Son of Man, and boldly announced that by His very presence in the world, "the kingdom of God is near." In response, people were to "repent and believe the good news!" (Mark 1:15).

His Kingdom message rang out as a message of hope. The people envisioned a kingdom of economic, political and military resources. To an oppressed nation, Jesus declared that the Kingdom had arrived.

Here is the most important truth He said about the Kingdom: "The kingdom of God is within you" (Luke 17:21).

His kingdom would not come with military might, political power or religious aristocracy. His kingdom would not be measured by lands conquered, subjects and slaves, wealth and power. His kingdom would not be centered in the Holy City (Jerusalem), on the seven hills of Rome, or in Babylon.

His kingdom would be established in the hearts of everyone who believed in Him and followed Him: "To all who received him, to those who believed in his name, he gave the right to become children of God" (John 1:12). If you have surrendered your life to King Jesus, then the kingdom of God is within you!

The Kingdom Within

Jesus said, "The kingdom of God is within you" (Luke 17:21). The Kingdom is simply the sphere of God's rule. Jesus delivers us from sin's rule and brings us under the rule of God.

Not only did Jesus announce the arrival of the Kingdom, He embodied the Kingdom and demonstrated its arrival by performing miracles. "But if I drive out demons by the Spirit of God, then the kingdom of God has come upon you" (Matthew 12:28).

While Jesus openly declared and demonstrated the Kingdom, He also spoke of its mystery. He privately told His disciples, "The secret of the kingdom of God has been given to you" (Mark 4:11). The "messianic secret" consisted of how the kingdom of God would come. His kingdom would not come through military force or a political insurrection but, rather, through His death, resurrection and ascension.

The Cross was the "secret of the Kingdom" of which Jesus spoke. The Cross was the eternal plan of God. He is the "Lamb slain from the foundation of the world" (see 1 Peter 1:19, 20).

Jesus told Pilate, "My kingdom is not of this world. If it were, my servants would fight. . . . But now my kingdom is from another place" (John 18:36). The way to enter the Kingdom is through the new birth. "No one can see the kingdom of God unless he is born again" (3:3).

The kingdom of God is not a matter of religious ritualism but, rather, "righteousness, peace and joy in the Holy Spirit" (Romans 14:17).

As citizens of the kingdom of God, we represent the King of Glory. Let us go into the world and introduce others to the King and invite them to share in His kingdom.

A Great Opportunity

According to legend, a man was out walking in the desert at night when a voice said to him, "Pick up a handful of pebbles and put them in your pocket. Tomorrow you will be both sorry and glad."

The man obeyed. He stooped down and picked up a handful of pebbles and put them in his pocket. The next morning he reached into his pocket and found diamonds, rubies and emeralds. And he was both sorry and glad. Glad that he had taken some—sorry that he hadn't taken more.

Opportunity! The word itself is filled with promise. America is known as the land of opportunity. The word *opportunity* comes from Latin, meaning "at the gate."

When opportunity knocks, we feel both the rush of exhilaration and the weight of responsibility. It has been said that there is no greater burden than a great opportunity.

At Jesus' ascension into heaven, the believers stood on the Mount of Olives and watched Him ascend in the clouds of heaven. Suddenly, two angels appeared with them. "'Men of Galilee,' they said, 'why do you stand here looking into the sky? This same Jesus, who has been taken from you into heaven, will come back in the same way you have seen him go into heaven'" (Acts 1:11). Instead of gazing, they were told to get going! "Go and make disciples of all nations" (Matthew 28:19).

No one knows when Jesus will return. Furthermore, we are not to be overly concerned with the matter. Instead, we are to seize every opportunity we have to advance the kingdom of God in every facet of society.

May we not be guilty of standing still, gazing up into the sky. Don't be a spectator in life. Don't waste time observing others' success, or paralyzed by fear, or preoccupied with the future. Stop gazing and get going!

Open Your Eyes   DAY 273

What you see is what you get. If you see the world as a frightening place, you will live in fear. But if you see the world as a place of opportunity, you will accomplish great things.

Jesus taught us to see the world as a place of opportunity. "Do you think the work of harvesting will not begin until the summer ends four months from now? Look around you! Vast fields are ripening all around us and are ready now for the harvest" (John 4:35, *NLT*).

We will accomplish only what we see. Our vision makes us or breaks us. Jesus' command to "open your eyes" implies that our eyes can be closed to opportunities. The KJV reads, "Lift up your eyes," implying that we need to get our heads out of the sand.

Jesus also told us to seize every opportunity while we have it: "All of us must quickly carry out the tasks assigned us by the one who sent me, because there is little time left before the night falls and all work comes to an end" (9:4, *NLT*).

He challenged us to possess an opportunity mind-set: "I know all the things you do, and I have opened a door for you that no one can shut" (Revelation 3:8, *NLT*).

William Carey saw the world as a place with an open door. In May 1792, a most significant event transpired in Nottingham, England. William Carey stood before a group of ministers and delivered what has been called the greatest missionary sermon in church history.

At that time, there were no missionary societies anywhere in the world. William Carey made a map of the world, placed it on the wall of his cobbler shop and began to pray for the whole world. He became so burdened for the lost that he left home and went to Bengal, India. He preached there for seven years before he had his first convert.

Over the years, Carey translated the Bible, or parts of it, into about 40 different Indian languages or dialects. Within a generation, scores of believers had answered Christ's call to carry the good news to the ends of the earth because Carey reminded us that Jesus has set before everyone an open door.

Competing Against Yourself   DAY 274

One of my life verses is John 3:27: "A man can receive only what is given him from heaven." We have all received something from heaven. Talents, intelligence, musical ability, physical health, material possessions, cultural opportunities—*everything* is a gift from God. These things are not yours to be used only for yourself; they are God's wonderful gifts to be used for His glory and for the good of others.

God never asks us to do more than we are capable of doing. But God expects us to live up to our potential and our privileges. The supreme question of success is this: Are you doing your best?

You don't have to compete against anyone else. Don't compare yourself with others. You're only competing against yourself. You are only expected to do your best, not outperform someone else.

Oscar Wilde wrote a troubling parable about Jesus. One day Jesus was walking through the streets of a city. In an open courtyard, He saw a young man overindulging his appetites by eating and drinking. "Young man," asked Jesus, "why do you live like that?" "I was a leper," he replied, "and You healed me. How else could I live?"

Jesus went on and saw a young girl dressed immodestly, flaunting her beauty. A young man was eyeing her lustfully. "Young man," asked Jesus, "why do look at her like that?" "I was blind," he said, "and You opened my eyes. How else should I look?"

Then Jesus asked the young lady, "Daughter, why do you live like that?" She replied, "I was a sinner, and You forgave me. How else should I live?"

These three people had received the grace of Christ, yet failed to live up to their potential and privileges.[21] The ultimate success is to be able to honestly say, "I have done my best."

Do Your Best! DAY 275

We talk a lot about living for God's glory, but what does it mean? It means doing your very best so that He will receive honor from your life.

Mediocrity and the status quo certainly bring no glory to God. "So whether you eat or drink or whatever you do, do it all for the glory of God" (1 Corinthians 10:31).

Here's Robert B. Horton's spin on it from BP America:

> Irony is for sophomores, and the tragic view of life is only for adolescents. How precious it is that we live at all! And work is what we do with our lives. Until the end, there is always something productive we can do. The daily test for every one of us is: Did we do what we chose to do as well as we could? Competence is the ethical content of work. The ethical person is conscientious—you do whatever you do to the best of your ability and sensitivity.

Bringing glory to God is the ultimate purpose of life. The glory of God takes us outside ourselves. We live for a higher purpose than pleasure, prosperity and position. Our very existence takes on eternal significance when we make it our aim to honor God.

While we all have many goals, let us put this one at the top of our list every day: "So we make it our goal to please him. . . . For we must all appear before the judgment seat of Christ, that each one may receive what is due him for the things done while in the body, whether good or bad" (2 Corinthians 5:9, 10).

Erma Bombeck said, "When I stand before God at the end of my life, I would hope that I would not have a single bit of talent left but could say, 'I used everything you gave me.'"

Sweating the Small Stuff   DAY 276

Success begins by doing little jobs well—and doing them right the first time. Look out for the enemy of procrastination. Do what needs to be done without having to be asked to do it. That's called *initiative*.

Some people ask God to give them a great task. God is watching to see how we handle little things. A popular book says, "Don't sweat the small stuff." But there are some small things we need to sweat. If you don't sweat the small stuff, chances are you won't ever enjoy life's larger privileges and pleasures. Successful people pay attention to details. After all, the big picture is nothing more than a collection of small details.

No job is too small for anyone. No job is beneath any person's dignity. The Incarnation teaches us this lesson. The eternal Son of God, the Creator, became a man. He left the glory of heaven and "took upon him the form of a servant" (Philippians 2:7, KJV). And Paul tells us that our "attitude should be the same as that of Christ Jesus" (v. 5). Jesus grew up working as a carpenter in His father's business. (That's a blue-collar job, by the way.) Later, He washed the feet of His disciples so that they would learn the lesson of humility.

No one starts at the top. You have to earn your way there by doing little jobs well. God will notice, and so will others. You can still earn your way to the top by being faithful in the little things of life.

When Jesus came to earth, "He emptied Himself" (v. 7, *NASB*). Of what? His glory . . . His power . . . His privilege . . . His position. He made Himself nothing. He accepted the limitations of being human. He found joy in the little things of life, even though He had the greatest task of all—to redeem the world from sin.

Walking on Water DAY 277

I love the story of Peter walking on the water (see Matthew 14:22-33). Maybe it was only for a few seconds. But he did it!

It was easier for Peter to remain in the safety of the boat with the other 11 disciples. They were afraid to take the risk. But Peter's impetuous nature, along with a little faith, was enough for him to get out of the boat.

Everybody wants to walk on the water. Everybody wants to experience the power of God. God will help you walk on the water—to accomplish great things that may even seem impossible. But He will not, under any circumstances, pick you up and put you on the water. You have to take that step by yourself.

Here, then, is the test of faith: *You'll never walk on the water until you get out of the boat!* God requires us to take a step of faith and run the risk!

And don't worry about failing. If you start to sink, just pray like Peter did: "Lord, save me!" (v. 30). He'll rescue you just like He did Peter. That's why you don't need to be afraid of failure. You always have a backup plan: *Lord, save me!*

People today want everything guaranteed up front. But life doesn't work that way. You have to walk by faith and not by sight! You have to take risks. Some people foolishly call the psychic hot line. They want to know the future. They want a guarantee about a job, or an investment, or whether or not they should marry a particular person. Think about it. If the psychic really knew your thoughts, he or she would call you!

Here's the only guarantee you will ever need: *God is faithful.* If you will get out of the boat of your comfort zone and take a step of faith, you will discover that you, too, can walk on the water.

Use It or Lose It

Jesus said, "Whoever has will be given more; whoever does not have, even what he has will be taken from him" (Mark 4:25). The rabbis taught that God gives wisdom only to him who possesses wisdom. The Jewish Rabbi Hillel said, "He who increases not, decreases."

We either develop or we deteriorate. We advance or we retreat. We gain ground or we lose it. But we never stand still. Quantity isn't the issue. Some people are always asking God for more. Americans are addicted to "more." But let me assure you, you don't need more money, more talent, more time, more position, more influence, more opportunity, or more of anything to succeed. You just need to use what you have. It's what you do with what you have that counts, not how much or how little you have.

One of America's greatest geniuses was George Washington Carver. He passed the test of *use*. One day he prayed, "Dear God, You are the Creator of the universe. Reveal the secrets of the universe to me."

But God answered, "George, that's too big for you to handle. But I will reveal to you the secrets of the peanut." Now that was more his size. From the universe to the peanut!

"Take it apart," God said. Washington humbly obeyed the Creator and discovered hundreds of elements in that little seed. "Now put it back together," God told him. As he did, he produced research linked to nutrition, plastics, oil, and endless products. He revolutionized Southern agriculture and industry by using what God had given him. You don't need a universe of talent, wealth, or resources to succeed. You just need a peanut!

Getting a Promotion

Employers and supervisors give important projects to productive workers. Lazy workers get fired. So, the next time a pile of work ends up on your desk, take it as a compliment. You're doing a good job. And somebody important is taking notice.

Promotion means more work and greater responsibility. It is a compliment for your employer to ask you to do more work. It shows his or her confidence in you. It is a compliment to your ability and to your contentious effort. Jesus said, "From everyone who has been given much, much will be demanded; and from the one who has been entrusted with much, much more will be asked" (Luke 12:48).

When you fulfill the responsibilities God has given you, He will promote you! We would rather get a raise than more work, but the greatest reward for a job well done is increased responsibility.

General Colin Powell recalls how he learned this lesson while mopping floors at a local soft-drink bottling plant:

> Someone once told me a story about three ditchdiggers. One leaned on his shovel and talked about owning the company. Another complained about the hours and the pay. The third just kept digging. Years went by and the first guy was still leaning on that shovel. The second guy had retired on disability after a phony injury. And the third guy? He owned the company.
>
> The moral is, no matter what you do, someone is always watching. So I set out to be the best mop wielder there ever was. One day someone let 50 cases of cola crash to the concrete, and brown, sticky foam cascaded across the floor. It was almost more than I could bear. But I kept mopping, right to left, left to right. At summer's end, the foreman said, "You mop floors pretty good." The next summer, he had me filling bottles. The third summer, I was deputy foreman. As I have learned, someone is always watching.[22]

A New Mind   DAY 280

Spiritual growth is a constant process of putting off old ways and putting on new ways. We put off the old self of sin and put on the new self of Christlikeness. This transformation begins in the mind. Paul says the key is "having a fresh mental and spiritual attitude" (Ephesians 4:23, *Amp.*).

In Barrie's *Peter Pan*, Peter is in the children's bedroom. They have seen him fly, and they want to fly too. They have tried it from the floor and from jumping off the beds, but they can't fly. John asks Peter, "How do you do it?"

Peter replies, "You just think lovely, wonderful thoughts, and they lift you up in the air." The only way to defeat evil thoughts is to think godly, positive and beneficial thoughts. Operate from the mind of Christ in you. "But we have the mind of Christ" (1 Corinthians 2:16).

In 1964, Norman Cousins, editor of the *Saturday Review*, was diagnosed with a crippling and rare disease which causes the degeneration of the connecting tissue holding bones together. Cousins was known for his humor and determination. He had a 1-in-500 chance of surviving. He was aware of how thoughts and feelings affect the body.

Proverbs 17:22 says, "A cheerful heart is good medicine, but a crushed spirit dries up the bones." He was on heavy doses of medication, but with the doctors' permission he stopped the medication, except for Vitamin C. He left the hospital and went home. He prescribed laughter for himself. When he felt pain, he watched comedies or had a nurse read him funny stories. Two hours of genuine "belly laughter" gave two hours of pain-free sleep. His debilitating state reversed and, in time, nearly completely recovered.

He was the first nonphysician to publish an article in the *New England Journal of Medicine*. His story is written in his book *The Anatomy of an Illness: As Perceived by the Patient*. After leaving *Saturday Review*, he joined the medical staff at UCLA Medical School, where he lectured on how attitudes and emotions affect disease.

Putting Off the Old Self   DAY 281

The Christian experience is a miracle followed by a process. The miracle is the new birth. We experience a sudden, dramatic transformation of heart when we receive Jesus as Savior. Truly "old things have passed away; behold all things have become new" (2 Corinthians 5:17, *NKJV*).

We then begin the process of following Him as Lord. In this process, we learn to "put off your old self, which is being corrupted by its deceitful desires" (Ephesians 4:22).

Transformation happens first in the mind with a change of attitude and perspective. "As he thinks in his heart, so is he" (Proverbs 23:7, *NKJV*). We begin by exposing and eliminating hidden, unproductive thoughts.

The human mind is like an iceberg. The smaller portion above the water is the conscious mind. The larger portion below the surface of the water, the subconscious mind, is the realm of stored memories filled with programmed thoughts, feelings and experiences. The mind stores between 10 and 15 trillion memories during an average lifetime. While we can't access the data at will, the unconscious mind affects our behavior in ways we do not realize. No wonder Paul wrote, "My own behavior baffles me" (Romans 7:15, *Ph.*).

Thoughts are programmed through personal experiences, perceptions, culture, family upbringing, stereotypes, and so forth. Change begins by confronting your thoughts and testing them against the truth. "You will know the truth, and the truth will set you free" (John 8:32).

The Holy Spirit exposes the subconscious motivators and defense mechanisms through prayer, introspection and counseling. "Let the word of Christ dwell in you richly" (Colossians 3:16).

Pray this prayer, "Search me, Oh God, and know my heart" (Psalm 139:23). When we seek Him, the Lord will show us the inner, hidden, repressed memories and thoughts that cause us pain and keep us bound in unproductive patterns.

Transformed   DAY 282

How does spiritual maturity take place? Paul tells us it happens as we are "transformed by the renewing of [our] mind" (Romans 12:2). This means we develop new ways of thinking that are in accordance with the Word of God.

We live in the age of the computer. But no computer can compare with the human brain. The brain has been called the most mysterious, intriguing area of our universe. The brain is a three-pound, jelly-like mound of tissue that looks like crinkled putty, but it is actually a collection of up to 100 billion neurons. Each neuron is as complex as a small computer. More than 100,000 chemical reactions occur every second.

Its nerve cells send impulses to the body at the rate of 200 mps, and it stores between 10 and 15 trillion memories in a lifetime. The left brain hemisphere controls logic, language and mathematics. The right brain hemisphere controls art, orientation to space, creativity, athletic coordination, mechanical abilities, and appreciates anything visual. The right brain controls the left side of the body and vice versa. Some say that since the right brain controls the left side, then only left-handed people are in their right minds.

Are we open to changing our minds? Transformation comes when we are willing to confront our unproductive ways of thinking. The light of Scripture has to shine on the darkened places of the unconscious mind, exposing our hidden thoughts, beliefs and prejudices. To expose your unconscious mind, simply expose it to Scripture. "Have nothing to do with the fruitless deeds of darkness, but rather expose them. . . . But everything exposed by the light becomes visible, for it is light that makes everything visible" (Ephesians 5:11, 13, 14).

What is the light that exposes the unconscious mind and brings healing? "The fruit of the light consists in all goodness, righteousness and truth" (v. 9). These things come to us through the Word of God. As we meditate on Scripture, a healing light shines in the darkened places of the mind, and we are transformed into the image of Christ.

Coping With Change — DAY 283

Leo Tolstoy said, "Everyone thinks of changing the world, but no one thinks of changing himself." About the only constant thing in life is change!

Some people handle change better than others. For some, change is alarming; it threatens the status quo. For others, change is an adventure filled with incredible possibilities.

I read recently, "When you're through changing—you're through."

Jesus' parable of the wineskins is a pithy commentary on how to cope with change. Jesus' entrance into the world marked a new day. The kingdom of God came in a new and dynamic way. His presence threatened the status quo of organized religion. Truth squared off with tradition. Things were beginning to change.

But not everybody welcomed the changes Jesus brought. We, too, tend to hold on to the way things are. We justify our resistance to change, boasting, "We never did it that way before."

Many religious leaders were steeped in traditionalism. Tradition, in and of itself, is not bad. But their traditions ran contrary to God's truth. Jesus told them point-blank, "You nullify the word of God for the sake of your tradition" (Matthew 15:6).

The Pharisees cherished old traditions. Consequently, they struggled to adjust their thinking to the new ideas of Jesus. So Jesus challenged them to think outside the box.

He told them this parable:

> "No one tears a patch from a new garment and sews it on an old one. If he does, he will have torn the new garment, and the patch from the new will not match the old. And no one pours new wine into old wineskins. If he does, the new wine will burst the skins, the wine will run out and the wineskins will be ruined. No, new wine must be poured into new wineskins. And no one after drinking old wine wants the new, for he says, 'The old is better' " (Luke 5:36-39).

The message is clear: If we want God to do a new work of grace in our lives (the wine) we have to be willing to make changes (the wineskins).

Wine and Wineskins — DAY 284

Jesus' parable of the wine and wineskins teaches the importance of change. "New wine must be poured into new wineskins" (Luke 5:38). Let's summarize the success points of the parable.

First, old wineskins cannot contain new wine. Translation: Old methods are insufficient for the implementation of new ideas.

Second, new wine belongs in new wineskins. Translation: New ideas require new methods if they are going to succeed.

Third, if you pour new wine in old wineskins, the skins will burst, and both the wine and the wineskins will be ruined. Translation: When new ideas are rigidly confined to old methods, both will eventually be ruined, and all will be lost. You cannot afford not to change.

Since we don't use wineskins anymore (Aren't you glad the good 'ole days are gone?), a word about wineskins is in order. Ancient wineskins were made from animal skins. Over a period of time, they became hard and brittle and, eventually, broke. The wineskins can't stretch. In the same way, people can become so rigid in their thinking that they, too, crack under the pressure of change.

Fourth, traditionalists pride themselves on old methods. "The old is better," they say (see v. 39). They feel safe in the comfort zone. "Don't rock the boat!" they caution. "I remember the way things used to be," they remark, musing over the past. Sadly, they don't even try the new wine. But over the course of time, when the new wine seasons, it becomes the best wine of all!

Tradition has its place. Many rich spiritual traditions provide our lives with an anchor for the soul. But tradition has its limitations. And it becomes a serious liability when we cherish tradition at the expense of new experiences with God.

The sage cautions, "Do not say, 'Why were the old days better than these?' For it is not wise to ask such questions" (Ecclesiastes 7:10). The old days weren't really any better than these days. They only seem that way to the traditionalist because he tends to romanticize history, forgetting the hard times and remembering only the good. It's called *selective memory*.

When God pours out the new wine of opportunity, be flexible and open. Welcome the newness of His grace. New wine needs a flexible container that can be shaped to contain it. When God stretches us, it is only to get us ready for new wine!

Attitude Rules   DAY 285

Our attitude toward change is more important than change itself. There are three attitudes we can adopt toward change.

First, *we can react with fear.* The unknown frightens us. What is fear? False Expectations Appearing Real. A study from the University of Michigan showed the following: Sixty percent of our fears are totally unwarranted; they never come to pass. Twenty percent of our fears are focused on our past, which is completely out of our control. Ten percent of our fears are based on things so petty that they make no difference in our lives. Of the remaining 10 percent, only 4 percent to 5 percent could be considered justifiable.[23]

Second, *we can react to change with resistance.* We try to keep things the way they are. We deny reality, telling ourselves everything is the same. Some friends of mine went through a major change in their lives that caught them completely by surprise. Their initial response was, "Nothing's changed. Everything's just the way it was before." I just thought to myself, *Whatever.* Then reality sank in. Things were anything but the same. Eventually, they made the right adjustments.

Here's a humorous story on resistance to change: One night, a ship's captain saw a light dead ahead on their course. He sent the signal, "Change your course 10 degrees east."

The light signaled back, "Change yours 10 degrees west."

Angry, the naval captain sent the message, "I'm a Navy captain! Change your course, sir!"

"I'm a seaman second class," came the reply. "Change your course, sir."

Now the captain was furious. "I'm a battleship! I'm not changing course!"

There's one last reply: "I'm a lighthouse. It's your call."

Decide now to face change with courage so that you can embrace new opportunities and not be trapped in traditions.

Develop or Deteriorate   DAY 286

Instead of being afraid of change, or resisting change, we need to *welcome change as an opportunity for a new beginning*—if not a new beginning, at least a new chapter in our lives. This is the third attitude we can adopt toward change. "But grow in the grace and knowledge of our Lord and Savior Jesus Christ" (2 Peter 3:18).

There is a vast difference between change and instability. Some people are unstable and are constantly changing their minds about what they want. That's not healthy change. Healthy change is productive, resulting in greater accomplishments and the fulfillment of goals.

While we can't control all the changes that come our way, we can learn to adjust. And adjustment is the key to keeping your act together when facing tough changes. If you can adjust, you can make it through anything.

Everything on earth exists under the dominion of one of two laws: the law of deterioration or the law of development. This means that everything that doesn't change and develop to a new and higher state will eventually deteriorate and die.

If you take your money and put it in your attic, in 10 years it will be worth considerably less than it is today due to inflation. Over time it loses purchasing power. Since it doesn't develop greater worth, it deteriorates in value.

Or take, for example, physical exercise. Without proper exercise through aerobics and weight lifting, the body deteriorates more rapidly. A leading cause of arthritis and osteoporosis is inactivity. You see, if the body lies dormant, the muscles atrophy, and the bones deteriorate.

All inanimate objects deteriorate because they are incapable of development. But we are living organisms and, as such, have been endowed by the Creator with creative power and unlimited potential. You can change. Hope means that life can change for the better. Your personality can change, along with your attitudes, values, beliefs, lifestyle and relationships.

By the grace of God, *you can change!*

Forward Movement   DAY 287

L ife as a series of seasons. The key to life is learning to pass successfully from one season to the next without getting stuck. Some people get stuck in a particular season of life because of trauma, tragedy, failure, disappointment, resentment, unforgiveness, bad habits or fears.

The movement of God's work in our lives is always forward. He continually leads us onward into new seasons. We "go from strength to strength" (Psalm 84:7), "from faith to faith" (Romans 1:17, *NKJV*), and "from glory to glory" (2 Corinthians 3:18, *NKJV*).

So, how do you adjust to change?

Change is tough to handle when it catches us by surprise. The reason it catches us by surprise is because we believe falsely that things will stay the same. When people live in fantasy and don't anticipate change, they are totally unprepared to handle it. They get depressed and are unable to move forward. Sometimes we fail to see the new things God is doing, and we miss the opportunities He brings our way. Never say, "It can't happen to me." These are famous last words.

Change can be stressful. The first time Barbie, the kids and I moved to another city, I realized how stressful change is. I mean, when you relocate, you've got to find a new dentist, a new family doctor, establish new friendships, move your funds to a new bank, try out new restaurants to figure out what's going to be your favorite place, and decide which grocery store you'll use. True, these may be small changes, but when you add them up together, they equal a lot of stress. Change means choices, and having to make too many choices at one time is stressful.

Instead of being afraid of change, embrace it with enthusiasm as a new season filled with new possibilities. God promises His people: "I will lead the blind by ways they have not known, along unfamiliar paths I will guide them; I will turn the darkness into light before them and make the rough places smooth. These are the things I will do; I will not forsake them" (Isaiah 42:16).

A New Season   DAY 288

Let's continue today with a strategy for managing change. *Change is easier to manage if it comes in small doses.* So, when possible, break significant changes down into smaller steps. You won't be as overwhelmed by having to make too many new adjustments, and you'll reduce the shock effect that often accompanies change. Big changes in our lives can be scary. So, instead of taking a giant step forward, take small, calculated steps to reach your goals.

Change is pregnant with new possibilities. A season of change can fill your life with new blessings. So, don't look at change as a negative; it is a new opportunity. Change is a lot like a pregnant woman.

A woman goes through many changes during the nine months of pregnancy. Her shape changes quite a bit, but the changes aren't bad. Each month brings her closer to the birth of her child. That's what change is like in life. You are not heading for D-Day—you are heading for a new beginning.

Welcome change as a friend instead of opposing it as an enemy. Change never travels alone—it carries with it unlimited possibilities.

So if change has entered your world, be on the lookout for exciting opportunities.

One of my favorite Biblical promises is found in the Book of Lamentations. I'll admit that that's an unusual place to find anything positive. Lamentations is a collection of lament by the prophet Jeremiah over the destruction of Jerusalem at the hands of the Babylonian army (586 B.C.).

After the invasion, the people were carried off into exile to Babylon. Jeremiah sat perched high above the ruins of the city and the destruction of Solomon's Temple, where he lamented their calamity. But in the midst of such negative change, he envisioned the possibilities of a new beginning: "Because of the Lord's great love we are not consumed, for his compassions never fail. They are new every morning; great is your faithfulness" (Lamentations 3:22, 23).

Changing for the Better   DAY 289

There are three types of change. First, *there are those changes that happen to us over which we have no control.* Life consists of a series of changes, both positive and negative. Such changes demand that we adjust. In fact, one of the keys to happiness and the ability to bounce back from adversity is the ability to adapt. *Maturity* is the ability to adapt. *Immaturity* is characterized by fantasy and refusing to accept and deal with life's realities.

Second, *there are those changes that God works in us as He conforms us to His likeness.* The Holy Spirit is God's change agent. This transformation "comes from the Lord, who is the Spirit" (2 Corinthians 3:18). Spiritual growth means change. In fact, the word *growth* is defined as "an increase in size, amount and degree; to come to be gradually; and to progress toward maturity."

Third, *there are the changes we make happen.* Are you a change agent? Now I am not advocating constant change. I think such a state of constant change breeds instability. Some people are constantly changing because they are searching to discover themselves and to find direction in life. Others change because they are discontent with the way things are, so they constantly experiment. They make life confusing and alarming for those in the wake of their misguided changes.

Let's talk about healthy change. There are times that we need to change. Such times come in our personal lives, in our careers and families, and in the church. There are times when God speaks to us by His Spirit and directs us to change. He leads us in a new direction. Do we follow? Do we have the faith necessary to change when God so directs?

When God calls us to make a change of direction, may our prayer be that of Samuel: "Speak [Lord], for your servant is listening" (1 Samuel 3:10).

Cling to the Changeless   DAY 290

We live in a world of constant change. Technology has caused our world to explode with infinite possibilities of change, creating a better world. We cannot even keep pace with the incredible changes in technology and science.

Change either frightens us or fills us with faith. Every morning is a reminder of new opportunities. David prayed, "Let the morning bring me word of your unfailing love" (Psalm 143:8).

The morning brings an assurance of God's unfailing love, the promise of new mercies, and the awareness of His abiding presence. So, embrace the changes you are facing with optimism and faith.

Fortunately, there are some things that will never change. To use Jesus' metaphor of wine and wineskins, the wineskins may change, but the wine remains the same from generation to generation. The wine being the grace of God.

The wine of God's truth never changes. In a day of moral relativism, build your life on the solid rock of Biblical truth. I believe God originally inscribed the Ten Commandments on tablets of stone to remind us of their unchangeable nature.

Most importantly, the wine of God's love never changes. "Who shall separate us from the love of Christ? . . . For I am convinced that neither death nor life, neither angels nor demons, neither the present nor the future, nor any powers, neither height nor depth, nor anything else in all creation, will be able to separate us from the love of God that is in Christ Jesus our Lord" (Romans 8:35, 38, 39).

In a changing world, remember, "Jesus Christ is the same yesterday and today and forever" (Hebrews 13:8).

Sacrificial Love

There is no love without sacrifice. Jesus said, "Greater love has no one than this, that he lay down his life for his friends" (John 15:13). How do you measure love? "This is love: not that we loved God, but that he loved us and sent his Son as an atoning sacrifice for our sins" (1 John 4:10). Real love costs greatly, but it pays rich dividends.

Russell H. Conceal shares this touching true story about the costliness of love in *Acres of Diamonds*. The account took place in the early 1900s.

A sobbing little girl stood outside a small but wealthy church where she had been turned away by an usher because it was "too crowded." The pastor noticed her crying and asked what was wrong. "I can't go to Sunday school," she said with tears in her eyes. She was dressed in shabby, unkempt clothes. The pastor guessed why she had been discouraged from attending, so he took her hand and escorted her to her Sunday school class.

When she went to bed that night, she thought about other children who had no opportunity to worship Jesus. Some two years later, this child was found dead in a poor tenement building. The parents called the pastor, who had been so kind to their daughter, to handle the funeral arrangements, which he gladly did.

As her body was being moved, a worn-out purse was found. It contained 57 cents and a note scribbled in a child's handwriting: "This is to help build the little church bigger so more children can go to Sunday school." She had saved the offering for two years. The next Sunday, he stood before his congregation with the crumpled red purse in his hand. He told the people about the little girl and read her note to them. He challenged his deacons to raise the funds to build a new church.

A local newspaper learned of the story and published it. A realtor read it and gave the church a parcel of land. When the church told him that they couldn't afford it, he sold it to them for 57 cents!

The members responded with generous contributions. Gifts even came from around the country in response to the published story of the little girl. Within five years, her 57 cents had increased to $250,000.

Today, the church that love built stands in Philadelphia. The Temple Baptist church seats over 3,000 worshipers, along with Temple University and a hospital. In one of the rooms of the Sunday school building is displayed a picture of the little girl who made history, along with a portrait of the pastor.

What's in It for Me?   DAY 292

A s Americans, we are conditioned to ask, "What's in it for me?" Have you considered the personal benefits of obeying God? "All these blessings will come upon you and accompany you if you obey the Lord your God" (Deuteronomy 28:2).

Obedience means to submit to God as the ultimate authority. As children, this is the first principle God wants us to learn. Parents are to teach their children to honor and obey them (see Ephesians 6:1-3). Even Jesus learned to obey as a young boy (see Luke 2:51). Later, "he learned obedience through the things he suffered" (Hebrews 5:8). If this was true of Jesus, how much more do we need to learn obedience?

Did you know that God looks at obedience to Him as worship? In fact, obedience is the highest form of worship. The Hebrew word for *worship* means "to bow down." The first use of the word *worship* in the Bible occurs in Genesis 22:5. Abraham took his son, Isaac, to Mount Moriah in obedience to the command of God to offer him as a sacrifice. Of course, God didn't want Abraham to sacrifice his son, and Abraham knew it. It was a test of his faith and his obedience. But he bowed his will to the will of God. "The boy and I will go and worship, and we will return," he told the servants who accompanied him on the lonely journey to Moriah.

Have you had your own personal Moriah experience where you bowed your will to the will of God? Remember, great blessings will come as you obey the Lord your God.

Faith in Action   DAY 293

O bedience to God equals faith in action. Obedience is predicated on trust. Once we trust God's wisdom, we will obey Him. "Trust in the Lord with all your heart and lean not on your own understanding; in all your ways acknowledge him, and he will make your paths straight" (Proverbs 3:5, 6).

God's ways are higher than our ways and His thoughts are higher than our thoughts (see Isaiah 55:8, 9). So you have to trust Him. Mary, the mother of Jesus, was told by the angel that she would give birth to the Messiah. Her response was simply, "I am the Lord's servant. . . . May it be to me as you have said" (Luke 1:38). What faith! What obedience! She did not understand, but she obeyed because she trusted God.

George Mueller was a remarkable man of faith. He dedicated his life to care for orphans in Bristol, England. One night after dinner, he prayed for the children and sent them to bed. They had no idea that there was nothing for breakfast the next morning or that the orphanage was out of money.

Mueller was confident that the Lord would provide, even though he didn't know how. Mueller went to bed committing them to God. The next morning, he went for a walk asking God to provide for their needs. He met a friend who asked him to accept some money for the orphanage. Mueller thanked him but never told him of their urgent need. God always provided for him and the children in that way. He found God to be faithful day after day. He truly knew the meaning of the prayer, "Give us this day our daily bread" (Matthew 6:11, *NKJV*).

Remember God's promise: "If you are willing and obedient, you will eat the best from the land" (Isaiah 1:19).

The Uncluttered Heart   DAY 294

This statement of Jesus has made a profound impact on me: "But the worries of this life, the deceitfulness of wealth and the desires for other things come in and choke the word, making it unfruitful" (Mark 4:19).

Spiritual growth comes to a grinding halt when the human heart gets too cluttered to hear God speak through His Word. Some people are pack rats. They keep everything. What we call junk, they call treasure. They usually end up having to buy a bigger house just to have a place to store all their stuff. Usually, the closets, basement, attic, and every nook and cranny is cluttered. Well, that's OK if you're a pack rat, but it's not advisable when it comes to your heart.

Keep your heart pure and clean, as a clear channel to hear the Word of God. "Who may ascend the hill of the Lord? Who may stand in his holy place? He who has clean hands and a pure heart" (Psalm 24:3, 4).

Spiritual clutter starts with worry. Worry chokes our lives. Instead of listening to the promises of God, we listen to fears. The English word *worry* comes from an Anglo-Saxon word meaning "to choke" or "to strangle." What a graphic picture of what worry does to us.

The heart also gets cluttered by the deceitfulness of wealth, which can be either a blessing or a curse. The Bible never makes an issue of how much wealth a person has, but it does make an issue about how much wealth has a person. If you don't control your wealth, and your attitude toward it, it will control you. But Jesus doesn't say that wealth clutters the heart, rather, He says it is the *deceitfulness* of wealth we need to guard against.

A prayer for today: *Lord, clean out our hearts and minds from the worries of this life and the lies of our age about happiness, that we may live in the light of Your truth and hear Your voice.*

Searching for Happiness DAY 295

Everyone wants to be happy, but there are a lot of false notions about what brings happiness. Jesus cautioned us against "the deceitfulness of wealth" (Mark 4:19). Money can't make a person happy. But the lack of it can make one very unhappy.

Happiness is a deep sense of satisfaction that comes from a relationship with God. Happy people have their two deepest emotional needs met—security and significance. The lie going around is that wealth can meet these needs. That's the deceitfulness of wealth. God is the only true source of security and significance.

The heart can also get cluttered with the pleasures of this life. Americans, by and large, are conditioned to be consumers. We just can't get enough—of anything. We demand more! We lack contentment and are possessed by an insatiable desire for more.

Contentment equals peace. "Better a little with the fear of the Lord than great wealth with turmoil" (Proverbs 15:16). But contentment is learned. By nature, we seek to have more. So Paul says, "I have learned to be content whatever the circumstances" (Philippians 4:11).

People stunt their potential because of the clutter. So, have a spiritual spring-cleaning. Clean out your heart; organize your priorities; get rid of the baggage so that you can hear the voice of God.

Buy the Truth   DAY 296

I'm sure you've heard people say, "Everything's for sale." Is it really? Should it be? Truth should never be sold. "Buy the truth, and sell it not" (Proverbs 23:23, KJV).

Truth has always been challenged by the skeptic. Jesus said, "Heaven and earth will pass away, but my word will never pass away" (Matthew 24:35).

I'm sure you've crammed for an exam. You learned the class material just long enough to dump it on an exam. A week later you couldn't pass that same test if your life depended on it. That's enough to get by for an exam, but not enough for life.

Hold on to the Biblical truth you have been taught. Jesus said we are to persevere in His Word (Luke 8:15). Jude said we are "to contend for the faith that was once for all entrusted to the saints" (v. 3). *Perseverance* means steadfastness and determination. Don't let the Word of God slip from your memory.

When we think of Christian martyrs, we tend to think of people who lived a long time ago—people like Paul, or Peter, or Joan of Arc. When the Columbine High School shootings occurred, one teacher and 12 students were dead and 23 wounded. The shooters were part of the Trench Coat Mafia.

Among the victims was Cassie Bernall, an outspoken witness for Christ. When the gunmen asked if anyone in the class was a Christian, she boldly said, "Yes." Others report that she told them, "There is a God, and you need to follow along God's path." Then she died. She had perseverance—the ability to suffer long.

Another girl died for her faith at Columbine that horrible day. Her name is Rachel Scott. Her murderer shot her first in the leg and then asked if she believed in God. When, like Cassie, she said, "Yes," he replied, "Then go be with Him now!"

The message is: *Buy the truth, and do not sell it.*

Tune In

We need to tune in to the prompting of the Holy Spirit and move when He moves. "Since we live by the Spirit, let us keep in step with the Spirit" (Galatians 5:25).

Young Samuel grew up to be one of the most powerful prophets of God who ever lived. Yet, when he was a boy, he was unfamiliar with the voice of God. He had to learn to tune in so that he could recognize God's voice and respond. Eli, the priest, taught Samuel to respond to the still, small voice of God by saying, "Speak, for your servant is listening" (1 Samuel 3:10). That's how you tune in—by desiring to hear from God and by being willing to respond obediently.

An American Indian was in downtown New York walking along with his friend who lived in New York City. Suddenly he said, "I hear a cricket." "Oh, you're crazy," his friend replied. "No, I hear a cricket. I'm sure of it." "It's the noon hour. You know there are people bustling around, cars honking, taxis squealing, noises from the city. I'm sure you can't hear it."

"I'm sure I do." He listened attentively and then walked to the corner across the street and looked all around. Finally, on the other corner, he found a shrub in a large cement planter. He dug beneath the leaf and found a cricket. His friend was astounded. But the American Indian said, "My ears are no different from yours. It simply depends on what you are listening for. Here, let me show you."

He reached into his pocket and pulled out a handful of change—a few quarters, some dimes, nickels, and pennies—and dropped them on the concrete. Every head within a block turned. "You see what I mean? It all depends on what you are listening for."

Create a Cycle of Blessing

Psychologist Alfred Adler, who coined the term *inferiority complex*, said that all human failure is attributed to the inability to grasp the fact that "it is more blessed to give than it is to receive."

One of the ways we partner with God in the work of the Kingdom is through giving. What do we have to give? We can give faith, hope and love. We can give our time, talent and treasure. We can give mercy, benevolence and kindness. We can give knowledge, counsel and wisdom. We all have a lot to give.

One of the reasons we work is to give. "He who has been stealing must steal no longer, but must work, doing something useful with his own hands, that he may have something to share with those in need" (Ephesians 4:28).

Prosperity doesn't just fall out of the sky, it is the result of giving. Wealth is meant to be put in circulation. When we give, we create a cycle of blessing and wealth. "Cast your bread upon the waters, for after many days you will find it again" (Ecclesiastes 11:1). Jesus said, "Give, and it will be given to you" (Luke 6:38).

Money reveals the condition of our hearts. "You write your autobiography in your checkbook," someone aptly said. Jesus said, "For where your treasure is, there your heart will be also" (Matthew 6:21).

Real prosperity starts with giving. Generosity is the pathway to true greatness.

Graceful Giving

One of the funniest movies I've ever seen is *The Money Pit.* Those of you who saw it are already remembering some of the classic scenes.

How do we get out of the money pit? While the Bible contains some 500 verses on faith and about 500 verses on prayer, it has nearly 2,000 verses on money. We can only do three things with money: Give it, save it, and spend it.

We are to "excel in this grace of giving" (2 Corinthians 8:7). There are three types of Biblical giving: the tithe, freewill offerings, and alms to the poor. Tithing is giving the first tenth of one's income. The tithe is holy, and it belongs to the Lord (Leviticus 27:30). "Honor the Lord with your wealth, with the firstfruits of all your crops" (Proverbs 3:9).

Offerings are given by the worshiper from a heart of gratitude to God. Alms are gifts to the poor. In the Old Testament, the tithe represents the rest of all we have. Tithing is not giving a tenth of our possessions. Instead, God allows us to have 90 percent of what He owns. God asks for the firstfruits, which expresses the devotion of all we possess.

Attitude precedes action. There is a proverb in the Apocryphal book of Sirach that says: "The gift of a grudging giver makes the eyes dim" (18:18). To the contrary, "God loves a cheerful giver" (2 Corinthians 9:7).

Giving shapes our character and makes us like God. "God so loved the world that he gave" (John 3:16). One of the greatest marks of maturity is generosity. As Jesus said, "It is more blessed to give than to receive" (Acts 20:35).

The Miracle of Provision   DAY 300

The cycle of blessing applies to all areas of life. Take the gift of encouragement for example. Those who sow it, reap it. Have you ever been in a planning meeting with a group of positive people? They generate plans and ideas. They bring out the best in others. But what a downer to get around a group of negative people and listen to their discouraging outlook.

The same is true of faith. Faith breeds faith. I love to be around people of faith. They say such things as these: "We can do it! If God be for us, who can be against us? No weapon formed against us will prosper!" Conversely, fear breeds fear. We reap what we sow.

Think about the miracle of Jesus feeding the 5,000 with five loaves and two fish. The miracle required the partnership of a little boy. The miracle of provision required two things—the power of Jesus and the boy's lunch. His lunch wasn't much until he placed it in the hands of Jesus. Then his lunch fed a multitude. But first, he had to give it.

The disciples didn't chase him down and take his lunch from him. There were 12 baskets left over. I wonder if the little boy got to take the leftovers home. Now that would have been a sight to see the look on his mother's face when she said, "Did you eat your lunch?" "Yes," he replied, "But I couldn't eat it all." He had more than enough. Not only did he have his need met, but he also met the needs of many others because he gave what he had. He put it in the hands of Jesus, and it was multiplied. The "more-than-enough" principle goes into operation when we partner with Christ in the Kingdom through giving.

Remember, *God loves a cheerful giver!*

Everyone Has Something to Give DAY 301

Have you ever heard someone pray, "Lord, bless those who have to give and those who have not to give"? The truth is, everyone has something to give!

Jesus commended a widow who put two small coins in the treasury while others were giving great wealth. He told His disciples, "This poor widow has put more into the treasury than all the others. They all gave out of their wealth; but she, out of her poverty, put in everything—all she had to live on" (Mark 12:43, 44). I'm sure she had another paycheck coming. She lived on a limited income. She was a wise manager of her money, but she understood the power of giving.

A missionary from Chile tells of how a pastor who served several extremely poor villages was confronted by the Holy Spirit that he was not teaching the people all of God's truth. He had failed to teach them about tithing. "But these people are so poor," he argued with God, "they have nothing to give."

"Teach them anyway," the Lord seemed to press upon his heart. So the pastor did. He slowly took them through the Scripture explaining God's plan of tithing. The next Sunday, the people arrived with their tithe—chickens, fruits, vegetables, eggs, leather goods, and all kinds of handmade articles. The pastor sold some of the goods and used the money for the work of the church. He gave some of the gifts to the destitute in the village and kept some for his own livelihood. Sunday after Sunday, the people gave.

A severe drought swept through the area, but, miraculously, the crops of the church members continued to flourish. Their fields were green and lush, while those in surrounding areas withered. Relative abundance replaced abject poverty. They began selling their crops and tithed on the income. The money they gave enabled them to build a church facility for the congregation. [24]

Don't wait to receive before you start giving. The principle is this: "Give, and it will be given to you" (Luke 6:38).

Practice the Golden Rule — DAY 302

Life principles are only beneficial if they are practiced. Such is the case with the Golden Rule: "Do to others as you would have them do to you" (Luke 6:31). While the Golden Rule is given by Jesus, its essence is found in Leviticus 19:18: "Love your neighbor as yourself." Treat others the way you want to be treated.

When Moses was giving laws for Israel to follow, he said: "Do not oppress an alien; you yourselves know how it feels to be aliens, because you were aliens in Egypt" (Exodus 23:9). You know how it feels to be hurt, rejected, mistreated, and so forth. So don't treat others that way.

Roy Lloyd, a founding board member of the International Forgiveness Institute, was a part of the 15-member delegation that went to Yugoslavia to try to get three captured American soldiers released. When members met with President Slobodan Milosevic, they were aware that negotiations were limited because they had nothing to offer him.

So they appealed for him to release them on the basis of forgiveness; to simply do what was morally right. After their appeal was made, all nine of Milosevic's top advisers told Milosevic to let the soldiers go free. But to complicate the process, on the very day that Milosevic promised to release them, tragedy struck. A busload of ethnic Albanians was hit by a bomb, killing dozens, and then NATO bombed the ambulance that was going to help the victims. But Milosevic kept his word, in spite of the bombing and in spite of the fact that he was a very wicked man who unleashed horrible suffering on others.

All three American soldiers practiced forgiveness upon their release. Each one was very religious, and one in particular, Christopher Stone, wouldn't leave until he was allowed to go back to the soldier who served as his guard and pray for him.[25]

Short-Term Faith

Have you had the unfortunate experience of coming out of one crisis only to face another one? That's how the Israelites felt after the Exodus. They had witnessed the power of God to deliver them from the crisis of slavery in Egypt. Hope replaced hopelessness. Faith replaced fear. Expectation replaced disillusionment. However, instead of leading them straight toward the Promised Land, God led them on the desert road toward the Red Sea. They were going from the frying pan of slavery in Egypt into the fire of the Red Sea.

They finally arrived at the edge of the sea, at Baal Zephon ("Baal of the North"). Pharaoh learned of their location and marshaled his forces. Soon the army of Egypt was breathing down their necks, ready to capture them and bring them back to Egypt. They were hemmed in on every side. Baal Zephon was a cul-de-sac. To the north awaited the army of Pharaoh. To the south lay the Egyptian desert called Mizraim. To the west were the cities of Rameses and Goshen, where they had once lived. To the east lay the Red Sea.

Fear quickly replaced faith. They were terrified by the sight of the Egyptian forces marching after them. They cried out to God and complained to Moses: "Was it because there were no graves in Egypt that you brought us to the desert to die? What have you done to us by bringing us out of Egypt? Didn't we say to you in Egypt, 'Leave us alone; let us serve the Egyptians'? It would have been better for us to serve the Egyptians than to die in the desert!" (Exodus 14:11, 12).

They suffered from "short-term" faith. As long as everything was going great, they had faith, but when events turned against them, they doubted God's promise and gave up all hope. Any way you look at it, the Red Sea experience is a living testimony to the God of miracles who makes a way for His people when there is no way.

All of us face impossibilities in this life. We run out of resources. We do everything we can in our own power but come up short. "Man's extremity is God's opportunity" is more than an adage—it is a fact of faith. And the Israelites learned that fact at the Red Sea.

Prime the Pump   DAY 304

Dr. Robert Schuller, in *Tough-Minded Faith for Tender-Hearted People,* tells the story of a remote road stop in the desert with a deserted gasoline station. Alongside it was an old-fashioned pump. A traveler dying of thirst came across the outpost. He ran to the well and, there, he saw a cup of water. But under the cup was a note that read:

> Dear Traveler: There's loads of water down in this well. Use this cup to prime the pump. Then drink all you want from the bottom of the well. When you've had all you want, fill the cup again for the next person who comes thirsting down the road. Whatever you do, don't drink from this cup, or there'll be no water to prime the pump ever again.

The thirsty traveler read the note and stared at the cup of water. Fearing this would be the only water he would get, he put the cup of water to his lips. Then he hesitated and, in a moment of faith, he followed the instructions. He poured the water down the dry pump, worked the handle as fast as he could, then suddenly, fresh water poured out from the well. When he had had all he wanted, he filled the cup and left it on the well with a note that said:

> You prime the pump when you spend your last ounce of energy
> on the hope that your energy will be renewed.

Hoarding is a great mistake. Some people try to hoard time, wealth and energy, but we can't keep any of these things. God has invested in us so that we may invest in others.

Life is meant to be lived in circulation, just as the hydrological cycle of evaporation and rain, as well as the cycle of breathing, sustains life. You can't breathe in oxygen and hold it and expect to live. You have to breathe out to replenish the atmosphere. Only then can you take another breath. In the same way, we have to breathe out life, love, wealth, time and talents. Everything is meant to be shared. In doing so, we receive what we need to live. "Give, and it will be given to you. A good measure, pressed down, shaken together and running over, will be poured into your lap. For with the measure you use, it will be measured to you" (Luke 6:38).

Real Change
DAY 305

The story is told about a machinist with the Ford Motor Company in Detroit who had, over a period of years, "borrowed" various parts and tools from the company and not had bothered to return.

While this practice was not condoned, it was more or less accepted by management, and nothing was done about it. The machinist, however, was saved and baptized at a revival meeting. He took his baptism seriously. So the very next day, he arrived at work with his truck loaded with all the tools and parts he had taken from the plant over the years.

He explained the situation to his foreman, and added that he'd never really meant to steal them and hoped he would be forgiven. The foreman was so astonished and impressed by his action, that he cabled Henry Ford himself, who was visiting a European plant, and explained the entire event in detail. Immediately, Ford cabled back: "Dam up the Detroit River," he said, "and baptize the entire plant!"

Baptism is an outward expression of an inward work. When we turn from sins and receive God's forgiveness, He gives us a new heart. "We were therefore buried with him [Jesus] through baptism into death in order that, just as Christ was raised from the dead through the glory of the Father, we too may live a new life" (Romans 6:4).

God gives us grace to die to the things that are wrong, unproductive and useless, so that we may walk in newness of purity, power and productivity. Ask Him to do this work in your heart today.

The Comforter
DAY 306

Jesus called the Holy Spirit the Comforter, or Counselor. "I will ask the Father, and he will give you another Counselor to be with you forever" (John 14:16). The word is *paraklete* (Greek) and means "one called alongside to help."

A missionary among a remote people group in Africa found it difficult to translate the word *Comforter* in their language. She couldn't find a comparable word, so she asked a number of people what word they would use. She explained that the Spirit comforts, guides, strengthens, helps, protects.

One day she asked a group, "Is there not a word that has this meaning?" Someone spoke up and said, "If someone would do all of that for us, we would say that he falls down beside us."

"What do you mean?" she asked. The man explained that porters travel long journeys with heavy loads on their heads. Sometimes they collapse from exhaustion. A porter may lie there all night exposed to cold, sickness, and danger of being attacked by wild animals. Sometimes, if he is fortunate, a person will pass by and rescue him. This friend, like the Good Samaritan, will stoop down, pick up the porter, and carry him to safety to a nearby village. "We would refer to such a friend as 'one who falls down beside us.'" That was the word for which the missionary sought.

Dalbey, in *Healing the Masculine Soul*, points out that *paraklete* is an ancient warrior's term. When Greek soldiers entered battle, two soldiers would draw together, back-to-back, covering each other's blind spots. One's battle partner was called his *paraklete*.

Face every challenge today with the confidence that your Helper and Battle Partner, the Holy Spirit, is with you.

Under God — DAY 307

The Supreme Court is considering whether or not the phrase "under God" in the Pledge of Allegiance is constitutional. Robert Destro of Catholic University of America presented an excellent summary of the political arguments in support of the phrase "under God" in an *amicus curiae* brief:

> All three branches of our federal government have long recognized the premise from which Jefferson argued his Declaration of Independence, namely that our freedom is grounded in an authority higher than the State. . . . If reciting the Pledge is unconstitutional simply because it refers to a nation "under God," then reciting the Declaration of Independence, which refers to the

Creator as the source of rights, is surely cast in doubt. And that would mean that publicly acknowledging the traditional grounding of our rights itself arguably violates those very rights. That would be an earthquake in our national ethos.

Aleksandr Solzhenitsyn brought our spiritual decline to our attention in his now-famous 1978 Harvard Commencement address, "A World Split Apart."

In the last three decades there has been an erosion of Christian values and ideals in Western Civilization. While we have safeguarded human rights, man's sense of responsibility to God and society grew dimmer and dimmer . . . we have lost the concept of a Supreme Complete Entity which used to restrain our passions and our irresponsibility. We placed too much hope in political and social reforms, only to find out that we were being deprived of our most precious possession: our spiritual life.[26]

What an assurance to know that we live "under God." The psalmist said, "He who dwells in the secret place of the Most High shall abide under the shadow of the Almighty" (91:1, *NKJV*).

Equipped for Life   DAY 308

In a *Newsweek* article titled, "How the Bible Made America," the authors noted that the Bible has for centuries "exerted an unrivaled influence on American culture, politics and social life. Now historians are discovering that the Bible, perhaps even more than the Constitution, is our founding document: the source of the powerful myth of the United States as a special, sacred nation, a people called by God to establish a model society, a beacon to the world."

They go on to report, "There were times, too, when Bible study was the core of public education, and nearly every literate family not only owned a Bible but read from it regularly and reverently." Because of this pervasive Biblical influence, the United States seemed to Europeans to be one vast congregation, as G.K. Chesterton said, "with the soul of a church."[27]

The University of Houston investigated more than 15,000 writings of the founding fathers from 1760 to 1805 to determine their original ideas and convictions. Three men quoted most often in these writings were Montesquieu, John Locke and William Blackstone. Yet the Bible was quoted *16 times* more frequently than any of these men. In fact, Scripture was quoted by our founding fathers in 94 percent of the documents that were examined.[28]

The Bible is the Word of God. When we internalize its truths in our hearts, we discover it is "useful for teaching, rebuking, correcting and training in righteousness, so that the man of God may be thoroughly equipped for every good work" (2 Timothy 3:16, 17).

Blessed of God DAY 309

W hen God created Adam and Eve, He blessed them and said, "Be fruitful, and multiply, and replenish the earth, and subdue it" (Genesis 1:28, KJV).

Everyone wants to be blessed of God. Moses said, "All these blessings will come upon you and accompany you if you obey the Lord your God" (Deuteronomy 28:2).

We praise God today for our rich blessings through Christ Jesus. "Praise be to the God and Father of our Lord Jesus Christ, who has blessed us in the heavenly realms with every spiritual blessing in Christ" (Ephesians 1:3).

The word *blessed* in Hebrew thought has five predominant meanings:

1. *The favor of the Lord. Favor* literally means "to speak well of." Isn't it reassuring to know that God thinks and speaks well about His people? While God does not show favoritism, and He loves all persons the same, He does grant favor and success to those who trust and obey Him. "If you are willing and obedient, you will eat the best from the land" (Isaiah 1:19).

2. *To convey gifts upon.* "Every good and perfect gift is from above, coming down from the Father of the heavenly lights" (James 1:17).

3. *The blessing opposes and nullifies the curse of the law and sin.* The word *curse* describes the consequences of sin and the absence of blessings. "Christ redeemed us from the curse of the law" (Galatians 3:13).

4. *The fullness of life.* You can experience more than just getting by. Jesus said, "I have come that they may have life, and have it to the full" (John 10:10).

5. *The enjoyment of life.* "When God gives any man wealth and possessions, and enables him to enjoy them, to accept his lot and be happy in his work—this is a gift of God" (Ecclesiastes 5:19).

May the Lord bless and keep you throughout this day.

Does Anyone Care?   DAY 310

In the stage play *1776*, John Adams is portrayed as pacing the floor during the session of the Continental Congress in Philadelphia. The debates were deadlocked, determining our country's course to either return to colonialism or emerge as a free nation.

His heart was filled with anguish, and his soul struggled with these lonely questions: *Is anyone there? Does anyone see what I see? Does anyone care?*

Apathy is the enemy of progress and change. Self-absorption makes us look out for number one. Narcissism asks, "What's in it for me?" Yet, of Jesus, we read: "When he saw the crowds, he had compassion on them, because they were harassed and helpless, like sheep without a shepherd" (Matthew 9:36).

Here's an anonymous commentary on the complacent:

Blessed are the pushers, for they get on in the world.

Blessed are the hard-boiled, for they never let life hurt them.

Blessed are those who complain, for they get their own way in the end.

Blessed are the blasé, for they never worry over their sins.

Blessed are the slave drivers, for they get results.

Blessed are the men of the world, for they know their way around.

Blessed are the troublemakers, for they make people take notice of them.

Every day we meet someone who is hurting. I read that we should be kind to everyone we meet because everyone is going through some kind of pain. Be on the lookout for someone today who needs the compassion of Christ coming through your listening ear, kind word, or act of kindness.

Sent From God   DAY 311

There is a comical scene in the movie *Blues Brothers* when Jake says to Elwood, "We're on a mission from God."

We need to see ourselves on a mission from God. Every day is an opportunity to advance the kingdom of God.

The last words of Jesus were, "Go into all the world" (Mark 16:15). Every believer is to go into his or her world at home, work, and play as a minister of the grace of God.

One fact stands out about John the Baptist: he was a man sent from God. "There came a man who was sent from God; his name was John. He came as a witness to testify concerning that light, so that through him all men might believe. He himself was not the light; he came only as a witness to the light" (John 1:6-8).

He emerged out of the desert after a long time of private preparation with God. John had that real spiritual authority that rests on a person who comes out of the presence of God with a message from God.

Alexander MacLaren said: "John leapt, as it were, into the arena full-grown and full-armed." He did not come with an opinion of his own but with a message from God. The prophetic voice must come first from being in the presence of God and then into the presence of men.

What is our message and our ministry? Jesus said, "Peace be with you! As the Father has sent me, I am sending you. . . . If you forgive anyone his sins, they are forgiven; if you do not forgive them, they are not forgiven" (20:21, 23).

Only God can forgive sins, but we are to share the good news with others that God has provided forgiveness of sins and eternal life. Today you are sent from God as His representative to minister peace and forgiveness.

Repentance Unto Life   DAY 312

Jesus brought a simple message of hope: "The kingdom of God is near. Repent and believe the good news!" (Mark 1:15).

Repentance is the gateway to God. It is central to one's relationship with God because we have all strayed from God's way. The Hebrew word *teshubah*, which is the noun for the verb *shub*, means "to turn." It is a turning from sin and toward God; a change in one's attitude toward God.

Jeremiah offers a definition of *repentance* by contrast: "They have turned their backs to me and not their faces" (2:27). The people turned to false gods: "But my people have exchanged their Glory for worthless idols. . . . Where then are the gods you made for yourselves? Let them come if they can save you when you are in trouble! For you have as many gods as you have towns, O Judah" (vv. 11, 28).

The Westminster Confession of Faith says, "Repentance unto life is a saving grace, whereby a sinner, out of a true sense of sin, and understanding of the mercy of God in Christ, turns from it unto God, with full purpose of and endeavor after, new obedience."

God delights in repentance: "As surely as I live, declares the Sovereign Lord, I take no pleasure in the death of the wicked, but rather that they turn from their ways and live. Turn! Turn from your evil ways! Why will you die, O house of Israel?" (Ezekiel 33:11)

Repentance brings restoration: "Restore me, and I will return, because you are the Lord my God" (Jeremiah 31:18).

Let us turn away from our sins and turn toward our God in love, devotion and worship, for He alone is the Lord our God who loves us with an everlasting love.

It's Never Too Late   DAY 313

It is never too late for a person to repent of sins and receive forgiveness and new life. King Manasseh was the most wicked king recorded in Israeli history.

The prophets summed up his reign in one statement: "He has done more evil than the Amorites who preceded him and has led Judah into sin with his idols" (see 2 Kings 21:9).

The king of Assyria captured Manasseh and led him away in bronze shackles to Babylon. "In his distress he sought the favor of the Lord his God and humbled himself greatly before the God of his fathers. And when he prayed to him, the Lord was moved by his entreaty and listened to his plea; so he brought him back to Jerusalem and to his kingdom. Then Manasseh knew that the Lord is God" (2 Chronicles 33:11-13).

That's a tough way to learn repentance! When he got back home to Jerusalem, he did three things: (1) He got rid of the foreign gods (idols); (2) He restored the altar of the Lord and offered thank offerings; (3) He told the people to serve the Lord.

It's never too late to repent and turn to the Lord. *Repentance* is one of the most hopeful words in the Bible. God gives us grace to repent. He enables us to turn away from those things that harm and destroy us and turn to Him in devotion. As long as individuals have breath, they can call on God and repent and receive forgiveness, cleansing, and new life.

Fruits of Repentance DAY 314

John the Baptist called for the evidence of repentance: "Produce fruit in keeping with repentance" (Matthew 3:8). Over the last few days, we have learned that *repentance* means "to turn; to turn away from sin and to turn toward God in devotion and worship and obedience."

What are the benefits or, in the words of John, the fruits of repentance?

A new relationship with God. Repentance and forgiveness go hand in hand. John brought a positive message of new life and righteousness. He not only called people out of their sins, but he told them to turn their lives toward God. It is written of John: "Many of the people of Israel will he bring back to the Lord their God. And he will go on before the Lord, in the spirit and power of Elijah, to turn the hearts of the fathers to their children and the disobedient to the wisdom of the righteous—to make ready a people prepared for the Lord" (Luke 1:16, 17).

A new sense of faith. Repentance means changing our false beliefs about God and accepting His revelation in Jesus. Faith and repentance go hand in hand. Jesus said, "Repent and believe the good news!" (Mark 1:15). Unbelief is the root of all sin. Jesus said of the Holy Spirit: "When he comes, he will convict the world of guilt in regard to sin . . . because men do not believe in me" (John 16:8, 9). Adam and Eve sinned because they did not believe God's word. Doubt always leads to disobedience. Repentance leads to new faith in God.

A new relationship with others. A person who is right with God will live at peace with others. "Follow peace with all men, and holiness, without which no man shall see the Lord" (Hebrews 12:14, KJV). Holiness toward God and peace toward others go hand in hand.

A new purpose in life. We turn from the kingdom of the self to the kingdom of God. Jesus said, "Repent, for the kingdom of heaven is near" (Matthew 4:17). The kingdom of God is embodied in Jesus the King. Turning our lives toward God and toward Jesus as Lord gives us a new center for living. Our lives are centered in Him and in His will. We then "seek first the kingdom of God and His righteousness" (6:33, *NKJV*).

Keep an Open Mind DAY 315

The drugstore chain CVS learned this lesson. In 1992 just 7 percent of its 10,000+ workforce was over age 55. They conducted a study of their older employees and found that they were less likely to call in sick than the younger employees, and they were still capable of performing demanding tasks. Seventy-year-olds could still lift boxes, and 90-year-olds could handle tough management jobs.

So CVS began recruiting workers 55 and over, and today its older workforce has more than doubled to 16 percent of the total employee population. Older workers, CVS finds, need less training in areas like customer service and show high degrees of loyalty and dedication to their jobs.[29]

How we think determines how we live. "As he thinks in his heart, so is he" (Proverbs 23:7, *NKJV*). Emerson said, "A man is what he thinks about all day long."

To think means "to produce or form in the mind; conceive mentally; to examine in the mind; meditate upon, or determine by reasoning (to think a plan through); to believe; consider; to bring to mind; remember; to have the mind preoccupied by; to expect or anticipate; to bring about by thinking (to think oneself sick); to exercise judgment and form ideas; to have a particular opinion or feeling" (Webster).

"A simple man believes anything, but a prudent man gives thought to his steps" (Proverbs 14:15). "The mind of sinful man is death, but the mind controlled by the Spirit is life and peace" (Romans 8:6). "We have the mind of Christ" (1 Corinthians 2:16). "Your attitude should be the same as that of Christ Jesus" (Philippians 2:5).

Change your mind—change your life!

When I Was a Child   DAY 316

"**D**addy, do all fairy tales begin with the words 'Once upon a time'?" The little girl asked.

"No," he replied. "A whole lot of them begin with the words 'If elected, I promise.'"

One of the marks of maturity is thinking in terms of facts, not fiction or fantasy. Maturity means accepting life the way it is, not the way we wish it were. Paul said, "When I was a child, I talked like a child, I thought like a child, I reasoned like a child. When I became a man, I put childish ways behind me" (1 Corinthians 13:11). Childish thinking dwarfs our character development.

Paul said, "Brothers, stop thinking like children. In regard to evil be infants, but in your thinking be adults" (14:20). We are not to pride ourselves on being streetwise. Don't value being "experienced" in sin. Young people often think they need to first experience everything in the world. The fact is, they need to be inexperienced in the things of the world but knowledgeable in the things of God. We need to grow up in our thinking.

A study by a Stanford University research team has shown that what we watch affects our imaginations, learning, and behavior patterns. By "repeated viewing" and "repeated verbalizing," we shape our future and determine our destiny.

I read: "Control your thoughts. Thoughts become words. Words become actions. Actions become habits. Habits become destiny."

Thoughts Change Circumstances   DAY 317

One of the most frightening feelings we can have is the feeling of being out of control. There are so many things that are beyond our control: circumstances, people, the economy, global conditions, the weather, illness; but one thing is always in our sphere of control—our thoughts. While we cannot always control the world around us, we can control the world within us. By the way we think, our basic attitudes come through, and they do make an impact on our circumstances. Let me show you how.

Thoughts determine how we respond and deal with circumstances. We respond with fear or faith. We respond with hope or despair. We respond with action or resignation to the way things are. The way we respond to circumstances has an effect on how circumstances turn out. We are to take charge of our reponses: "Be joyful always; pray continually; give thanks in all circumstances, for this is God's will for you in Christ Jesus" (1 Thessalonians 5:16-18).

Thoughts determine how people respond to us. They pick up whether we are positive or negative, encouraging or discouraging, whether we whine or win! The way people relate to us is often a mirror of the attitudes we project without even realizing it.

Thoughts of faith change the world. Jesus said we could move mountains with faith (see Matthew 17:20). We have a commission to bring change: "Go and make disciples of all nations" (28:19). Faith begins as a thought, followed by words and then by action. Circumstances change when you handle them with faith. Everything is not predetermined. If you don't like your life, then you can do something about it! If you don't like the return, change the investment strategy!

Commitment   DAY 318

The success of any endeavor, relationship or organization is determined by people's commitment level. *Commitment* means "to be dedicated to a cause; to be willing to make necessary sacrifices; to demonstrate ownership; and to fulfill one's responsibilities."

Commitment rises and falls on the way we think. If we take a laissez-faire attitude about things, we will flounder. If we think somebody else will do the work, we will fail to do our part. But if we make the commitments necessary, we will be successful in whatever we do. Marriage takes commitment. Getting a good education takes commitment. Living holy in a secular age takes commitment. Financial freedom takes commitment. Building a ministry takes commitment.

Here's an important point: Emotional commitments never last. We often make premature or impulsive commitments in a moment of passion or haste. We mean well at the time, but then we get away from the moment, emotions subside and we ask ourselves, "What have I done?"

We need to make intellectual commitments. Think it through. Weigh the pros and cons. Seek counsel. Commitments that last are made in the mind, followed by a decision of the will. Then there are feelings of joy and satisfaction.

Jesus said, "No one who puts his hand to the plow and looks back is fit for service in the kingdom of God" (Luke 9:62). He also challenged us to "count the cost" before starting a project, lest we start and not have what it takes to finish (see 14:28-30).

Now for a final thought: "Do not be quick with your mouth, do not be hasty in your heart to utter anything before God. God is in heaven and you are on earth, so let your words be few" (Ecclesiastes 5:2).

The lesson for today is this: *Think it through!*

Lessons From a Mayfly DAY 319

I don't remember where I read this description of the mayfly, but I find it thought-provoking. Half the life span of a mayfly is about 12 hours.

"My goodness! I met such and such a man, and he swung a flyswatter at me!" one mayfly says to another. "I was almost crushed to death, and you know, I've never met such a cruel man during my half-life."

It had only lived 12 hours and couldn't stop talking. But already, half of its life had passed. By 7 or 8 in the evening, it faced the twilight of its life and, in a short while, death. Some mayflies survive for 20 hours, some 21, and some live to the ripe old age of 24 hours. They may talk of their lifelong experiences, but what is that to us?

We need an eternal perspective on life. God has a different view of our lives, just as we see the mayfly's life span differently than it does.

The writer of Ecclesiastes says: God "has also set eternity in the hearts of men; yet they cannot fathom what God has done from beginning to end" (3:11).

We need to measure our lives in terms of eternity. Only then can we make sense of our lives and be equipped to handle changing circumstances. "Therefore we do not lose heart. . . . For our light and momentary troubles are achieving for us an eternal glory that far outweighs them all" (2 Corinthians 4:16, 17).

Jesus kept an eternal perspective on the Cross: "For the joy set before him [He] endured the cross" (Hebrews 12:2). He measured the suffering of the Cross in light of eternal salvation for humanity.

Three Steps for Direction   DAY 320

We all want to know that God is directing the course of our lives. He promises to guide us: "Your ears will hear a voice behind you, saying, 'This is the way; walk in it'" (Isaiah 30:21). Jesus said the Holy Spirit "will guide you into all truth" (John 16:13). And Paul wrote: "For as many as are led by the Spirit of God, they are sons of God" (Romans 8:14, *NKJV*).

Here are three action steps for spiritual direction:

First, *trust in the Lord*. Expect Him to guide. Hearing His voice is a natural experience. It is only logical that God would speak to us if prayer is a conversation with God. It is logical that we would hear Him speak in our minds and that His voice would sound like words in our minds. God created the brain to work in this fashion, and He reveals Himself to us in ways we can understand.

Should we expect God to bring us His word in the form of an old man with a long, white beard looking like he came out of *The Lord of the Rings*, who carries an ancient leather scroll sealed with seven seals, with a word for our lives? No, God speaks in the mind.

Second, *"lean not on your own understanding"* (Proverbs 3:5). This does not mean that we should not use reason. We should. God gave us the power of reason, but He also reveals truth to us at times that makes no sense to us. Of Abraham, we read that he "obeyed and went, even though he did not know where he was going" (Hebrews 11:8). When we know God is directing, we are to trust and not be limited by our own understanding. God sees the big picture—the end from the beginning.

Third, "*in all your ways acknowledge Him, and He shall direct your paths*" (Proverbs 3:6, *NKJV*). We cannot just ask for direction for a particular decision and not surrender the totality of our lives to the Lord. We are to acknowledge Him in all our ways and seek His will for all areas of life.

The result: "He shall direct your paths." The *NIV* says, "He will make your paths straight."

Pertinent Questions

As a pastor, I am asked often how to know the voice of God. Here are the most common questions:

1. *How can I know it is God's voice?* When God speaks, the result is peace. "Let the peace of Christ rule in your hearts" (Colossians 3:15). God never leads us to do anything that is contrary to His Word.

2. *How much of a decision is my part versus God's part?* Both are important. We have to take charge of our lives and make good decisions based on counsel, Scripture and experience.

3. *How can I recover from a bad decision?* One thing you can do is plant a new harvest. A person "reaps what he sows" (Galatians 6:7). If you have reaped a poor harvest, then plant new seeds of faith, wisdom and responsibility. Don't waste time trying to dig up the bad harvest, just plant a new one.

4. *What do I do when a good decision turns into a bad decision?* Examine the steps of the downward path. How did you end up where you are? Maybe your predicament is the result of someone else's choice, and there was no way to avoid it.

5. *How do you deal with opposition from those you respect?* You are an adult. It is your life. You are accountable to God to do the best you can. There is a difference between people giving us advice and trying to control us or live our lives for us. You have the freedom to make a mistake and to make the wrong decision.

6. *How do you practice patience when direction is clear, but the timing is not now?* God says, "Though [the vision] tarries, wait for it; Because it will surely come" (Habakkuk 2:3, *NKJV*). What possible good can come from getting in a hurry?

7. *How much of the past should we take into account when making a decision?* "Forget the former things; do not dwell on the past" (Isaiah 43:18). Learn what you can learn and move on. Let experiences be redemptive, not ruin your life or self-confidence.

8. *How do I distinguish the voice of God from my conscience or emotions?* Check the content. Are you just trying to convince yourself or justify your actions? When God speaks, there is substance and content to what He is saying. God doesn't waste words or give trivial counsel.

9. *Is there a set path for a person's life, or multiple choices?* God gave us choices so that there are options. God does give ministry callings. We are chosen for salvation, but not every detail of life is predetermined. God wants you to think things through and make good decisions. God is glorified when we use the mind He gave us.

Now for a final thought: *Meditate on Scripture.* "Let the word of Christ dwell in you richly" (Colossians 3:16). As you do, your mind will be more in tune with the voice of God.

The Lord Is My Shepherd   DAY 322

For the next several days, we are going to look at the portrait of God painted in Psalm 23. This is the most inspirational and influential psalm of the Psalter. A *psalm* is simply a song of praise. For ages, this psalm continues to stand in a category of its own as a literary masterpiece. No greater portrait of God has ever been painted by the hand of an artist or captured in the words of a lyricist than those of David, the king of Israel.

Of all this psalm gives us, it provides a correct view of God. We come to see God as our shepherd, the One who cares for us and watches over us. We are not cosmic orphans in the universe. Neither is God watching us from a distance. He is carefully watching over our lives to lead us in paths of righteousness, "through the valley of the shadow of death" and, one day, to dwell in His house forever.

David begins, "The Lord is" (v. 1). Who is the Lord, and what is my relationship to Him? Let's consider the Trinity: God the Father is the author of life. The Hebrew name *Elohim* found in Genesis 1:1 means

"God is Creator." *Adonai* means "Sovereign Lord." *El Shaddai* means "Provider." *Yahweh* means the "self-existent God" who reveals Himself and who binds Himself to His creation through His oath of faithfulness.

David sees God as a shepherd, an image he was familiar with, since his own father was a shepherd. God is the shepherd of Israel (Isaiah 40:11). Jesus is the Good Shepherd (John 10:11).

We are owned by God; we belong to Him by virtue of Creation (Psalm 24:1) and redemption (1 Corinthians 6:19, 20; 1 Peter 1:18-20). We are the object of His infinite love. We bear His mark. Sheep are branded or marked by their owner (Ephesians 1:13). To bear His mark is to joyfully submit to His claim of ownership in our lives.

I Shall Not Want   DAY 323

The confident affirmation of a sheep is that it is completely satisfied and content with its lot in life and the care of the shepherd. To not *want* means to have no lack of basic care and provision and to be fully content in God's care, not craving or desiring anything more.

Here we have a balanced view of material and spiritual provisions. David, when hounded by King Saul, wandered in deserts and mountain caves. But through it all, God was his source of contentment. David knew his share of failures as a husband and a father. He knew the meaning of depression and anguish of heart, yet, he could say, "I shall not . . . want" (Psalm 23:1). God provides grace so we can handle these things. The greatest wealth is to be rich in grace and faith.

The shepherd gets up early to prepare the day for his sheep. He stays with them throughout the day as they graze and rest. In the evening he inspects them for wounds or pests and cares for each one.

Sheep are very fearful animals. So the shepherd makes them lie down. Four conditions have to be present for sheep to lie down: They have to be free from all fear; free from friction within the flock; free from pests, such as parasites and flies; and free from hunger.

The presence of the shepherd in the pasture brings peace to the flock. Green pastures were the work of the shepherd's labor, time and skill. David was a shepherd in the dry, semiarid climate of Palestine. He had to carefully prepare green pastures. Even so, God prepares green pastures for us as He makes us lie down. We have perfect peace knowing our God will provide everything we need.

Beside Still Waters

DAY 324

The way we see God has a profound effect on the way we live out our faith. David says, "He leads me beside the still waters" (Psalm 23:2, *NKJV*). Stillness is one of our greatest needs because we battle so much stress.

In one terse statement, David gives us an eternal truth on which to base our lives: "The Lord is my shepherd, I shall not . . . want" (v. 1). This promise tells us that God loves us and cares for us. We overcome fear as we set our hearts at rest in His love.

Water is a basic necessity of life. The body of the sheep is 70 percent water. Water determines the vitality and strength of the sheep. Thirst indicates the need of the body for an outside supply. In 63:1, David said he thirsted for God. Jesus said, "Blessed are those who . . . thirst for righteousness, for they will be filled" (Matthew 5:6). Jesus also said, "If anyone thirsts, let him come to Me and drink . . . [for] out of his heart will flow rivers of living water" (John 7:37, *NKJV*).

There are three sources of water for the sheep: dew on the grass, deep wells, and springs or streams. Sheep will only drink from still waters. The shepherd takes rocks to build a dam across a small stream to form a still pool for the sheep. The sheep's fear of rushing water will keep it from drinking.

Jesus said: "I am the good shepherd. The good shepherd lays down his life for the sheep. . . . I know my sheep and my sheep know me" (John 10:11, 14).

We need the Good Shepherd to lead us because we have a tendency to stray from Him. Isaiah said, "We all, like sheep, have gone astray, each of us has turned to his own way" (53:6). Yet, God in Christ leads us to still waters where we can rest and renew our spiritual strength for life's journey.

Paths of Righteousness DAY 325

Everyone wants to know God's will. God promises to guide us. This is a predominant theme of Psalm 23. He leads us beside still waters, and He leads us in paths of righteousness (vv. 2, 3).

Sheep have no sense of direction. If lost, a sheep cannot find its way home like a dog, or cat, or horse. They lack an inner sense of direction. Sheep also have poor eyesight. They can only see about 10 or 15 yards ahead. The fields of Israel were covered with narrow paths over which the shepherd led his sheep to pasture. Some of these paths led to a precipice over which a sheep could easily fall to its death. Isaiah says, "We all, like sheep, have gone astray" (53:6). Great danger awaits us when we stray from the path of righteousness.

Sheep are also creatures of habit. Once they find a path, they will follow it until it is a rut and will graze the same hills until the land is barren. They will eat the grass down to the root, even destroying the roots if not directed by the shepherd. These well-worn areas can quickly become infested with parasites of all kinds. So, the shepherd has to keep them on the move. What is interesting about sheep is that they are filled with excitement when they are led to new pastures. Newness brings excitement and anticipation.

God leads us by the inner voice of the Holy Spirit who speaks in our minds. He doesn't drive us. We, then, are called to follow Him in trust and obedience. Even as Israel followed the cloud by day and the pillar of fire by night through the wilderness, God always leads us in paths of righteousness. As God directs us, He also goes with us. It is His living presence that guides us. The shepherd always stays with the sheep. God leads us for His name's sake. The reason God guides us is so that we will find our purpose in life and live for His glory.

Through the Valley of the Shadow DAY 326

The journey of life is filled with dangerous places like the valley. While there is an actual valley of the shadow going from Jerusalem to the Dead Sea, this valley is also figurative of more than just physical death. The phrase can be translated "the glen of gloom." Remember, to get to the mountain peaks, you have to cross through the valleys. Every mountain has its valleys, ravines and draws.

Why take the route of the valley? The shepherd leads the sheep to the mountain peaks by way of the valleys for three reasons: (1) because the valley is the easiest grade, (2) it is well watered, and (3) it has the best forage along the route.

God's presence is with us in the valley, so we can say with David, "I will fear no evil for you are with me" (Psalm 23:4). Note that David says, "I walk through." The important word is *through*. We do not stay in the valley, we pass through as the shepherd leads.

The valley, a dangerous place for the sheep, is subject to the attacks of predators, mud slides, thunderstorms and heavy rains, and falling rocks. Yet, the abiding presence of the shepherd keeps the sheep calm and assured, fearing no evil.

"My Presence will go with you, and I will give you rest" (Exodus 33:14).

The Rod and the Staff   DAY 327

David's lyric, "Your rod and your staff, they comfort me" (Psalm 23:4), is rich with meaning. The shepherd's rod is a source of *protection* for the sheep against animals of prey. David tells how he slew a lion and a bear when protecting his sheep. The shepherd's rod was a hard, heavy club about 3 feet long. It is an extension of the shepherd's own right arm, a symbol of his strength and power.

The sheep is defenseless by itself. Yet, in the shepherd's presence, the sheep finds comfort. The staff is also a symbol in Scripture of the authority of God in the hands of His people. Moses stretched forth his shepherd's staff over Egypt and displayed the miracles of God. The rod, then, represents spiritually the Word of God.

The rod was also used to *discipline* and correct a wayward, rebellious sheep that insisted on going his own way. The rod was also used to *examine and count* the sheep. This is referred to as "passing under the rod" (see Ezekiel 20:37). The shepherd makes a careful examination of each sheep to ensure its greatest care.

The staff was about 8 feet long with a crook on the end. The shepherd will use the staff to pick up a newborn lamb and bring it to its mother. This way, the lamb will not be rejected by the mother by smelling the scent of the shepherd's hand on the lamb. In the same way, the Spirit of God works to bring lost humanity into fellowship with God.

The staff is used to guide the sheep through dangerous areas by gentle prodding. Sometimes the shepherd will hold the staff next to the side of the sheep just to remind them of the shepherd's touch. Finally, the staff is used to lift a sheep out of a dangerous area if it slips on a treacherous slope.

In the Presence of My Enemies   DAY 328

David celebrates the provision and protection of God in the lyric, "You prepare a table before me in the presence of my enemies" (Psalm 23:5). God prepares what we need in advance just as the shepherd prepares for the sheep. The word *prepares* is important because we learn from it that God is proactive, not reactive, in His work in our lives.

We are crisis-oriented, reacting to one situation after another, but God is calculated in what He does for us. The shepherd prepares the pastureland by removing the weeds and poisonous plants that grow throughout Israel. Also, he removes the thorny plants that prick the noses of the sheep. He gathers up the weeds and plants and burns them, purging the pasture. The Holy Spirit destroys the weeds in our hearts so that the Word of God can grow and flourish in our minds and hearts.

The table of the Lord is fulfilled in Holy Communion. What a price Jesus paid to prepare this table for us in the presence of our enemies. The Communion service serves to remind us that Jesus, "the Chief Shepherd and Bishop of our souls" (see 1 Peter 5:4; 2:25), has provided everything we need for life and godliness.

The Anointing   DAY 329

Sheep are often wounded in the process of traveling and grazing. Cuts to the head or nose occur while the sheep graze among thorns.

Sheep get tired from the heat of the day and the long treks across slopes and plains. The shepherd's oil was used to bind up the wounds of the sheep.

There is another interesting use of oil or ointment. During the summer, swarms of insects and parasites disturb the sheep. Especially troublesome, according to Philip Keller in *A Shepherd Looks at Psalm 23,* are the nose flies or nasal flies. They get into the nasal cavity and lay eggs, which causes severe inflammation in the sheep's head. Shepherds will apply the ointment in advance to protect the sheep from such parasites. A shepherd will also smear the heads of the rams with oil so that when they become combative, they will slip off each other when they butt heads to keep them from injury.

The oil represents the Holy Spirit in His healing ministry. The oil also represents consecration for service (see Exodus 29:7; 1 Samuel 16:13). The anointing work of the shepherd is an ongoing experience, just as the Holy Spirit continues His work of empowerment for service and healing for our spiritual wounds. He gives "the oil of gladness" for times of depression and discouragement (Isaiah 61:3).

My Cup Runs Over — DAY 330

I have always found great meaning in the lyric "My cup runneth over" (Psalm 23:5, KJV). God always provides *more than enough.* He gives blessings so great we cannot contain them. The cup of which David speaks is a cup of contentment. The shepherd gives the sheep water to drink when they arrive home every evening, satisfying their deepest thirst. Paul said, "I have learned to be content whatever the circumstances" (Philippians 4:11).

It is also a cup of joy. The overflowing cup speaks of the fact that God gives His people more than enough to satisfy their desires: "Now to him who is able to do immeasurably more than all we ask or imagine" (Ephesians 3:20). In God's presence is the "fullness of joy" (Psalm 16:11, *NKJV*). Jesus said, "These things I have spoken to you so that My joy may be in you, and that your joy may also be made full" (John 15:11, *NASB*).

Finally, David references a cup of wine. Philip Keller reflects on his own experience as a shepherd. When the cold, chilling winter would come, he kept with him a bottle containing a mixture of water and brandy. This was used to soothe the lambs that might become too cold or wet from the frost.

Joy comes from this next lyric: "Surely goodness and mercy shall follow me" (Psalm 23:6, *NKJV*). Now there's a positive outlook on life!

The word *surely* deserves comment. He could have said "perhaps," or "maybe," or "I hope so." But he said "surely." David has a deep-settled assurance that God cares for His people. The entire psalm is a declaration of what he knows God will do for him. He does not ask God for anything in the psalm, he simply affirms as fact the provisions of God in his life.

The House of the Lord   DAY 331

In a world of evil, injustice, unfairness and unexplained suffering, David is confident that God's goodness and mercy will be his lot in life. Goodness and mercy follow his every step. On every side and at every turn, he expects the goodness and mercy of God to be showered upon him. The compassion of the shepherd was fully expressed when the Good Shepherd laid down His life for the sheep.

We neither deserve the mercies of the Lord, nor do we always discern them; but still they follow us. This lyric also means that the impact of our actions toward others is to be goodness and mercy. This is the legacy we are to leave as we walk through this life.

Finally, our hope is "I will dwell in the house of the Lord forever" (Psalm 23:6). David, speaking as a sheep, reflects on all that the Shepherd provides: green pastures, still waters, the table, anointing, an overflowing cup, and the mercy of God. The house belongs to the Shepherd. David has no wish to belong to any other than to the Good Shepherd.

Forever is a long time! Yet, our hope is that we will dwell in the Lord's house forever. David is one of the few Old Testament writers to speak so openly about eternity and life after death (see also Psalm 16:10, 11).

While eternal life is in view here, he is also thinking of "forever" as a here and now. We are to live our lives in the presence of the Good

Shepherd. The ultimate fulfillment of this promise is when we come to rest eternally in God's presence.

As Mr. Feeble Mind says in John Bunyan's classic, *Pilgrim's Progress:* "But this I am resolved on: to run when I can, to go on when I cannot run, and to creep when I cannot go. . . . My mind is beyond the river that has no bridge, though I am, as you see, but of a feeble mind."

Take Captive Every Thought   DAY 332

Albert Einstein said, "I want to know the thoughts of God. The rest are just details." How we think and what we think about determines how we live. Our thoughts shape our attitudes, values, beliefs, philosophy of life, and lifestyle.

Paul writes, "Be transformed by the renewing of your mind" (Romans 12:2). Transformation begins with new thoughts. "Let this mind be in you which was also in Christ Jesus" (Philippians 2:5, *NKJV*). Peter says, "Prepare your minds for action. . . . Be clear minded and self-controlled so that you can pray" (1 Peter 1:13; 4:7).

We are in a battle for the mind. "For though we live in the world, we do not wage war as the world does" (2 Corinthians 10:3). We have spiritual weapons—the weapon of prayer and the Scripture—enabling us to "take captive every thought to make it obedient to Christ" (v. 5).

The question is, what thoughts do we need to take captive? We need to take captive worldly thoughts. In the movie *The Edge,* Anthony Hopkins turns to Alec Baldwin and says, "Just because you feel lost doesn't mean your compass is broken." Our compass is our faith in Christ and the Scripture.

The word used here for *world* in Greek is not the earth. The word *cosmos* means "the world without God, which is organized on wrong principles—pagan society as a whole; this present age of sin and suffering." The world is a system of attitudes, values, and lifestyles contrary to the will of God.

We march to a different drumbeat than the world. We are citizens of heaven and live by the eternal values of the Word of God. The Word, not the world, dictates how we live.

Love Not the World

John tells us that there are three thoughts of the world we need to take captive and allow them no room in our minds: "Do not love the world or the things in the world. If anyone loves the world, the love of the Father is not in him. For all that is in the world—the lust of the flesh, the lust of the eyes, and the pride of life—is not of the Father but is of the world. And the world is passing away, and the lust of it; but he who does the will of God abides forever" (1 John 2:15-17, *NKJV*).

The lust of the flesh is the attitude that governs everything by materialistic standards; indulgence; seeks pleasure at all costs; and tends toward shallow living with no real spiritual life.

The lust of the eyes refers to the person overly concerned with the outward show; ostentatious; covetousness; and the false notion that happiness is based on what we see. Adam and Eve disobeyed God when they "saw that the fruit was pleasant to the eyes" (see Genesis 3:6).

The pride of life means empty pride. It describes the person who lays claim to possessions and achievements not his own; bragging and boasting of what one has and does. But the glory belongs to God.

God says, "Let not the wise man boast of his wisdom or the strong man boast of his strength or the rich man boast of his riches, but let him who boasts boast about this: that he understands and knows me, that I am the Lord, who exercises kindness, justice and righteousness" (Jeremiah 9:23, 24).

Our citizenship is in heaven (Philippians 3:20). We govern our lives by a higher law than the principles of the world system. We take captive every worldly thought and make it obedient to the truth of God's Word. "Forever, O Lord, Your word is settled in heaven" (Psalm 119:89, *NKJV*).

Runaway Thoughts

Anxiety is blind, apprehensive fear; a generalized foreboding; a sense that the worst-case scenario will happen. Imagined fears of catastrophes and personal disaster haunt us. We suffer panic attacks and phobic seizures.

The antidote to anxiety is to take captive every thought and make it obedient to the promises of God. "Do not be anxious about anything, but in everything, by prayer and petition, with thanksgiving, present your requests to God. And the peace of God, which transcends all understanding, will guard your hearts and your minds" (Philippians 4:6, 7).

We need to face our fears with four questions:

1. What is the best thing that can happen today?
2. What is the worst thing that can happen today?
3. What can I do today to make sure that the best thing does happen?
4. What can I do today to make sure that the worst thing doesn't happen?

When you face your fears instead of running from them, you take them captive to thoughts of faith.

The burst of thunder sent the 4-year-old flying into her parents' bedroom. "Mommy, I'm scared," she said. The mother, half awake and half unconscious, replied, "Go back to your bed. There's no reason to be afraid. God is there with you." The little girl stood there for a moment and said softly, "Mommy, I'll sleep here with Daddy. You go sleep with God."

There's a medieval legend about a traveler on his way to a European village. He picked up an aged woman on the side of the road. As they were traveling in the horse and carriage, he was terrified when he realized that she was the dreaded plague, Cholera. She assured him that she would only kill 10 people in the village. She even offered the traveler a dagger and said, "You can kill me if more than that die." Arriving in the village, over 100 were dead. The angry traveler lifted the dagger to kill the plague, but she protested, "Wait. I killed only 10. Fear killed the rest."

The message of God to us is, "Fear not, for I am with you" (Isaiah 41:10, *NKJV*).

A Healthy Mind   DAY 335

Jesus is the most hopeful person who has ever lived. His message is one of hope: "Repent, for the kingdom of heaven is near" (Matthew 4:17).

What is a healthy and hopeful mind? A University of Chicago research report studied "high-stress/low-illness" people and found three characteristics:

1. *A positive attitude toward change and challenge.* For those who are healthy, change is an opportunity to grow. Others escape in a world of TV, tranquilizers, alcohol and oversleeping.

2. *A commitment to their goals, relationships, and significant causes that take them outside of themselves.*

3. *A feeling of being in control of their lives.* Faith gives us a sense of control over our attitudes, values, beliefs, feelings and actions. We are in the hand of God.

When writer Anthony Burgess was 39, his doctors found a brain tumor and gave him a year to live. He made a vow to write 10 novels in that last year so his widow could live on the royalties. At the end of the year, he had completed five and a half novels, and the brain tumor had completely disappeared. He lived to age 76 and wrote about 50 novels and at least 15 nonfiction works. He was so prolific, even his publisher was unsure of the exact number of his books at the time of his death.[30]

Facing Death With Faith   DAY 336

When John Wesley was asked to explain the success of the Christian gospel, he said, "Our people die well." Only in Christ is the crisis of death resolved. He has promised us who believe in Him: "Because I live, you also will live" (John 14:19).

We tend to experience dread over our finiteness. We worry about death and feel that life is pointless if we have no faith. Even Paul writes, "If only for this life we have hope in Christ, we are to be pitied more than all men" (1 Corinthians 15:19).

But in Christ we have hope beyond this life. "And this is what he promised us—even eternal life" (1 John 2:25). Jesus said, "Do not let your heart be troubled. . . . In My Father's house are many dwelling places. . . . I will come again and receive you to Myself, that where I am, there you may be also" (John 14:1-3, *NASB*).

Alan Jones, in *Soul Awakening,* takes a triumphant attitude toward death:

> To live our life from the point of view of our death is not necessarily a capitulation to despair, to withdrawal, to passivity. Rather, it can become the basis for our being and doing in the world. The more we refuse to look at our own death, the more we repress and deny new possibilities for living. We are all going to die, and our life is a movement to that sure end. Believers find that meditation on this simple fact has a wonderful way of clearing the mind! It enables them to live every single moment with new appreciation and delight. When I say to myself, "This moment may be my last," I am able to see the world with new eyes.

"O Death, where is your sting? Oh Hades, where is your victory? . . . But thanks be to God, who gives us the victory through our Lord Jesus Christ" (1 Corinthians 15:55, 57, *NKJV*).

May our hearts today be filled with praise and honor to God for His goodness. One of the Hebrew words for *praise* in the Bible means "to boast and to brag about God"!

People God Uses

We all share the desire to be used of God for His glory. But we feel unqualified. We think we don't have enough Biblical knowledge or spiritual maturity, or perhaps we have done too many things wrong in life.

Well, what kind of people does God use? If there was ever a person who was surprised that God not only called him into service but did, indeed, use him in a powerful way, it was a first-century fisherman from Galilee known as Simon Peter.

Peter was introduced to Jesus by his brother Andrew. When Jesus met him, He changed his name from *Simon* to *Peter* (see John 1:40-42). Why the name change? *Simon* means "a reed." Here was a man blown by the winds of public opinion and shaken in his beliefs by the pressure of others. But Jesus saw something more in him, so He called him *Peter,* meaning "a rock"—one who would be strong and steadfast in his loyalty to Jesus and his commitment to the call of God.

Peter's journey with Jesus was one of being transformed from a *reed* to a *rock*. Peter was in the fishing business with his brother, Andrew. They were partners with their close friends, James and John.

On the day Peter was called by Jesus, these fishermen had just spent a grueling night fishing but didn't catch anything. They were tired and frustrated. Around the shoreline, a crowd had gathered. The new controversial teacher, which some were saying was the Messiah, was preaching the Word of God. Simon listened from a distance.

Jesus started His preaching in the synagogues, but He wasn't restricted to the synagogues. The world was His parish; the countryside, His sanctuary; every man's heart, His pulpit.

The first step to being used by God is to be flexible in God's hands so that He can change you from a reed to a rock. The words of the hymn put it this way:

> Have Thine own way, Lord! Have Thine own way!
> Thou art the Potter, I am the clay.
> Mold me and make me after Thy will,
> While I am waiting, yielded and still.

Launch Out Into the Deep   DAY 338

Today we continue looking at Jesus' calling on Peter's life. Peter and his partners had fished all night and caught nothing. After addressing the crowd from the shore of Galilee, Jesus noticed the men, along with their boats, on the shoreline.

He asked to use Peter's boat so that He could address the people off-shore. After delivering His message, Jesus made an unusual request of Peter: "Launch out into the deep" (Luke 5:4, *NKJV*).

Did He merely mean the deep of Galilee? Not really. He was calling Peter into deeper waters with God. He was calling him to an adventure of faith. Christ had a plan for Peter's life that was bigger than his fishing business.

Jesus challenges you, "Launch out into the deep." There is more to life than fishing. There is more to life than the pleasures of the world, the pursuit of power, the achievement of fame, and the accumulation of wealth. Life is more than daily routines—eating and drinking, sleeping and waking, working and resting, making money and preparing for retirement.

There are deep waters in God that will fill your life with eternal purpose. "For we are God's workmanship created in Christ Jesus to do good works which God has prepared in advance for us to do" (Ephesians 2:10). We are salt to preserve (Matthew 5:13), light to illuminate (v. 14), a city set on a hill (v. 14), witness to testify (Acts 1:8), letters to be read by others (2 Corinthians 3:2), mirrors to reflect His glory (v. 18), jars of clay containing a heavenly treasure (4:7), ambassadors to represent Christ (5:20), priests to intercede for others (1 Peter 2:9), and ministers of the grace of God (4:10).

So, launch out into the deep!

God Uses Ordinary People   DAY 339

The apostle Peter was a fisherman—an entrepreneur with a family business. Yet, Jesus called him. This was one of the distinctive features of Jesus as a Rabbi. Traditionally, parents would save up enough money and then seek out a rabbi to teach their son whom they wanted to study the Law of God. Not so with Jesus. He sought out His followers, and He was no respecter of persons. To the Pharisees, He said, "The tax collectors and prostitutes are entering the kingdom of God ahead of you" (Matthew 21:31).

The day that Jesus called Peter to follow Him gives us three great lessons about His calling on our lives:

1. *Jesus initiates the search.* God searches for us. Jesus is the Good Shepherd who leaves the 99 sheep to look for the one lost sheep (Luke 15:1-7). Jesus said, "The Son of Man has come to seek and to save that which was lost" (Luke 19:10, *NKJV*).

2. *Jesus accepts us just the way we are.* Jesus didn't tell Peter to change anything when He first called him. He simply said, "Follow Me." The promise of Christ to those who follow Him is, "I will make you." We do the following; He does the making. Charlotte Elliott wrote a magnificent hymn expressing this dynamic truth, titled "Just As I Am."

3. *Jesus takes what we have and uses it for His glory.* Peter knew how to fish. Jesus told him, "I will make you a fisher of men" (see Matthew 4:19). The Lord takes our talents when we submit them to Him, and He shows us how to use our talents in ways to advance the kingdom of God. Every talent and skill you have can be an asset in Christian ministry.

A friend once told me that God uses FAT people. The first time he said it I asked him what in the world he was talking about. He said, "FAT people—Faithful, Available, Teachable."

Nevertheless, at Your Word   DAY 340

Perseverance is more important than ability in the success equation. Although Peter was tired from fishing all night and coming up empty, he was willing to throw the nets in again because of Jesus' instruction. "Master, we've worked hard all night and haven't caught anything. But because you say so, I will let down the nets" (Luke 5:5).

I have had the opportunity to go fishing with friends in Canada. If there's one thing I've learned about fishing, it is to cast your line in one more time. Fishermen are a patient and persevering breed. I don't really have the patience for fishing. I get frustrated quickly when the fish aren't biting. But a good fisherman always goes back into the same waters that discouraged him and tries again.

One of the greatest faith statements in the Bible is nestled in this beautiful passage: "Nevertheless at thy word I will let down the net" (KJV).

If there is one word you need in your vocabulary, it's the word *nevertheless*. It means that in spite of doubt, discouragement, disillusionment, failures of others, and personal setbacks, I will obey the Lord. I will let down the net one more time. I will try it again, even though I have failed.

Sir Lionel Wood met the king of France at a social gathering. The king casually asked Wood to come by the palace the next day and have lunch with him. Forgetting he had made the invitation, as the king entered the dining hall the next day, he was shocked to see Lionel Wood present.

"You didn't respond to my invitation yesterday, so I didn't expect you," the king remarked.

Sir Lionel replied, "A king's invitation needs no response, it only needs to be obeyed."

In Search of Humility   DAY 341

Humility is the one virtue we know we need; but if we ever suggest we have it, we only prove we don't. We certainly don't want to be like the guy who wrote a book titled *Humility and How I Achieved It.*

Humility simply means to recognize your need of God. One of the reasons why Jesus used Simon Peter is because he was humble. When Peter took Jesus out in his boat and Jesus worked a miracle of a great catch of fish, Peter recognized Christ's divinity, fell at his knees, and blurted out, "Go away from me, Lord; I am a sinful man!" (Luke 5:8).

Humility is a mark of all God's servants. Abraham said, "I am but dust and ashes" (Genesis 18:27, *NKJV*). Jacob confessed, "I am not worthy of the least of all Your mercies" (see 32:10). Job came to the place where he could say, "I repent and abhor myself" (see Job 42:6).

When Isaiah saw the Lord in a glorious vision, he lamented, "Woe to me! . . . I am ruined! For I am a man of unclean lips" (Isaiah 6:5). Paul said, "I am the chief of sinners and the least of the apostles" (see 1 Corinthians 15:9; 1 Timothy 1:15).

John Bradford, the faithful martyr for Christ, used to sign some of his letters with these words: "A most miserable sinner, John Bradford."

Humility before God transforms us into servants to others. We relinquish the desire and the drive to rule over others, to control, to dominate, to intimidate, and to exercise authority over them.

The disciples themselves got caught up in the quest for power. Jesus taught them the way of humility and service: "If anyone wants to be first, he must be the very last, and the servant of all" (Mark 9:35).

If we expect God to use us in His service, we must come by the way of humility. Salvation is deliverance for both sin and the self. The self is now in submission to Jesus as Lord. Humility is the key to promotion in the kingdom of God. The way up is the way down. "Blessed are the poor in spirit, for theirs is the kingdom of heaven" (Matthew 5:3).

Visionary People

When Jesus met Peter, He gave him a vision of what he could be and what he could do for the kingdom of God. Peter felt unworthy to be in the presence of Divinity. But Jesus said to him, "Do not be afraid; from now on you will catch men" (Luke 5:10). The response of Peter and also Andrew, James and John was, "So they pulled their boats up on shore, left everything and followed him" (v. 11). One can only imagine the magnetism Jesus exuded when He called people into service.

Vision inspires loyalty. "They left everything." This doesn't mean they abandoned their families. These men traveled with Jesus on ministry tours and then returned home to raise their families. But when they left everything, they redefined their relationship to material things. They knew the difference between treasures on earth and treasures in heaven. They gained an eternal perspective in a temporal world. They were free from encumbrances so they could follow Jesus. You have to be free before you can follow.

"They followed Him." The word *follow* is the defining action of a disciple. "Follow Me," says Jesus to every person. Following is an act of faith, commitment, determination and love. The disciple says, "Lord, I will follow You wherever You lead." To follow is an act of surrender to Christ's will and direction. Following means that we remain close to Jesus in continued fellowship. To follow someone, you have to be where they are. They clung to every word Jesus spoke. They paid attention to every action He took. They listened intently to every prayer He offered.

Incredible things happen when people get a vision of greatness for their lives. They accomplish more than they ever dreamed they were capable of doing.

We start off just fishing, but when Christ becomes Lord of our hearts, our goals and our careers, we end up fishing for men.

God's Vision for Your Life

Proverbs 29:18 gives us a vital principle for life: "Where there is no vision, the people perish" (KJV). Getting a long-range vision for your life will empower you with a workable plan and a meaningful purpose.

Norman Vincent Peale told the story of a friend who grew up very poor in a Midwestern city. His father told him that he could go through the lower grades and then he would have to go to work to help support the family. One day he was walking down one of the main business streets of the city where he lived. He passed a newspaper office and saw a man sitting behind a desk with his coat off, vest unbuttoned, tie loose, sleeves rolled up, and the young boy was struck immediately as though transfixed.

He asked the policeman at the corner, "Who is that man?"

"That man," replied the officer, "is the editor of that newspaper, and he is just about the most powerful influence in all this area."

"How did he get that job?" asked the boy.

"I don't know. He probably worked for it," the officer answered.

Right then the boy envisioned himself as the editor of that paper. The image was formed in his mind; he had no doubt about it at all. That was his future. And he went to work. At first he got a job delivering papers. Then he got on one of the trucks that took the papers out. Next, he moved into the Advertising Department and advanced rather rapidly. But this wasn't the normal path that led to the editorial chair.

The day came when the editor's position became open, and the publisher called him in and said, "Roger, I don't know why I'm going to make you this offer. You are the best advertising man we've ever had, but I have an overwhelming feeling that you were intended to be the editor of this paper. So, I appoint you editor in chief."

"Thank you, sir," Roger said, "but God gave me the job years ago." The publisher listened in astonishment to Roger's story. He had a dream of what he could be, and it came to pass.

That day on the shores of Galilee, Peter got a vision of the person he could be in Christ, and it came to pass.

Walking in Truth   DAY 344

A couple of years ago, Barbie and I were flying back from the National Prayer Breakfast in Washington, D.C. I struck up a conversation with the guy sitting next to me. He, also, was from Atlanta.

He asked what I did, and I told him I was a pastor. He asked me where, and I told him about our church. I then asked if he and his family attended church, and he replied, "I haven't attended church since I was confirmed." I asked why not, and he said he was always busy with work or playing golf on Sundays. So I encouraged him to attend church and to grow in his faith.

Then out of the blue, he asked, "So, as a minister, do you always walk the straight and narrow?"

"What do you mean?" I responded.

"Do you always play by the rules?" I told him that I did, but the question struck me as odd. Barbie and I discussed it later and agreed that his question was a reaction to another widely publicized scandal that had just hit the press about some ministry gone awry.

Walking the straight and narrow is about maintaining integrity. The word *integrity* means "uprightness of character; probity; honesty; the condition of being sound and whole; the state of being complete and undivided." In mathematics, an integer is a whole number. We live one life, not a double life. Shakespeare said, "To thine own self be true." So, what does it mean to have integrity?

Integrity is the outward expression of inward character. Christ's character spoke volumes. The Pharisees told Jesus, "We know you are a man of integrity" (Matthew 22:16). The Greek word translated for *integrity* is *alethia,* meaning "truth." The KJV of the verse says, "We know that thou art true." Character is what you know you would do if you knew you would never get caught.

Integrity Plus   DAY 345

Let's continue our look at integrity as modeled by Jesus. The Pharisees told Jesus, "We know you are a man of integrity" (Matthew 22:16). The Greek word translated for *integrity* is *alethia,* meaning "truth." The KJV translation reads, "We know that thou art true."

Integrity is not swayed by men. We often care too much about the opinions and judgments of others. We get into trouble trying to please everybody. Do not be swayed by the pressure of men to conform or by the persecutions of men.

John Bunyan, who wrote *Pilgrim's Progress,* was imprisoned for preaching in the 1400s. While in prison, his captors brought his daughter to him, who begged him to come home. "You can leave now and go home to your family if you will stop preaching," they told him.

He replied, "If you let me out tonight, you will find me tomorrow morning preaching in Bedford Square."

Integrity never shows favoritism. The Pharisees also acknowledged in reference to Jesus, "You aren't swayed by men, because you pay no attention to who they are" (v. 16). Peter said in Acts, "I now realize how true it is that God does not show favoritism but accepts men from every nation who fear Him and do what is right" (10:34, 35). We discriminate on the basis of who people are and whether they are like us or different from us, or what they can do for us. God is without favoritism, and we are to follow suit.

Here is God's will for us: "I have no greater joy than to hear that my children are walking in the truth" (3 John 4).

The Power of Sharing   DAY 346

The Christian life can be practiced in small, ordinary ways that produce great spiritual benefits. One of the most important virtues is sharing with others. As kids, our parents teach us to share. "Share with God's people who are in need. Practice hospitality" (Romans 12:13).

One of the spiritual highlights of my life was hearing Mother Teresa deliver a speech at the President's National Prayer Breakfast in February 1994. Here is a part of her message on the virtue of sharing:

> Those who are materially poor can be very wonderful people. One evening we went out, and we picked up four people from the street. And one of them was in a most terrible condition. I told the Sisters: "You take care of the other three; I will take care of the one who looks worse." So I did for her all that my love can do. I put her in bed, and there was such a beautiful smile on her face. She took hold of my hand, as she said one word only: "Thank you"—and she died.

I could not help but examine my conscience before her. And I asked, "What would I say if I were in her place?" And my answer was very simple. I would have tried to draw a little attention to myself. I would have said: "I am hungry, I am dying, I am cold, I am in pain," or something. But she gave me much more—she gave me her grateful love. And she died with a smile on her face.

I had the most extraordinary experience of love of neighbor with a Hindu family. A gentleman came to our house and said: "Mother Teresa, there is a family who have not eaten for so long. Do something." So I took some rice and went there immediately. And I saw the children—their eyes shining with hunger. I don't know if you have ever seen hunger. But I have seen it very often. And the mother of the family took the rice I gave her and went out. When she came back, I asked her: "Where did you go? What did you do?" And she gave me a very simple answer: "They are hungry also." What struck me was that she knew. And who were "they"? A Muslim family. And she knew. I didn't bring any more rice that evening because I wanted them, Hindus and Muslims, to enjoy the joy of sharing.

The 11th Commandment   DAY 347

I once read about the 11th commandment—*Thou shalt not worry!* What an apropos commandment for our times. The American fear level is rising to an all-time high with terrorist attacks, school shootings, the Middle East conflict, and the war in Iraq.

Jesus said it would be this way in the last days: "Men's hearts failing them for fear, and for looking after those things which are coming on the earth: for the powers of heaven shall be shaken" (Luke 21:26, KJV). His words read like the headlines of today's paper.

The future of the world lies in the hands of God. As Billy Graham said of the Bible, "I have read the last chapter, and we win!" The will of God shall be accomplished. Good will triumph over evil. History is *His story* as He "works out everything in conformity with the purpose of his will" (Ephesians 1:11). We will inherit a new heaven and a new earth.

We will live with Christ in eternity. So, in the words of Jesus, when you see the signs of the times unfolding, "Look up and lift up your heads, because your redemption draws near!" (Luke 21:28, *NKJV*).

Whatever happens in world events or in the daily struggles of your life, the commandment of the Lord is, "Thou shalt not worry." The psalmist understood the 11th commandment: "Fret not thyself " (37:1, KJV).

I like the way that reads in the Old English. To *fret* means "to get all steamed up; to be hot and bothered; to get wound up as tight as a drum; to be filled with fear, frustration and anger over things that are beyond your control."

The Way out of Worry   DAY 348

The way out of worry is the way of trust. Do you trust God with your life? Your family? Your problems? Your finances? Your career? Your relationships? Your ministry? Are you trusting, or are you striving? Isaiah tells us what God will do for us when we trust Him: "You will keep in perfect peace him whose mind is steadfast, because he trusts in you" (26:3).

Is your mind steadfast on the Lord? Do you trust Him in the tough times as much as you do in times of triumph? Can you say with conviction, "Yea, though I walk through the valley of the shadow of death, I will fear no evil: for thou art with me" (Psalm 23:4, KJV)? Or, do you only trust Him when you're on the mountain peak? Remember, God is with us in the valley just as He is on the mountain.

Jesus issues a command to us when we face uncertain times and wonder whether or not God will provide for us: "Do not worry about your life, what you will eat or drink; or about your body, what you will wear" (Matthew 6:25). He forbids us to worry. Instead, He tells us to make better use of our emotional energy. Trust God. Order your life by spiritual priorities. Take care of the things in your control and leave the rest to your heavenly Father. "But seek first his kingdom and his righteousness, and all these things will be given to you as well" (v. 33).

Corrie ten Boom, survivor of Hitler's death camp, defines *trust* as, "Don't doubt in the dark what God has shown you in the light." It's easy to lose faith in the darkness of adversity, suffering or discouragement. But God is faithful in the darkness as He is in the light.

So, obey the 11th commandment, *Thou shalt not worry.*

Life Is Not a Spelling Bee

When my son, David Paul, was in fourth grade, he and another classmate were selected to represent their fourth-grade class in the spelling bee contest for grades kindergarten through fifth grade.

The students were to repeat the word out loud and then spell it. However, if one letter was wrong, the student could not even amend the spelling. He or she was omitted from the competition. For over an hour the students spelled and misspelled until only two fourth-grade boys were left out of a group of about 60 or more students—my son and another boy. On and on they spelled until all the words were used up.

Then the judges took out a big, yellow book of words used for school competition. They both continued to spell until, finally, because we had gone beyond the allotted time, the judges called it a tie and awarded both boys first place.

During the competition I could not help but notice the expressions of some of the children when they misspelled a word and walked off the platform. One boy in particular became teary-eyed at his failure and walked off with a dejected look. He expected to win, but he didn't. He expected to have a perfect performance, but he didn't. In the spelling bee, the rule is firm—one mistake, and it's over. There is no second chance. There is no opportunity to correct your spelling when you misspell a word. It's all-or-nothing.

The good news is that life is not a spelling bee. We get more than one chance. Every mistake doesn't exempt us from life. We need to strive for success, not perfectionism. Making mistakes and failing are important parts of one's personal development. "Whatever your hand finds to do, do it with all your might" (Ecclesiastes 9:10).

Perfectionism Pitfalls

Perfectionism is the process of measuring one's worth on the basis of a flawless performance. What I do, then, tells me who I am. We often call the perfectionist a "workaholic," or the nice guy who always tries to please everyone, or the martyr who makes limitless sacrifices.

The pitfalls of perfectionism are many. The perfectionist believes,

"I have to be perfect to be worthwhile." The problem usually begins at home with overdemanding parents who relate to their children with conditional love. As we grow up we learn to act in certain ways to get people to love us.

Perfectionists overreact to failures and mistakes. One mistake, and the perfectionist says, "I'll never get it right." "I should have done this," or "I mustn't do that again." Such "should" statements create feelings of frustration and guilt.

Perfectionists operate from all-or-nothing thinking. It's the straight-A student who falls apart when she makes a B. Or, the top athlete who wants to quit because he had a bad game performance. The perfectionist fears mistakes and overreacts to them. They want to blame someone or something.

Perfectionists suffer from the saint/sinner syndrome. The saint has to do everything right all of the time or else he feels like the worst sinner in history. Only Jesus was perfect. When we put our faith in Him, He gives us His righteousness as a gift. "Therefore, having been justified by faith, we have peace with God through our Lord Jesus Christ" (Romans 5:1, *NKJV*).

To be *justified* means to have righteousness in God's sight and to be pardoned from all sin. It's a gift we receive, not a merit we earn. When we rest in the finished work of Christ, we are free to enjoy life, to excel within reason, and live free from perfectionism.

Relax!   DAY 351

Let's continue with our analysis of perfectionism and God's answer for this malady. Here are a few more symptoms if you're diagnosing yourself.

The perfectionist overworks and is unable to relax; is a control freak; is both self-critical and critical of others; gets frustrated with self and others because perfection is never achieved; is oriented toward the future because of dissatisfaction with the present; tries to correct the past and undo mistakes; procrastinates due to the fear of failure; battles depression due to unrealistic guilt and a negative view of self.

The perfectionist has three main concerns: (1) Diet—which is very clean; (2) time—obsessive about punctuality; and (3) money—anxious about security. The emotional nemesis of the perfectionist is rejection. He or she fears criticism, rejection or disapproval. The perfectionist believes (incorrectly, I might add) that a perfect performance insulates him or her from these painful experiences.

Believe it or not, perfectionists have some very positive traits. Their goal-directedness, attention to detail, and persistence at success result in tremendous achievements. The drawback is their inability to relax and to cope with failure, and their relentless pursuit of perfection, which can never be achieved.

Perfectionism does not increase one's efficiency but, rather, hinders it. One study of 150 salespersons showed that the 40 percent who were deemed perfectionists felt that they were under greater stress and suffered anxiety and depression, but they were not more successful at sales than the nonperfectionists. The discouragement and pressure characteristic of perfectionists can lead to a decrease in creativity and productivity because of their self-imposed tension and fear of failure.[31]

So the message is, *Relax!* Don't overstate successes or exaggerate your failures. Stay off the roller coaster and maintain your balance. "Let your gentleness be evident to all. The Lord is near" (Philippians 4:5).

All of Grace   DAY 352

The most important spiritual question of the human heart is, How can a person be right with God? Paul's letter to the Romans answers this ageless question in one word—justification. Paul uses the verb *justify* 22 times in his writings (mostly in Romans 3:21—5:1).

Justification means God pardons us from our sins on the basis of Christ's atoning death on the cross. He then credits to our lives the righteousness of Christ as a free gift. In Romans 4, Paul uses the verb *credit* nine times. "God made him who had no sin to be sin for us, so that in him we might become the righteousness of God" (2 Corinthians 5:21).

Good works or keeping the law of God can never justify a person. "No one will be declared righteous in his [God's] sight by observing the law; rather, through the law we become conscious of sin" (Romans 3:20).

Righteousness is God's gift to us, provided on the basis of Christ's atoning death on the cross: "All have sinned and fall short of the glory of God, and are justified freely by his grace through the redemption that came by Christ Jesus" (vv. 23, 24). Look at that—we are justified *freely.* A free gift, given extravagantly. The cry of the Reformation was "Sola gratia"—all of grace!

On what basis does God justify us? "Through the redemption that came by Christ Jesus. God presented him as a sacrifice of atonement, through faith in his blood" (vv. 24, 25). To be redeemed means to be freed from the slavery of sin. *Atonement* means "to cover." God covers our sins. The word *blood* is a synonym for *life* in the Bible (see Leviticus 17:11). We are redeemed because Jesus laid down His life for us. He suffered the penalty of sin on the cross. God has now pardoned the world.

So, accept by faith God's gift of righteousness and live as a new person who has peace with God.

Aim for Perfection

While we know that perfection is a pitfall, many Christians are under the delusion that they can be perfect. But doesn't Jesus say, "Be perfect, therefore, as your Father in heaven is perfect" (Matthew 5:48)? Yes, but the word *perfect* (Greek, *teleios*) means "to finish, to complete or to mature," and the context is love. "Grow up in love," is Jesus' command. Paul told the Corinthians, "Aim for perfection" (2 Corinthians 13:11). The word *perfection* here is *katartizesthe* and means "to restore, to mend, or to make fit," speaking of making good their deficiencies. It is a call for progress, not perfection in the way we use the word today.

I caught an announcer on a Christian radio station talking about the Christian life as a striving for perfection. She remarked, "We aren't always perfect." I thought to myself, *Are we ever perfect?* Is the Christian life a constant vacillation between perfect days and imperfect days? Christ is our only perfection. "You have been given fullness in Christ" (Colossians 2:10).

I once dedicated a baby named Ashley. The problem was that I prayed a beautiful dedicatory prayer dedicating her as a *boy*! After the service, the family said, "That was a beautiful prayer—the problem is that the baby is a girl."

You can imagine how stupid I felt. I apologized repeatedly. They were gracious, laughed it off, and said, "We took it as a sign from God that she'll be the first president of the United States." Coincidentally, we ended up at the same restaurant after church, and I went through the apologies again.

The secret of power in ministry is not perfection, it's dependency on God. "We have this treasure in jars of clay to show that this all-surpassing power is from God and not from us" (2 Corinthians 4:7). One of the most destructive lies a person can believe is that you have to be perfect to be worthwhile or to be used by God. If God only uses perfect people, He doesn't have any candidates to select from here on earth.

He uses "jars of clay" that open to receive His power. So open your heart to Him as a jar of clay and pray, "Lord, pour into me, and I will pour out to others."

Leaders Need Failure DAY 354

Leaders never really accomplish anything until they have survived a significant failure. Failure defines character. This principle is classically illustrated in Peter's denial of Jesus. Jesus told Peter that he would deny Him, but Peter didn't believe it. He thought himself invincible.

Jesus' only encouragement to Peter was prayer: "But I have prayed for you, Simon [Peter], that your faith may not fail. And when you have turned back, strengthen your brothers" (Luke 22:32).

Doesn't seem like much, does it? That's like you being on the verge of bankruptcy and a millionaire friend says, "I'll pray for you." What you need is financial assistance, not prayer. I'm sure that's how Peter must have felt. Why didn't Jesus intervene? Because He knew that failure is a part of growth and that Peter had to go through the experience. Sometimes, we try to intervene too much and end up enabling people to stay in their problem instead of suffering the consequences of their actions so that they can grow up.

Peter's denial and recovery made him the man of courage he came to be to preach the first sermon in the Christian church on the Day of Pentecost. He withstood his opponents, saying, "We must obey God rather than men" (Acts 5:29). He died for his faith, nailed upside down on a Roman cross. Failure was a painful, yet necessary part in the formation of a faith that could stand the test.

Take the Risk

When you fail, try again. I meet so many people who allow their failures to keep them from trying again. Maybe you failed at marriage, or the ministry, or business. You have one of two options: live like a hermit in a cave or come out and take the risk again.

After Peter denied Christ and watched his Lord be crucified, he went out and wept bitterly. His depression drove him out of the ministry and back to his fishing business after Jesus' resurrection. But the risen Lord went to Peter early one morning when Peter was out fishing. He met him on the shore of the Galilee and asked him one question: "Peter, do you love Me?"

Peter was deeply moved and replied, "Lord, You know I love You."

Jesus said, "Feed My sheep." He never questioned Peter's loyalty. He never mentioned Peter's denial to him. He never chided him, saying, "I told you that you would deny Me." He only extended him the opportunity to start over again (read John 21). Peter did, and so can we.

Taking the Risk

To laugh is to risk appearing the fool.

To weep is to risk appearing sentimental.

To reach out for another is to risk involvement.

To expose feelings is to risk exposing your true self.

To place your ideas, your dreams, before a crowd is to risk their loss.

To love is to risk not being loved in return.

To live is to risk dying.

To hope is to risk failure.

But risks must be taken.

Because the greatest hazard in life is to risk nothing.

If you risk nothing and do nothing, you dull your spirit.

You may avoid suffering and sorrow, but you cannot learn, feel, change, grow, love, and live.

Chained by your attitude, you are a slave.

You have forfeited your freedom.

Only if you risk are you free.

—Author unknown

Flee, Follow, Fight

All Raymond Raines wanted to do was whisper a prayer over his lunch. But every time the fourth-grader bowed his head, his teacher sent him to the principal's office. When his mother complained to the principal of Waring Elementary School (St. Louis), she was told that praying is not permitted in public school.

The enemy of faith is *secularism*, which means "this-worldly." How can we live spiritual lives in a secular culture? Paul gives a strategy: "Flee from all this, and pursue righteousness, godliness, faith, love, endurance and gentleness. Fight the good fight of the faith" (1 Timothy 6:11, 12).

Flee. Smart people run from danger. There are things in life from which we are to run. When Potiphar's wife grabbed Joseph by his cloak and tried to seduce him, Joseph "left his cloak in her hand and ran out of the house" (Genesis 39:12). "Flee the evil desires of youth," Paul tells Timothy, his son in the faith (2 Timothy 2:22). The desires and misguided plans of our youth are many. We need to outgrow them and move on toward maturity.

Follow. The Greek word *dioko* means "to pursue intently, to seek eagerly, to run swiftly." When Christ called the blind man, Bartimaeus, "Throwing his cloak aside, he jumped to his feet and came to Jesus" (Mark 10:50). What eagerness to answer the call of Christ! The best way to get past your mistakes is to run after Christ.

Fight. The gift of faith is free, but the life of faith is a fight. Your faith in God and in Christ is going to be opposed and tested. The Greek word *agonizomai* means "to agonize, to contend, to struggle." Paul said, "I labor, struggling with all his [Christ's] energy, which so powerfully works in me" (Colossians 1:29). He calls it "a good fight," which is taken from the ancient Olympic Games. The *good* fight means that which is beautiful and pleasing to the crowd; the beauty of the techniques used in competition.

Others are depending on you and me fighting the good fight of faith, standing true to our convictions, and holding fast to Christ, because they will follow in our steps as we follow Him.

God's Funeral

In late 1983, Michael Harrington, a prominent leader in Washington politics, authored a book titled *The Politics at God's Funeral*. He postulates that God is dead, and we need to bury Him. Our long-accepted moral and social values, based on the Bible, need to be permanently rooted out of our culture and replaced with a secular value system in which each person determines his or her own values. Instead of absolute truth, the only truth needed is personal and situational truth. He calls for a united effort to create a new society based on the "death" of God.[32]

It reminds me of the guy who was in the New York City subway and noticed graffiti which read: "God is dead." Signed: Nietzsche. He took a can of spray paint, painted over it, and wrote: "Nietzsche is dead." Signed: God.

Can man live without God? The Lord's message through the prophet Jeremiah is apropos to our times: "My people have committed two sins: They have forsaken me, the spring of living water, and have dug their own cisterns, broken cisterns that cannot hold water" (Jeremiah 2:13).

God alone is the spring of living water. A person can live four days without water. Water is basic to life. Jesus says, "Whoever drinks the water I give him will never thirst. Indeed, the water I give him will become in him a spring of water welling up to eternal life" (John 4:14). Only a meaningful relationship with God can bring true satisfaction, security, and significance to life.

We have made modern cisterns to take the place of faith in God. The cisterns of secularism, humanism and materialism are cracked and broken and cannot hold water.

They cannot provide us meaning and eternal life. "Consider then and realize how evil and bitter it is for you when you forsake the Lord your God" (Jeremiah 2:19).

Here is God's invitation: "Return, faithless people; I will cure you of backsliding." Our answer must be, "Yes, we will come to you, for you are the Lord our God" (3:22).

On Eagles' Wings   DAY 358

When God brought the Israelites out of Egypt, He told the people, "I carried you on eagles' wings and brought you to myself" (Exodus 19:4).

In what ways does God carry us like an eagle carries her young? The female golden eagle best fits this description. Eagles live in most of the Northern Hemisphere. They serve as a symbol of power and courage because of their large size, aerial skills, and inaccessibility of nests in wild, mountainous country. The eagle has been a symbol for certain Roman legions, France under Napoleon, and the great seal of the United States.

The eagle's nest is usually built on cliff ledges, although some build in trees. They keep the same nest and, year after year, add new sticks until nests become as large as 6 feet in diameter and 5 feet high.

They produce few eggs and usually raise only two nestlings. The male hunts food and brings it to the nest. The mother feeds the young. Once they mature, the mother hunts as well as the male. The female eagle grows up to 3 feet long, with a 7-foot wingspan. The males are smaller, as with most birds of prey. They fly upward to 85 mph and downward to 140 mph.

Eagles exhibit grandeur in flight, rise above the clouds, transcend dangers below, build nests on high, mate for life, travel independently (not in flocks), and provide for and protect their family.

So God says, "I carried you out of Egypt on eagles' wings." Moses also writes of God: "He shielded him [Israel] and cared for him; he guarded him as the apple of his eye, like an eagle that stirs up its nest and hovers over its young, that spreads its wings to catch them and carries them on its pinions" (Deuteronomy 32:10, 11).

Spend time reflecting on the times God has carried you out of a problem and into His promise.

Stirring Up the Nest   DAY 359

Let's continue our reflections on the eagle, as it teaches us about God's care. The time comes to stir up the nest so that the eaglets can learn to fly.

The eagle constructs the nest from thorns, jagged stones, and pointed sticks, then covers the interior with feathers, wool, and fur from animals she has killed. The nest is soft and comfortable for the nestlings. However, the time will come when she will stir up the nest. She removes the wool, feathers and fur, picking it out piece by piece and throwing it to the wind. The now-developing eaglets find themselves pricked by the sharp edges of the sticks and thorns.

The mother eagle no longer brings food and places it in their mouths. It doesn't take long for them to venture out of the comfort of the nest, to spread their wings and soar to become what they were destined to become. The psalmist said, "[God] satisfies your desires with good things so that your youth is renewed like the eagle's" (103:5). Isaiah says, "Those who hope in the Lord will renew their strength. They will soar on wings like eagles" (40:31).

When God says, "I carried you on eagles' wings" (Exodus 19:4), He is reminding us of His care for us as an eagle cares for her young. But then there are times when He stirs up the nest so that we can learn to fly on our own. God uses the challenges and difficulties of life to stir up the nest so that we mature in our faith.

This is what James had in mind when he wrote: "Consider it pure joy . . . whenever you face trials of many kinds, because you know that the testing of your faith develops perseverance. Perseverance must finish its work so that you may be mature and complete, not lacking anything" (1:2-4).

If God is stirring up your nest, take the risk of faith and start flying. You weren't made to stay in the nest of comfort; you were made to soar above the clouds!

In the Desert   DAY 360

"God did not lead them [the Israelites] on the road through the Philistine country, though that was shorter. . . . God led the people around by the desert" (Exodus 13:17, 18). We typically like shortcuts—the easy way; the quickest route.

Yet, at times, God leads us into the desert. What a strange place for God to lead us. We would never dream of taking a vacation in a desert. We want a resort . . . theme parks . . . fine restaurants . . . beautiful beaches. While all of that has its place, sometimes we need a desert where we can get alone with God. The soul needs R&R just like the body.

Israel's experience in the desert shows us how God uses desert experiences in our lives . . .

- *To display His power.* They learned that God alone could, and would, bring them through. God never leaves us in the desert. He always brings us through. In the desert we learn to rely on His power and provisions.

- *To destroy our enemies.* The psalmist said: "To him who led his people through the desert . . . who struck down great kings . . . and killed mighty kings" (136:16-18). Armies sought to annihilate the Hebrews, but God's victory was won in the desert. God takes us into a desert experience to conquer enemies of our souls.
- *To receive His Word in undisturbed solitude.* Elijah heard the "still small voice" of God while in the desert where God led him (1 Kings 19:12, *NKJV*). Jesus was led by the Holy Spirit into the desert for 40 days of prayer and preparation before He launched His ministry (Matthew 4:1-11). He "often withdrew to lonely places and prayed" (Luke 5:16).
- *To test us.* God examines our hearts and prepares us to face life's challenges. "Remember how the Lord your God led you all the way in the desert . . . to test you in order to know what was in your heart. . . . He humbled you, causing you to hunger and then feeding you with manna . . . to teach you that man does not live on bread alone but on every word that comes from the mouth of the Lord" (Deuteronomy 8:2, 3).

Make the most of your desert. It is valuable time for solitude, reflection, and drawing closer to God.

Listening to God   DAY 361

Everyone desires to hear from God. Since prayer is a dialogue with God, it is only logical to assume that He desires to speak to us. The primary way we hear God is through the Scripture. He also speaks in our hearts, through spiritual gifts, and through the counsel of others.

But often the channel of communication is not clear. There are barriers that prevent us from hearing God. My mother used to say, "Get the wax out of your ears and listen."

Peter Drucker points out that 60 percent of business failures are due to poor communication. If you have seen the film *Cool Hand Luke*, you can recall Struther Martin, who played the prison warden, saying to Luke, played by Paul Newman, "What we have here is a failure to communicate."

The quality of our relationships is determined by the level of our communication. In the same way, the quality of our spiritual life depends on our communication with God.

The most important parable Jesus ever taught concerning the kingdom of God is the parable of the sower, which teaches us how to listen to God (see Mark 4:1-20). The word *hear* appears seven times in this parable.

A word about why Jesus used parables is in order. The word *parabole* (Greek) means "to place beside." Jesus placed the common alongside the uncommon so that people could understand spiritual truth. William Barclay says that a parable is earthly stories with a heavenly meaning. The goal of a parable is to overcome spiritual resistance so that people can hear the Word of God.

The lesson for today is, "If anyone has ears to hear, let him hear" (Mark 4:23).

Heart Conditions   DAY 362

Let's continue looking at Jesus' parable of the sower. The sower is Jesus, who actively sows the Word of God in people's hearts. The seed itself is the Word of God.

The Word is like a seed in three ways: (1) It has life-giving power. "My words are spirit and life" (see John 6:63). (2) It has fruit-bearing quality. Just one seed can produce a great harvest. (3) The Word of God, like a seed, must be planted and nourished. "Humbly accept the word planted in you, which can save you" (James 1:21).

Jesus says that the seed fell on four different types of soil which represent conditions of the heart.

The unguarded heart: the seed on the path. The path itself was hardened, so the seed could not take root. The birds of prey came and took the seed. When the Word of God is not accepted, it can be taken away and needs to be sown again.

The shallow heart: the seed on rocky places. Rocky places in Israel consist of a thin layer of soil over a rock base of limestone—shallow soil. The seed sprang up quickly, showing the absence of a root system and moisture. The result of the shallow heart is spiritual instability in times of testing: "Since they have no root, they last only a short time. When trouble or persecution comes because of the word, they quickly fall away" (Mark 4:17).

The cluttered heart: the seed among the thorns. Thorns first appeared on the earth after the Fall and are reminders of the Curse (Genesis 3:18; Hebrews 6:8). Three kinds of thorns choke our spiritual growth: "the worries of this life, the deceitfulness of wealth and the desires for other things" (Mark 4:19).

The receptive heart: the seed on good soil. The good heart is one that hears the Word, accepts it, and produces a crop. Hearing God is predicated on our desire to act on what God reveals to us.

Consider Carefully What You Hear | DAY 363

One could make the case that the phrase Jesus said more than any other was, "If anyone has ears to hear, let him hear" (Mark 4:23). This was His appeal after many of His messages. The *Phillips* translation reads, "If a man has ears he should use them!"

When Jesus finished teaching the parable of the sower, He knew that people could be in the presence of God, hear His Word preached or taught, and still not really hear. There is a difference between hearing audibly and hearing spiritually.

We all know how to tune people out when we want to. Husbands tune their wives out when they're watching a football game. Teenagers can tune out their parents when they want to. We all practice selective hearing.

We often tune out parts of a sermon or passage of Scripture without realizing we're doing it. So, Jesus teaches us to cultivate the right attitude toward the Word of God so that we can truly listen and learn.

Hearing God requires a relationship with Him. "My sheep hear My voice," said Jesus (John 10:27, *NKJV*). Hearing is predicated on a sincere desire to hear from God. "Speak, [Lord], for your servant is listening" (1 Samuel 3:10).

At the close of the parable, Jesus said: "Consider carefully what you hear. . . . With the measure you use, it will be measured to you—and even more. Whoever has will be given more; whoever does not have, even what he has will be taken from him" (Mark 4:24, 25). Here are five lessons for life:

1. We cannot give what we do not have.
2. What we receive is meant to be shared.
3. What we receive is what we become.
4. What we do not use, we lose.
5. What we use is returned in an abundant measure.

Let this be our prayer: "Open my eyes that I may see wonderful things in your law" (Psalm 119:18).

The Past Is Prologue DAY 364

W hen Dwight D. Eisenhower was president, he used to tell the story of a government employee who had just arrived in Washington, D.C. He was passing by the National Archives Building in a taxi when he noticed the motto carved on the building: "The past is prologue."

Since cab drivers are presumed to be all-knowing about their cities, the government worker asked what the motto meant. "Oh, that's just bureaucrat talk," he replied. "What it means is, 'You ain't seen nothing yet.' "

Our heavenly Father is the God of new beginnings. Just when we think it's the end, His grace breaks in with a new beginning. Man fell into sin, but grace came in the Garden. The Flood destroyed the earth, but a new chapter in the human story began. Jesus, the Messiah, died on the cross, but then came Sunday, and He rose again!

Let's go back in history for a minute. Judah was in exile to Babylon. The Temple was destroyed. Jerusalem laid in waste from the invasion. Hope was gone. But then came the Word of God to the exiles, and hope was reawakened. God would raise up Persia to overthrow Babylon and allow the people to return home. God had not forgotten them in their suffering and exile. He would come to them. He was their God and their eternal hope.

Isaiah brought God's Word of hope to the exiles: "He who made a way through the sea, a path through the mighty waters . . . [says] 'I am making a way in the desert and streams in the wasteland'" (43:16, 19).

God says, "I am the Lord, your Holy One, Israel's Creator, your King" (v. 15). He is their Creator, which means He made them out of nothing; the One who created them, watched over them and sustained them. The God who formed us will also lead us, guide us, and fulfill His will for us. He then recalls to their minds the Exodus. Just as He brought them through the sea, He will bring them through the hot desert sands of Arabia back to Judah.

What a promise for today: *God will make a way!*

The Passion-Driven Life   DAY 365

An English minister by the name of Charles Kingsley said, "We act as though comfort and luxury were the chief requirements of life, when all we need to make us really happy is something to be enthusiastic about."

I walked into a Starbucks recently to get breakfast, which is simply a hot chocolate. The young woman behind the counter wore a Starbucks T-shirt that read: "Our first passion is coffee."

I noticed a billboard on the interstate for an Italian restaurant with the slogan, "Pasta is our passion." What are you passionate about?

Our level of success is largely determined by our passion—ardent affection, jealousy, intense desire, zeal. The sufferings of Christ on the cross is called His Passion.

The greatest passion one can have is spiritual passion for the advancement of the kingdom of God. Paul says, "Fan into flame the gift of God, which is in you" (2 Timothy 1:6). The word *fan* (Greek, *anazopureo*) comes from three words: *ana*, meaning "again"; *zoe*, meaning "life"; and *pur*, meaning "fire." Paul says in effect, "Rekindle your spiritual passion."

King Jehu said, "Come with me and see my zeal for the Lord" (2 Kings 10:16). When Isaiah prophesied the coming of the Messiah, he said, "The zeal of the Lord Almighty will accomplish this" (9:7).

"Always be zealous for the fear of the Lord" (Proverbs 23:17). Of the Messiah, we read: "He put on righteousness as his breastplate . . . and wrapped himself in zeal as in a cloak" (Isaiah 59:17). Jesus was "consumed with zeal for the house of the Lord" (see John 2:17). Finally, Paul says, "For the love of Christ compels us" (2 Corinthians 5:14, *NKJV*).

We don't serve the Lord out of fear, guilt or duty. The love of Christ compels us to a life of worship and service. If you're bored, let me encourage you to do something you are passionate about and to pour yourself into it with all your might.

God Makes a Way

As the waters of the Red Sea parted, the Israelites passed through on dry land. They were learning that God makes a way where there is no way. We, too, have to enter the sea of impossibility. We have to take the step of faith. He parts the waters, but we have to pass through the problem. Notice that they walked, not ran. They were at peace, walking at the pace of faith.

Then, the cloud of God's glory lifted from Pharaoh's army, allowing them to enter the sea. The waters enveloped them, sweeping them away in one swift blow from the hand of God. There is archaeological evidence of the Red Sea miracle. One of the most memorable demonstrations of the miracles of God in human history was the parting of the waters of the Red Sea.

The Israelites stood on the other side of the sea and witnessed God's miracle power. They sang the first song recorded in the Bible: "Your right hand, O Lord, was majestic in power. Your right hand, O Lord, shattered the enemy" (Exodus 15:6).

God again proved faithful to His word. God not only promised to deliver them from slavery, but also to bring them safely into a land flowing with milk and honey. Finally, a long, dark chapter of slavery had come to an end. The night of oppression had given way to the dawn of a new opportunity. All their pain, suffering and hopelessness was buried in the waters of the Red Sea along with their enemies.

Unfortunately, it would require many more acts of God before the people would come to trust God. Over and over, they found it easy to complain to Moses and doubt God's ability to bring them into the new land. They, like us, were slow learners when it comes to trusting God.

Are you under pressure? Are you hemmed in on every side? Have you come to the end of yourself? Then meet the God who makes a way where there is no way.

I leave you with the promise of the Lord: "When you pass through the waters, I will be with you; and when you pass through the rivers, they will not sweep over you. . . . For I am the Lord, your God" (Isaiah 43:2, 3).

ENDNOTES

[1] Taken from "To Illustrate . . . ," *Leadership*, Fall 1986: 42.

[2] Denis Waitley, *10 Seeds of Greatness* (Old Tappan, NJ: Revell, 1983) 106-7.

[3] Cited in *The Pastor's Weekly Briefing*, Vol. 2, No. 38.

[4] Waitley, 77.

[5] *U.S. News and World Report*, Dec. 19, 1994: 64.

[6] Charles R. Hembree, *Fruits of the Spirit* (Grand Rapids: Baker, 1969) 125-6.

[7] Taken from the *Challenge*, a monthly supplement of the *Orthodox Observer*, an official publication of the Greek Orthodox Archdiocese of North and South America.

[8] William Barclay, *The Gospel of John*, Vol. 1 (Philadelphia: Westminster, 1975) 6-8.

[9] Barclay, 34-7.

[10] Michael Green, *Who Is This Jesus?* (Nashville: Thomas Nelson, 1992) 116-7.

[11] Green, 114.

[12] Taken from Catherine Marshall-LeSourd, *Adventures in Prayer*, 1975.

[13] *U.S. News and World Report*, Dec. 9, 1996: 17.

[14] Arnold Dallimore, *Spurgeon* (Chicago: Moody, 1984) 94.

[15] Tim Kimmel, "Robbed of Rest," *Focus on the Family*, Feb. 1988: 2-5.

[16] A.W. Tozer, *The Knowledge of the Holy* (Lincoln: Back to the Bible Broadcast, 1961) 6.

[17] J.B. Phillips, *Your God Is Too Small* (Basingstoke: Macmillan, 1961) 7.

[18] Lyrics and music by Annie Herring, Latter Rain Music, © 1988, ASCAP.

[19] *Christianity Today*, July 2003: 14.

[20] Craig B. Larson, ed., *Illustrations for Preaching and Teaching* (Grand Rapids: Baker, 1993) 109.

[21] Barclay, *The Parables of Jesus* (Louisville: Westminster John Knox Press, 1970) 141.

[22] *The Executive Speechwriter Newsletter* (Vol. 14, No. 3), 7.

[23] Waitley, *10 Seeds of Greatness* (Old Tappan, NJ: Revell, 1983).

[24] Pat Robertson, *The Secret Kingdom* (Nashville: Thomas Nelson, 1982) 109-11.

[25] Gary Thomas, "The Forgiveness Factor," *Christianity Today*, Jan. 10, 2000: 44.

[26] Rai Whitlock, "One Nation Under God—Sort Of," *Christianity Today*, Jan. 2004: 34.

[27] Kenneth L. Woodward and David Gates, "How the Bible Made America," *Newsweek*, Dec. 27, 1982: 44-51.

[28] Sekulow and Fourier, *And Nothing but the Truth* (Nashville: Thomas Nelson, 1996) 29.

[29] Adapted from "They Don't Retire Them, They Hire Them," by Joe Mullich on Workforce Online.

[30] *Speaker's Idea File*, Aug. 1996: 2.

[31] David D. Burns, "Aim for Success, Not Perfection," *Reader's Digest*, March 1985: 71-4.

[32] James T. Draper and Forrest E. Watson, *If the Foundations Be Destroyed* (Nashville: Oliver-Nelson, 1984) vii.